T0364259

SPIRIT OF LUXURY AND DESIGN

A Perspective from Contemporary Fashion and Jewellery

Edited by
Jie SUN   Elizabeth FISCHER

ORO
EDITIONS

TONGJI
UNIVERSITY
PRESS

CONTENTS

FOREWORD

ACKOWLEDGMENTS

CHAPTER 1
INTRODUCTION

CHAPTER 2
FUTURE & INSPIRATION
Design, Art, Craftsmanship, Material and Culture

CONTENTS

CHAPTER 3
BELONGING & INTERDISCIPLINARY
Sustainability and New Technology

Introduction
Jie SUN

CONTENTS

CHAPTER 4
DIALOGUE & COMMUNICATION
Curation

CHAPTER 5
CONCLUSION

ABOUT THE EDITORS

FOREWORD

Contemporary fashion and jewellery is a market based on positive feedback loops in which, pieces are built, and, like other academic and professional disciplines, receive criticism and feedback; it is an evolving field constantly adapting to changing discussion and challenges. It can even be spectacular, radical, and conceptual, provoking the imagination and perspectives on design, art, and innovation. Jewellery is also very personal; it is a medium through which one can tell their story, evoke memories, and reflect personality and character—it is a statement.

The development of fashion and jewellery research continues to evolve as avant-garde design on the periphery of the field is accepted, studied, and developed further before becoming an accepted part of the field. Jewellery, and the design of these artifacts and fashion, has become a remarkable growth industry. Most academics and practical research on the subject focuses on the fields of fashion and dress (Evans, 2003; Kawamura, 2011, 2018; Johnson, 2003; Breward, 1998, 2015, 2016), textile technology and crafts (Fletcher, 2014; Sikarskie, 2020), textile pattern design (Emery, 2014), clothing and material culture (Miller, 2005), fashion and culture (Kaiser, 2013; Baudel, 2004; Laver, 2020), fashion history and theory (Taylor, 2004, 2013; Riello, 2010; Granata, 2012; Fukai, 2015; Burns, 2019), market economics (Entwistle, 2009; Griffith, 2000; Flynn, 2009; Burns et al., 2016), sociology (Tseelon, 1995; Fliigel, 2004; Paoletti, 2015), and aesthetics (Gaimster, 2011), museums (Anderson, 2013; Melchior, 2014; Petrov, 2019)—skewing heavily toward textiles and clothing. However, fashion—as an interdisciplinary pursuit—involves many aspects, not just clothing and textiles. Fashion research based on clothing and textiles often shies away from jewellery and related items.

Relatively independent from mainstream "fashion," jewellery has its own history and development. The research on jewellery that proliferats usually focus on human history and archaeology (Chadour-Sampson, 2019; Awais-Dean, 2018; Scarisbrick, 2019), traditional crafts and techniques (Revere, 2018), gem stones and materials (Pointon, 2010), brand (Müller, 2015), contemporary art jewellery (Strauss, 2007; Skinner, 2013; Deckers et al., 2017), fashion and jewellery histories (Cera, 2019; Papi, 2016), and the modern and contemporary jewellery (Besten, 2011). Other fashion accessories such as footwear and bags (Høy, 2019; Steele, 2017; Pasols, 2012), human history (Wilcox, 2012), technology and crafts (Goonetilleke, 2017; Volken, 2019), and clothing accessories (Mauriès, 2017) mostly focus on luxury brands. The design of jewellery, watches, footwear, and bags is different from the design methods and processes of textiles—including a different frame of mind and sociological reasoning. Overall, there is a lack of discussion and research of the value and roles of jewellery and related objects in fashion and design. Research is critical in the current social culture, economy, and with material science and technological changes, and must go beyond industrial product design (Koskinen, 2011), architecture and environment (Colletti, 2017; Schaik, 2017), experiential design (Austin, 2020), fashion design, sustainable design (Stubbins, 2010), and research methodology (Plattner, 2017).

This book has come about after two years of development following the First WoSoF World Symposium for Fashion,

Jewellery, Accessories in Shanghai at the end of 2018 and the research and discussions had with scholars invited to Tongji University for the development of this book. There remains an academic divide between fashion and the role and value of jewellery design, and related accessories, when discussing contemporary fashion design theories and methods, making this forum necessary to further the field and support cross-disiplinary learning. The First WoSoF World Symposium for Fashion, Jewellery, and Accessories is part of the WoSoF World Fashion, Jewellery, and Accessories Innovation Design Project, which aslo includes the WoSoF Exhibition for Fashion, Jewellery, and Accessories and the publication of *Spirit of Luxury and Design: A Perspective from Contemporary Fashion and Jewellery* (this book).The whole WoSoF global fashion and jewellery innovation project has been successful thanks to the sponsorship of School of Design and Innovation at Tongji University, co-organized with Genève School of Art and Design, Switzerland, the Universidad Politecnica in Madrid, Spain, and the Institut Français de la Mode Paris, France.

WoSoF Exhibition for Fashion, Jewellery, and Accessories was held at the Tianjin Academy of Fine Arts' museum with roughly 60 pieces of work exhibited. Professor Elizabeth Fischer (Switzerland, Genève School of Art Design), Professor Guillermo García-Badell (Spain, the Universidad Politecnica in Madrid), and I jointly selected 30 cutting-edge designers from China, Switzerland, and Spain. These designers' works mainly focus on jewellery, bags, glasses, and shoes, which showcase the emerging design practices in the field as relates to materials, new technology, innovative craftsmanship, and design methods. On the third day, after the grand opening of the exhibition in Tianjin, the First WoSoF World Symposium for Fashion, Jewellery, and Accessories kicked off in Shanghai, where 17 speakers from nine countries—including China, the United Kingdom, the United States, France, Switzerland, the Netherlands, German, Australia and Italy gathered. The exhibition and symposium addressed centered on the question: "How does jewellery and related fashion items (shoes, hats, bags, glasses, watches, etc.) represent fashion design and contemporary culture?" Discussions addressed three topics: art, design, material, and culture; sustainability and new technology; curation and management.

This book consists of five chapters organized according to these topical groups. The first chapter discusses the role of contemporary design in the development of fashion luxury goods. In Chapter Two, "Future & Inspiration," 14 articles address fashion and jewellery as they relate to art, design, materials, and culture. In Chapter Three, "Belonging & Interdisciplinary," four articles continue the discussion of jewellery as it relates to sustainable development and new technologies on the development of jewellery design. Chapter Four focuses on the curation of exhibitions. And Chapter Five, "The Future is Now," draws a conclusion to the book and the WoSoF World Fashion, Jewellery, and Accessories Innovation Design Project. My hope is that this book can encourage readers from different backgrounds to re-examine jewellery and related fashion items as a distinct field of fashion and design and leads to new innovation within the industry.

Jie SUN

National Distinguished Expert, Professor at Tongji University, Shanghai, China

Reference

Anderson, F. 2013. "Museums as Fashion Media." In *Fashion Cultures Revisited: Theories, Explorations and Analysis*, edited by Stella Bruzzi and Pamela Church-Gibson. London and New York: Routledge.

Awais-Dean, N. 2018. Bejewelled: Men and Jewellery in Tudor and Jacobean England. London: British Museum.

Austin, T. 2020. *Narrative Environments and Experience Design: Space as a Medium of Communication.* London and New York: Routledge.

Baudel, C. 2004. "The Painter Modern Life." In *The Rise of Fashion*, edited by Daniel Leonhard Purdy, 213–21.Minneapolis: University of Minnesota Press.

Breward, C. 1998. "Cultures, Identities, Histories: Fashioning a Cultural Approach to Dress." In *Fashion Theory* 2(4), 301–13.

Breward, C. 2015. *Fashion (Oxford History of Art)*. Oxford: Oxford University Press.

Breward, C. 2016.*The Suit: Form, Function and Style*. London: Reaktion Books.

Burns, L. D. 2019. *Sustainability and Social Change in Fashion.* New York: Fairchild Books.

Burns, L. D., K. K. Mullet, and N. O. Bryant. 2016. *The Business of Fashion: Designing, Manufacturing, and Marketing.* New York: Fairchild Books.

Besten, L. D. 2011. *On Jewellery: A Compendium of International Contemporary Art Jewellery.* Stuttgart: Arnoldsche Verlagsanstalt.

Chadour-Sampson, B. 2019. *The Power of Love: Jewels, Romance and Eternity.* Singapore: Unicorn Publishing Group.

Cera, D. F. 2019. *Adorning Fashion: The History of Costume Jewellery to Modern Times.* London: ACC Art Books.

Colletti, M. 2017. *Digital Poetics: An Open Theory of Design-Research in Architecture (Design Research in Architecture).* London and New York: Routledge.

Deckers, P. K. Paton, and L. D. Besten. 2017. *Contemporary Jewellery in Context: A Handshake Blueprint.* Stuttgart: Arnoldsche Verlagsanstalt.

Evans, C. 2003. *Fashion at the Edge: Spectacle, Modernity and Deathliness.* New Haven, CT and London: Yale University Press.

Entwistle, J. 2009. *The Aesthetic Economy of Fashion: Markets and Value in Clothing and Modelling.* New York and Oxford: Berg Publishers.

Emery, J. S. 2014. *A History of the Paper Pattern Industry: The Home Dressmaking Fashion Revolution.* London: Bloomsbury.

Fletcher, K. 2014. *Sustainable Fashion and Textiles: Design Journeys.* 2nd ed. London and New York: Routledge.

Fliigel, J. C. 2004. "The Great Masculine Renunciation and its Causes" In *The Rise of Fashion*, edited by Daniel Leonhard Purdy, 102-08. Minneapolis: University of Minnesota Press.

Flynn, J. Z., and I. M. Foster. 2009. *Research Methods for the Fashion Industry.* New York: Fairchild Books.

Fukai, A., T. Suoh, and M. Iwagami. 2015. *Fashion: A History from the 18th to the 20th Century.* Cologne: TASCHEN.

Granata, F. 2012. "Fashion Studies In-Between: A Methodological Case-Study and an Inquiry into the State of Fashion Studies." In *Fashion Theory* 16(1), 67–82.

Gaimster, J. 2011. *Visual Research Methods in Fashion.* Oxford: Berg Publishers.

Griffith, I. 2000. "The Invisible Man." In *The Fashion Business: Theory, Practice, Image*, edited by Nicola White and Ian Griffiths, 69–90. Oxford: Bloomsbury.

Goonetilleke , R. S. 2017. *The Science of Footwear (Human Factors and Ergonomics).* London and New York: Routledge.

Høy, J., and C. Frost. 2019. *The Book of Rolex*. London: Acc Art Books.

Joost, G., K. Bredies, M. Christensen, and A. Unteidig. 2016. *Design as Research (Board of International Research in Design).* Basel: Birkhäuser.

Johnson, K. P., S. J. Torntore, and J. B. Eicher. 2003. *Fashion Foundations: Early Writings on Fashion and Dress.* Oxford and New York: Berg Publishers.

Koskinen, I., J. Zimmerman, T. Binder, J. Redstrom, and S. Wensveen. 2011. *Design Research Through Practice: From the Lab, Field, and Showroom.* Cambridge: Morgan Kaufmann Publishers.

Kaiser, S. B. 2013. *Fashion and Cultural Studies.* London: Bloomsbury Academic.

Kawamura, Y. 2011. *Doing Research in Fashion and Dress: An Introduction to Qualitative Methods.* London: Bloomsbury.

Kawamura, Y. 2018. *Fashion-ology: An Introduction to Fashion Studies (Dress, Body, Culture).* London: Bloomsbury Visual Arts.

Laver, J. 2020. *Costume and Fashion: A Concise History.* London: Thames & Hudson.

Miller, D., and S. Kiichler. 2005. *Clothing as Material Culture.* Oxford and New York: Berg Publishers.

Müller, F. 2015. *Piaget: Watchmaker and Jeweler Since 1874.* New York: Abrams Books.

Mauriès, P. 2017. *Yves Saint Laurent Accessories.* London: Phaidon Press.

Melchior, M. R. 2014. *Fashion and Museums (Dress, Body, Culture)*. London: Bloomsbury Academic.

Riello, G., and P. McNeil. 2010. *The Fashion History Reader: Global Perspectives*. London: Routledge.

Raposo, D., J. Neves, and J. Silva, eds. 2020. *Perspective on Design: Research, Education and Practice*. Cham: Springer.

Revere, A. 2018. *Professional Jewellery Making*. Brunswick: Brynmorgen Press.

Papi, S., and A. Rhodes. 2016. *20th Century Jewellery & the Icons of Style*. London: Thames & Hudson; Revised Edition, Reduced Format edition.

Paoletti, J. B. 2015. *Sex and Unisex: Fashion, Feminism, and the Sexual Revolution*. Indiana: Indiana University Press.

Petrov, J. 2019. *Fashion, History, Museums: Inventing the Display of Dress*. London: Bloomsbury Visual Arts.

Pointon, M. 2010. *Brilliant Effects: A Cultural History of Gem Stones and Jewellery*. New Haven, CT: Yale University Press.

Pasols, P. G. 2012. *Louis Vuitton: The Birth of Modern Luxury*. New York: Abrams Books.

Plattner, H., C. Meinel, and L. Leifer. 2012. *Design Thinking Research: Measuring Performance in Context*. Cham: Springer.

Stubbins, K. 2010. *Sustainable Design of Research Laboratories: Planning, Design, and Operation*, London and New York: Wiley.

Strauss, C. 2007. *Ornament as Art: Avant-Garde Jewellery from the Helen Williams Drutt Collection*. Stuttgart: Arnoldsche Verlagsanstalt.

Skinner, D. ed. 2013. *Contemporary Jewellery in Perspective*. New York: Lark Books.

Steele, V., G. O'Brien. 2017. *Louis Vuitton: A Passion for Creation: New Art, Fashion and Architecture*. New York: Rizzoli.

Schaik, L. V., and A. Johnson. 2020. *By Practice, by Invitation: Design Practice Research in Architecture and Design at RMIT, 1986-2011*. Barcelona: Actar Publishers.

Sikarskie, A. 2020. *Digital Research Methods in Fashion and Textile Studies*. London: Bloomsbury Visual Arts.

Scarisbrick, D. 2019. *Diamond Jewellery: 700 Years of Glory and Glamour*. London: Thames & Hudson.

Taylor, L. 2004. *Establishing Dress History*. Manchester and New York: Manchester University Press.

Taylor, L. 2013. *Fashion and Dress History: Theoretical and Methodological Fashion Revolution*. London and New York: Bloomsbury.

Tseelon, E. 1995. *The Masque of Femininity: The Presentation of Women in Everyday Life*. London and Thousand Oaks: Sage Publications.

Volken, M. 2014. *Archaeological Footwear: Development of Shoe Patterns and Styles from Prehistory till the 1600's*. SPA Uitgevers.

Vaughan, L. 2017. *Practice-based Design Research*, London: Bloomsbury Visual Arts.

Wilcox, C., J. Clark, A. Phillips, C. Evans, A. D. L. Haye. 2012. *Handbags: The Making of a Museum*. New Haven, CT: Yale University Press.

ACKNOWLEDGMENTS

Here, I especially want to thank Professor Elizabeth Fischer, who has worked closely with me during this whole project, and who is also one of the editors of this book, as well as Professor Guillermo García-Badell (Spain) and Ms. Marie-Pierre Gendarme (France). I would also like to thank the distinguished guests who participated in the symposium and fully supported this book: Associate Professor Jean-Marc Chauve (France), Dr. Maarten Floris Versteeg (the Netherlands), Dr. Elizabeth Shaw (Australia), Ms. Katharina Sand (Switzerland), Ms. Naomi Filmer (UK), Ms. Nichka Marobin (Italy), Ms. Mala Siamptani (UK), Mr. Volker Koch (Germany), Professor Christine Lüdeke (Germany), Professor Cristina Giorcelli (Italy), Associate Professor Emilie Hammen (France), Professor Paula Rabinowitz (US), Ms. Donatella Zappieri (Italy), Professor Hector Navarro (Spain). In addition, Professor Yong-il Jeon (South Korea), Mr. Akio Seki (Japan), Mr. Eelko Moorer (the Netherlands), and Dr. Chiara Scarpitti (Italy) contributed to this book.

Thanks to Professor Yongqi Lou, vice-president of Tongji University (previous dean of College of Design and Innovation), for his trust and support for my work. At the same time, there are colleagues in the organizing committee of the exhibition and the preparation group of the symposium who I want to thank for their contributions in different work stages: Associate

Professor Dongdong Zhuang from Tianjin Academy of Fine Arts; Ms. Dongyang Chen, Ms. Shijian Zhao, and Ms. Shuai Yuan from College of Design and Innovation Tongji University; Ms. Qing Zhu from Shanghai How Art Museum (former); Ms. Jialin Yuan and Ms. Yuantian Zhou from Tongji University Press. I would also like to thank swissnex China, the Science Consulate of Switzerland in China, the Swiss Science Consul Dr. Felix Moesner, and Mrs. Yiwen Sun for their strong support of this project.

CHAPTER

1

INTRODUCTION

From Luxury
to Contemporary
Fashion Design

Jie SUN

National Distinguished Expert, Professor, College of Design and Innovation,
Tongji University, Shanghai, China

A New Frame for the Understanding of Luxury within Fashion

German sociologist and philosopher Peter Sloterdijk once said in his monograph:

Luxury makes humankind possible and it is also through luxury that our world is born. Humans are, and have been since the very beginning, animals that mutually indulge and exonerate themselves by taking care of each other and by treating themselves with more security than any other living creature could ever dream of enjoying. Humankind arises through its secession with Mother Nature (Sloterdijk, 1993).

In his theory, Sloterdijk made an interpretation of luxury from the anthropological point of view (Elden, 2011), which is that the origin of human society is more conceptualized based on the pursuit of better individual/group existence. However, in his interpretation, he clearly explained the three characteristics of luxury: 1) desire (the pursuit of beauty and better); 2) culture and sociality; and 3) exclusivity (rarity).

In Chinese, the word "luxury" can be translated and understood as different parts of speech according to different contexts and situations, such as: luxury as positive vocabulary, representing exquisite and high-quality; luxury as negative vocabulary, representing excessive indulgence and material consumption. Relatively speaking, in terms of Luxury's understanding of these two, the word luxury has a more neutral meaning, and it reflects a special role and value in society, economy and culture. Of course, the understanding and cognition of luxury is definitely not a plane, but three-dimensional and multi-dimensional.

Let's understand our perception of luxury in a different way. Simply put, it may include our feelings about something (Berry, 1994). For example, when a person sees rosy clouds and the setting sun in a city that is often rainy or cloudy, it may make him or her feel that this matter is a luxury, but there is another condition here, that is, the person has aesthetic ability and can recognize the value of this matter. That is to say, if there is no awareness of scarcity (aesthetic appeal/culture) and reality (in a place where it often cloudy or rainy) as necessary conditions, then pure beauty cannot build luxury. This means that the inherent beauty of an event or thing is not enough to create a luxury perception (or deep impression) for an individual, unless the individual has accepted a certain culture and is made to be aware of the uniqueness and scarcity of things. Beauty, culture, and scarcity construct the perception of luxury. Obviously, the value cognition of scarcity has become the key, and it is also relatively subjective and private. However, this value recognition of scarcity (preciousness) is precisely created by culture, and is not necessarily directly related to material and money.

Obviously, the perception of luxury can be divided into two intersecting dimensions: a market-economy understanding and a social-culture understanding. From the perspective of market economy, luxury is mainly manifested in some explicit and established market mechanisms (Okonkwo, 2010), such as brand logos, websites, visual systems, social media, and so on. However, from the social-culture point of view, it is more manifested in some hidden cultural cognition and social relations, which usually create particularity (rarity) in different groups, social circles, classes, and social relations (Armitage, 2016). It is not difficult to understand that when we think of an item as a luxury, it is not only because of the scarcity in its material value, but also because of the scarcity of its hidden value at the social-cultural level (Adams, 2012). Therefore, the existence of luxury needs to have the factors of its market economy, and at the same time, it also needs to be able to show its cultural value and scarcity in social relations. The core of luxury is value and cognition of value. When an item is recognized as luxury, it will show its value, implying that it is more important than other things. On the other hand, luxury goods also reflect and promise the quality of things, which are not only exquisite craftsmanship and high quality, scarcity (unique/limited edition), and wonderfulness, but also accompanied by rich and colorful sensory and self-cognition experiences. The power of luxury can provide more and more efficient added value.

The relationship between fashion and luxury goods is ambiguous (Barthes, 2010). On the one hand, fashion and luxury goods are essentially opposite. Luxury is unique and exclusive, but fashion is popular and mass. It seems that luxury must deny fashion. On the other hand, the existence of fashion luxury goods is indeed the object of consumption "luxury." Consumption driven by fashion is essentially a materialization of the discourse power of capital in the market economy structure. Fashion is the repeated commercialization and materialization of culture by this discourse power in one stage. At the same time, as a primitive impulse, fashion pursues "popularization," which needs to be accepted by a group of people, so that an esoteric concept or way of life and behavior can be turned into a desirable commodity in society, and culture can be materialized and measured by the market (Kapferer, 2015).

Fashion needs to be recognized by the society before it can be pursued, while luxury goods must oppose this default recognition in principle. Luxury goods must remain mysterious to a certain extent in order to play their role as an elite cultural symbol. They must distinguish scarcity through a special way and method (Tungate, 2009). Because the higher the social exclusivity of any kind of products or services, the easier it is to be regarded as luxury, even if its cost is very low. It is for the same reason that the more fashionable a product or service is, the less it can be consumed as luxury, even if it is very expensive. While at the same time, once the elite cultural power of luxury goods is widely spread and consumed, the idea disappears—there is no further concept of a luxury good. However, within the capital economy, luxury goods must succumb to fashion before they can obtain sufficient profits. Therefore, a new fashion, or a new and more advanced luxury form (expression) of luxury goods, must appear, and fashion luxury is borne, a "scarce product" with a unique time cycle and market operation rhythm in a certain region (Calefato, 2012). Under such circumstances, contemporary art and design have become a bridge between fashion and luxury goods, constantly creating the appeal of fashion luxury goods to the market.

Design and Art Are the Driving Forces of Fashion Luxury Goods

"I love luxury. And luxury lies not in richness and ornateness but in the absence vulgarity. Vulgarity is the ugliest word in our language."

–Coco Chanel

In this sentence, Ms. Chanel implies the artistic quality driving forces the meaning of luxury rather than the others, and the core role of artistic design and taste in the construction of fashion luxury goods (Bourdieu, 2010). Economic and management scientists Chevalier and Mazzalova (2012) once proposed that the composition of fashion luxury goods must meet three standards. First, it must have strong artistic connotation and sophisticated design (Roberts, 2015);

1

2

1. *Portrait of Aldo Cipullo Photography © Manifesto*
2. *Bernstein's photograph of Aldo Cipullo's Love Bracelet at the Museum of Modern Art, New York City*

second, it must contain high-quality craftsmanship (handicraft or technology); and third, it must be recognized in the global context (internationalization). The connection between art design, craftsmanship, and luxury goods is not new, both of which require a high-level of skill, experience, and relatively expensive/rare materials (Adamson, 2013). Before the mid-20th century, consumption and use of luxury goods were regarded as symbols of material finance. However, with the development of science and technology and the influence of a globalized economy, the global middle class is increasing; more and more individuals have the ability to consume "luxury goods" that exceed their basic needs. Luxury goods are regarded more as the needs of improving personal quality of life and socialization of individuals.

The cross-border/cooperative design between modern and contemporary artists, avant-garde designers, and fashion luxury brands is nothing new (Silverstein, 2008). In the past ten years, it has reached an unprecedented level and continues to do so. There are some traditional fashion luxury brands that have brought opportunities for innovation and development because of such cooperation. For example, if Cartier did not cooperate with Italian jewellery designer Aldo Cipullo, perhaps Cartier really does not have much innovation in design (Chaille, 2019; Ricca, 2012). The jewellery series with Aldo Cipullo (see left) was adored by celebrities such as Princess Diana, the famous singer Frank Sinatra, and American movie star Angelina Jolie. In addition to the new peak of the brand's social influence, the selling price of Cartier's basic bracelet (4,450 pounds/about 43,000 RMB) has increased nearly tenfold (39,900 pounds/about 380,000 RMB), which has brought huge economic benefits to Cartier. There are also some fashion luxury brands that even identify this cooperation as one of the important cores of their own product innovation and strategic development. The short-term project cooperation mode continues to make their brands become the focus of media and society, and their products are constantly sought after (Dubois et al., 2005). Louis Vuitton and Jeff Koons, a famous American contemporary artist, launched a series of handbags in 2017. As one of the most respected figures in the contemporary art, Koons recreated the masterpieces of modern painting masters such as Da Vinci, Titian, Rubens, Fragonard, and van Gogh in many iconic handbag designs of Louis Vuitton. He also transformed the Louis Vuitton Monogram logo into its own initials. Each bag design is equipped with an inflatable rabbit shape (one of the classic symbols used by Koons in his artistic career for 40 years). To pay tribute to the classical masters, he also presented their life and portrait bronzing inside the bag. Louis Vuitton has many similar cooperation projects, such as graffiti design presented by Stephen Sprouse, a designer from New York in 2001, Murakami Takashi, a Japanese pop artist in 2003, Richard Prince, an American designer in 2008, Yayoi Kusama, a Japanese artist in 2012, Daniel Buren, a French contemporary artist in 2013, Frank Gehry, a famous American deconstructionist architecture master in 2014, and so on.

So, how does contemporary art and design catalyze fashion luxury goods? First of all, compared to traditional art forms, contemporary visual art, as a medium that can reach more and more places around the world, has the characteristics of more diversified value trends and the spread of globalization communication in its development. Contemporary art, like contemporary fashion, is becoming more and more non-exclusive and more and more easily seen by consumers. They have been well transformed and popularized through a large number of cultural institutions, such as the wide spread of museums, galleries, various media channels, avant-garde trends, and viewpoints in visual arts, or artists themselves (Berthon, 2009). The exposure and social influence of contemporary artists and designers have also gained unprecedented social attention, and contemporary art has become more "civilian." Secondly, from a material point of view, contemporary art, as a commodity, represents an absolute luxury. The actual purchase of contemporary art works is not regarded as a cultural product, but as capital and "special currency," which is extremely expensive and rare. The consumption of artworks far exceeds the purchasing power of the public. However, contemporary artists and designers have gained high recognition in the society, and the public is still eager to participate in that art world and to connect with their favorite artists and works in some way. Therefore, as a result, the time for the birth of "fashion luxury goods" appeared. With the cooperation with artists, luxury brands effectively transformed and attached their artistic views or ideas to their own luxury products through design. Art and design became the driving force for their product innovation and expanded its market audience, constantly innovating their products and always standing at the forefront of fashion, which is highly respected by the public (Giron, 2014). At the same time, due to the popularity of global cultural tourism in the post-industrial era, luxury brands can also build their own cultural and art institutions as platforms, such as the Fondazione Prada (Milan/Shanghai) and La Fondation

Louis Vuitton, Paris have created art museums under their own group, that is, collecting and displaying works of famous contemporary artists and designers to expand the added value of the brand culture, and using its own commodity visual language and promotion strategies to discover unique artists or enhance the reputation of cooperative artists (Mooij, 2014).

In addition to the cooperation between designers and artists as original creators and luxury brands to drive the fashion of luxury goods, many issues of contemporary design and art are also applied in the innovation process of luxury goods. For example, sustainable design is one of the most important topics in design theory, including sustainable material and energy design, product design, product service system design, distributed economy design, social innovation design, circular economy design, and so on. For example, in 2019, the Prada brand curated an exhibition called "Conceive a Sustainable World" in Shanghai Prada Rong Zhai , showing the public that the raw materials of its new products all come from the "re-nylon" produced by recycling waste such as "ghost fishing nets" in the ocean (see p. 26). Although nylon fabrics have always been the gene and symbol of the Prada brand, the pioneering fabric of "re-nylon" is completely recyclable and can be recycled indefinitely. Prada is expected to complete the whole transformation from pure nylon to recycled nylon by 2021. Here, sustainable design gives new fashion life to the series products of this classic brand.

Relationship between Fashion Design and Luxury

Throughout the development of society and the change of driving force for innovation, from being led by technology and driven by manufacturing in the middle of last century, to being market-oriented and brand-driven at the end of last century, in the 21st century, it is guided by the needs of society and individuals. Our life and society don't need more basic necessities, but need higher quality of life, service, content, products, collaborative creation, etc. Design has become a very important driving force for innovation at this stage. Design has more and more powerful values and functions than as tools for sales, technical optimization or industrial production. People can see this very clearly: the influence of design can effectively change personal ideas and social life, create not only economic or humanistic values, even update and promote

1

02

2

1/2. *Prada Bag made by ECONYL ® "re-nylon"*
   Photography © PRADA

the development model of society, or it can change the way of communication between society and human beings. Fashion design is based on the needs of current and future lifestyles.

Fashion and design are not only the driving forces of cultural and creative industries in economic growth. Meanwhile, fashion luxury goods also play the driving role in economic growth (ENCATC, 2014). Although in the current global turmoil, the stock market crash, regional economic slowdown, and global political instability are linked, the impact on the demand for luxury goods and consumption seems to be huge. But, the global luxury goods market is expected to reach 920 billion euros in 2018 and to exceed 1.3 trillion euros by 2025, including luxury experience (restaurants, hotels, cruises, resorts, wine and spirits, furniture, lighting, automobiles, ships, smartphones, and technology), the growth rate of which is 5%. The market value of personal fashion luxury goods exceeds 260 billion euros (*Bain's Annual Luxury Goods Worldwide Market Study'17th edition*), which is an increase of 6% over the previous year (D'Arpizio, 2018). It is estimated that by 2025, the growth rate will slow down to 3%~5% per year, reaching 320 to 365 billion euros. The economic growth rate of both sectors is higher than that of the global economy.

On the one hand, millennials and the post-'90s "Generation Z" occupy about 32% of the market share, and they are promoting the transformation and innovation of the entire luxury goods industry. It is estimated that by 2025 their consumption will account for 50%. Their understanding of life and self-awareness lead to very different expectations of luxury brands and products of these two groups from those of their predecessors. Millennials are looking for innovations in design and unique products that reflect their personality and values. Geographically, China is still the main force, accounting for 33% of the total market, and is expected to rise to 40% by 2025, accounting for 75% of the market growth from 2018 to 2025 (MFG, 2019). Therefore, the cooperation between the brand and the designer has become the key to new luxury goods.

On the other hand, according to the report "Value share of the global personal luxury goods market in 2019, by product category" (O'Connell, 2020), from the consumption category of global personal fashion luxury goods, clothing, and textiles accounted for 27%, perfume and cosmetics accounted for 22%, and jewellery and related fashion items (watches, shoes, and bags) accounted for 51%. However, in the study of fashion, the attention paid to the design and practice of jewellery and related items is very limited. Of course, it also shows its great research potential.

Conclusion

As the opening chapter of this book, this chapter discusses the role and development potential of contemporary design in the development of fashion luxury goods, and reflects the lack of design research on jewellery and fashion-related products in fashion research, especially when this theme is put into the context of contemporary luxury goods. Design is an expression of values and attitudes, and a tangible form of guiding the thoughts and desires of individuals and members of society. In the contemporary society, when science, technology, and craftsmanship reach a stage, whether products and services become luxurious or not, its quality, uniqueness, artistry, and rarity are all achieved through design. Luxury goods become luxurious because they are designed, not because they are luxury goods.

Reference

Armitage, J., and J. Roberts. 2016. *The Spirit of Luxury (Special Issue)*. *Cultural Politics* 12(1).

Adamson, G. 2013. *The Invention of Craft*. London: Bloomsbury Press.

Adams, W. H. 2012. *On Luxury*. Lincoln, NE: Potomac Books.

Bourdieu, P. 2010. *Distinction: A Social Critique of the Judgement of Taste*. London: Routledge.

Berthon, P., L. Pitt, M. Parent, J. P. Berthon. 2009. "Aesthetics and Ephemerality: Observing and Preserving the Luxury Brand." In *California Management Review*, 52.

Barthes, R. 2010. *The Fashion System*. London: Vintage Classics.

Berry, C. J. 1994. *The Idea of Luxury: A Conceptual and Historical Investigation (Ideas in Context)*. Cambridge: Cambridge University Press.

Chevalier, M., and G. Mazzalovo. 2012. *Luxury Brand Management: A World of Privilege*. Singapore: John Wiley and Sons.

Chaille, F., M. Spink, C. Vachaudez, T. Coudert, and V. Petit. 2019. *The Cartier Collection: Jewellery*. Paris: Flammarion.

Calefato, P. 2012. *Luxury: Fashion, Lifestyle, Excess*. L. Adarns (trans.). London: Bloomsbury.

D'Arpizio, C. 2019. *Luxury Goods Worldwide Market Study, Spring 2019*. www.bain.cn

Dubois, B., S.Czellar, and G. Laurent. 2005. "Consumer Segments Based on Attitudes towards Luxury: Empirical Evidence from Twenty Countries." In *Marketing Letters* 16: 115–28.

Elden, S. ed. 2011. "World, Engagement, Temperaments," In *Sloterdijk Now*. New York: Polity Press.

ENCATC. 2014. Paris. *European Cultural and Creative Luxury Industries: Key Drivers for European Jobs and Growth*. www.encatc.org. The European Cultural and Creative Industries Alliance (ECCIA), www.eccia.eu.

Giron, M. 2014. "Sustainable Luxury." In *Sustainable Luxury and Social Entrepreneurship*, edited by M. Gardetti and M. Giron, 2–21, Sheffield: Greenleaf.

Kapferer, J-N. 2015. *Kapferer on Luxury: How Luxury Brands Can Grow Yet Remain Rare*. London: Kogan Page.

Mooij, M. D. 2014. *Global Marketing and Advertising: Understanding Cultural Paradoxes*, 4th edition, Thousand Oaks. CA: Sage.

MFG (Matter of Form Group). 2019. *The Luxury Report: The State of the Industry in 2020 and Beyond*. https://matterofform.com/the-luxury-report

Okonkwo, U. 2010. *Luxury Online: Styles, Strategies, Systems*. London: Palgrave Macmillan.

O'Connell, L. 2020. *Value Share of the Global Personal Luxury Goods Market in 2019*, by Product Category. https://www.statista.com/statistics/245655/total-sales-of-the-luxury-goods-market-worldwide-by-product-category/

Roberts, J., and J. Armitage. 2015. "Luxury and Creativity: Exploration, Exploitation, or Preservation?" In *Technology Innovation Management Review*, 5(7):41–49.

Ricca, M., and R. Robins. 2012. *Meta-Luxury: Brands and the Culture of Excellence*. Basingstoke and New York: Palgrave Macmillan

Sloterdijk, P. 1993. *Weltfremdheit*. Frankfurt: Suhrkamp.

Silverstein, M. J., and N. Fiske. 2008. *Trading Up: Why Consumers Want New Luxury Goods and How Companies Create Them*. London: Penguin.

Tungate, M. 2009. *Luxury World: The Past, Present and Future of Luxury Brands*. London: Kogan Page.

CHAPTER

2

FUTURE & INSPIRATION
Design, Art,
Craftsmanship,
Material, and Culture

Introduction

Elizabeth FISCHER

Professor, Dean of Fashion and Jewellery Design, HEAD—Genève School of Art and Design, HES-SO Geneva, Switzerland

The essays in this chapter show how design in fashion and jewellery has opened new avenues, both in their respective fields but also through what could be called cross-pollination, with various types of interactions between the two domains. A telling example is given by Donatella Zappieri (jewellery business and creative consultant), who explains how Italian jewellery has come to play a defining role in trends and fashion since the 1980s. Guillermo Garcia-Badell (director of the fashion studies program at the Universidad Politecnica in Madrid) teaches students that design, in whatever field, is a holistic discipline, transcending boundaries and involving a mix of approaches, from the technical to the technological, from craft-based to concept-driven, combining both scientific and humanistic knowledge. Independent curator Nichka Marobin's compelling visual narrative on the affinities between objects of art, fashion, and jewellery offers a vivid testimony to the vitality that comes out of interconnecting disciplines. Naomi Filmer (designer and senior lecturer in the MA Fashion Artefact at London College of Fashion), supports students in pushing the boundaries of design and fashion to explore more deeply and dynamically the body as the site and means for confronting ideas of wearing and adorning, in an industry where art, craft, design, and performance overlap with each other. Questioning the designer's practice provides means to assess creative methods (Mala Simptani, visiting lecturer at London College of Fashion) to address pressing issues in sustainability (Volker Koch, director of product at Silent Goods) or to re-contextualize strong craft and design traditions in relation to new techniques and technologies (Yong-il Jeon, professor at Kookmin University in South Korea; Akio Sake, chief curator, Tokyo Metropolitan Teien Art Museum).

In this framework, identity and the body remain the core focus of fashion and jewellery. As indicated by Naomi Filmer, "accessories have evolved beyond adornment, and become key to expressing ways of thinking for design and living." The essay by Eelko Moorer (designer and head of the MA program in footwear at London College of Fashion) is a case in point, showing how the practice of footwear design can become a tool for critical thinking in design. The way fashion and accessories situate the body and the individual in society are evoked in history by Emily Hammen (lecturer at Institut Français de la Mode Paris), Paula Rabinowitz (emerita professor at University of Minnesota), and Cristina Giorcelli (professor, University of Rome III). These three essays show the power of fashion and accessories in daily life through their symbolic meanings in literature, film, and other iconography. Finally, Christine Lüdeke (designer, professor at Pforzheim University) explains "how the making and wearing of jewellery, accessories, and fashion provide amplifications of the body and of the self—whether physical or immaterial: the body provides the context, the body is the context."

As the body is central to jewellery and fashion, the context, we need to know what body we are referring to today. Before coming to this point, I will provide a brief overview of the historic relationships between fashion and jewellery in relation to the body, as primary objects of material culture and of our symbolic system. "Diamonds are forever" and "Fashion is fickle," if we are to believe those two sayings, which refer to the realm of luxury, jewellery, and fashion, stand worlds apart. Mainstream jewellery and fashion, however, share a lot in common as products that human beings use on a daily basis. Clothing, accessories, and jewellery are situated on the human body and in direct contact with it. Furthermore, all of them provide some functional or communicative extension to the body. In this way, they constitute our contemporary daily equipment (Farren and Hutchinson, 2004), the things we cannot live without to be able to function in society. These intensely personal items act as a primary means to express at once individual and social identity and to perform our daily tasks.

Initially, the importance that jewellery and accessories have acquired during the 20th century is due to the fact that Western mainstream daily dress progressively boiled down to variations of the uniform of blouse, shirt, or T-shirt paired with trousers, in a restricted range of colors: black, blue, gray, and white, worn in Western culture by both men and women. The feminine wardrobe includes the by now compulsory LBD or little black dress, worn in formal and informal occasions, easy to dress up or down, as introduced by Gabrielle Chanel in 1926. Hence, accessories and jewellery have become distinguishing elements of a person's attire and, by extension, social identity. They have become contemporary conversation pieces through social media, with people flaunting what they buy and wear on the web.

For the last 30 years accessories have brought in the most income for high and low brands. In the hierarchical relationship between clothing, considered essential, and accessories, considered secondary, sales have tipped in favor of accessories. Jewellery is now in the fore, indispensable in the performance of fashion on the catwalk and in the street (Evans, 2007, 231–33; Brand and Teunissen, 2007; Fischer, 2013). By means of aggressive marketing, jewellery and accessories have become a way of expanding a brand's message, sold to the audience as coveted "must haves."

The technological developments ushered in by the 21st century have had a major impact on the role of accessories. Wearables and connected items (mobile phone, headphones, iPods, computers, digital tablets, and so forth) have become indispensable equipment for the contemporary "supermodern" human being in an era of connected flows, speed, permanent mobility and an overabundance of information (Augé, 1995, 35–36; Bolton A., 2002, 7). Younger and older generations have wholeheartedly adopted the culture of equipment in dress with accessories and wearables. Mobile devices are kept permanently close at hand as an extension of their owner's identity. They are the depository of our social selves, harbouring all our contacts, pictures, messages, and personal timelines. The day's outfit comes with the universal 21st-century necklace, i.e., fine white cables that link earpieces to portable electronic products. Engineers at Logitech, a Swiss company specialized in state-of-the art computer peripherals, have found that today's challenge is to accessorize the person rather than the wearables[1]. The focus has therefore shifted to the wearable as part of fashionable equipment, while the necessary engineering, functionality, and ergonomics, indispensable to this type of product, remain in the background. The same process that transformed eyeglasses from medical necessity to fashion accessory is at play. This revolution has come about through embracing the design culture of the fashion industry (Pullin, 2009).

Thus, in contemporary fashion, accessories and jewellery are not mere adornments of clothing and/or the body, rather they have become the most necessary items of human beings' daily equipment. As C. Giorcelli has noted, Derrida's view on the necessity of the ornament with respect to what it supplements offers a fruitful interpretation of the role played by accessories in contemporary dress and for individuals today, as an artifact that fills in a lack, enabling an entity to become truly complete (Giorcelli, 2011).

A parergon comes against, beside, and in addition to the ergon, the work done (fait), the fact (le fait), the work, but it does not fall to one side, it touches and cooperates within the operation, from a certain outside. Neither simply outside nor simply inside. Like an accessory that one is obliged to welcome on the border, on board (au bord, à bord). ...The parergon inscribes something which comes as an extra, exterior to the proper field...but whose transcendent exteriority comes to play, abut onto, brush against, rub, press against the limit itself and intervene in the inside only to the extent that it is lacking from itself (Derrida, 1987, 53–56).

Derrida derived his notion of paragon and ergon from Kant's *Critique of Judgement* in which Kant discusses, among other things, picture frames and the dress of Greek statues as examples of parergon. For Kant the picture (the ergon, the work) becomes a picture only once

---

1. Conversation with Jean-Michel Chardon, engineer in product development and technology strategy at Logitech, 2016.

it is framed (the frame as parergon), just as the Greek statue (ergon) needs drapery (parergon) to be perceived as a statue. In this way the parergon has a definite impact on the existence of the ergon as a whole. "In other words, although an accessory, the parergon influences the ergon. What is more, for the parergon to exist, the ergon must lack something. Neither inside nor outside, neither superfluous nor necessary, the accessory is thus almost indispensable" (Giorcelli, 2011) for contemporary individuals' performance in society.

What is the contemporary individual lacking today, how is it incomplete? Human beings evolved as permanent bipeds, with the result that our feet and hands acquired different functions: our feet provide stability and locomotion, while our hands have specialized in the playful and practical manipulation of materials and tools (Warnier, 1999). One can argue that the need for equipment (i.e., any object/tool required by an individual for a specific activity) arose from this unique evolution. From very early on, human beings resorted to artifacts as means of agency in their daily life.

In the supermodern context ushered in by the end of the 20th century, dominated by a fascination for performance and connected technology, our bodies are perceived as inadequate. They need to be enhanced so we can live longer, so that signs and effects of aging or sickness are counteracted. The ethics of sports competitions now dominate leisure activities: sportswear is devised to enhance athletic performances, while functional clothing designed for outer wear is modelled on the extreme conditions of scientific expeditions to the Artic or to the desert, to the marine abysses or to outer space. New accessories are needed to help face global warming and pandemics, from fans, hats, masks, and other protective wear, to electronic devices constantly monitoring our health and whereabouts. Designers today work with this inadequate body as the norm, a body that has to negotiate the transitional spaces of worldwide urban life, spanning numerous time zones. They are required to create:

practical, functional clothing...[which] facilitates bodily movement, provides shelter against the inclemency of the weather as well as against noise and pollution from traffic, affords physical protection against street crime and psychological protection against the gaze of passers-by and the neutered gaze of the surveillance camera. Designers of supermodern clothing look to high-performance sportswear and military dress to achieve these functions. They also incorporate wearable electronics. Supermodern clothing promotes the idea that we can anticipate all contingencies, that our clothes can be complete and completely functional (Bolton, 2002, 7).

We have come a long way from the biped using artifacts for our daily activities. With connected electronic device and wearables, our selves have become ubiquitous, our body remaining in one place while our mind is transported elsewhere by the miracle of technology. We can interact with someone at the other end of the world while remaining seated on our office chair or on living room sofa. We seem to live in the age of speed: speed of information, speed of travel. However, we paradoxically spend most of our time in a seated position. We have in effect become sedentary beings more than ever before, our minds disconnected from the body. Furthermore, our fashion culture imposes an idealized and increasingly disembodied vision of the self, fragmented among the myriad of screens that surround us. Though a large part of our world now occupies an immaterial dimension, we are still material girls and boys. Personal equipment has become essential in order to overcome our bodily failings. We still depend on the material and design culture of accessories, which are primarily situated on our body, to provide us with the agency we need both in the real and virtual dimensions of our existence.

Reference

Augé, M. 1995. *Non-Places: Introduction to an Anthropology of Supermodernity*. London: Verso.

Bolton, A. 2002. *The Supermodern Wardrobe*. London: V&A Publications.

Brand, J., and J. Teunissen. 2007. *Fashion & Accessories*. Arnhem: ArtEZ-Press.

Derrida, J. 1987. *The Truth In Painting*. Translated by Geoff Bennington and Ian McLeod. Chicaago: University of Chicago Press.

Evans, C. 2007. *Fashion at the Edge: Spectacle, Modernity, and Deathliness*, 2nd ed. New Haven, CT and London: Yale University Press.

Farren, A., and A. Hutchinson. 2004. "Cyborgs, New Technology and the Body: The Changing Nature of Garments." In *Fashion Theory*, 8(4): 464.

Fischer, E. 2013. "The Accessorized Ape." In *Contemporary Jewellery in Perspective*, edited by D. Skinner, 202–08. New York: Lark Books.

Giorcelli, C. 2011. "Accessorizing the Modern(ist) Body." In *Accessorizing the Body, Habits of Being I*, edited by Christina Giorcelli and Paula Rabinowitz, 3-4. Minneapolis and London: University of Minnesota Press.

Pullin, G. 2009. *Design Meets Disability*. Cambridge: MIT Press.

Warnier, Jean-Pierre. 1999. *Construire la culture matérielle: L'homme qui pensait avec ses doigts*. Paris: PUF.

Jewellery and Fashion

Their Intrinsic Bond through Art, Design, and Savoir-faire

Donatella ZAPPOERI

Jewellery and Luxury Goods Strategic Consultant, Italy

The Role of Jewellery in Fashion

Historically, jewellery was a symbol of wealth and adornment. Currently in society, its scope has widened, becoming a means of self-expression—a symbolic identifier— embodying various meanings in addition to being subject to multiple interpretations.

Today, the very concept of jewellery has transcended semantic barriers: jewellery is an ornament to wear, to appreciate, to treasure, and to adore, regardless of the value of its material content.

This multiplicity inherent to jewellery has been rendered possible not only due to social shifts in modern culture, but also because of innovations in materials and technological expertise. This allows for a sophisticated form of creativity and a pure homage to aesthetics.

Jewellery holds an important role in the fashion universe and I would like to bring you through an overview on the different trends that mainly originated in Italy starting from the '80s until nowadays and that influenced the international scenario.

All these trends originated thanks to specific socio-cultural changes in lifestyle, habits and mannerisms, and were supported by the capability of skilled artisans and jewellery makers who were able to interpret these concepts and give life to beautiful pieces of jewellery that went on to influence the international market.

The Italian territory boasts a manufacturing tradition of invaluable strength and capacity of skilled work, nurturing a strong and solid relationship between the designer and the product developer throughout the entire production process. There are five important jewellery districts, each specializing in specific production techniques. They are specifically, Valenza, Arezzo, Firenze, Vicenza and Naples.

From Benvenuto Cellini's invention of a lost wax technique in the first half of the 1500s until today, modern production keeps the sophisticated and ancient methods alive, coupling them with state-of-the-art technologies that allow a perfect representation of the design.

These techniques do not impact the pureness of the design process. Instead, they are a vital expression of the aesthetics the designer wishes to impart. This is the strength of "Made in Italy" jewellery: a perfect alchemy between the idea and the making, re-establishing the perfect bond between ideator and manufacturer.

'80s General Scenario

Trends '80s

From a social-cultural perspective, the '80s represented the "gimme" decade[1], a time of over-the-top abundance without restraint. Those who were "in" worked 12 hours a day and to build a career, for which they needed the right look to be "dressed for success." This was the decade that introduced the term "Yuppies," and the years defined by power dressing seen on TV in *Dallas and Dynasty.*

Fashion designers like Giorgio Armani gained tremendous popularity by creating a new look for the career woman, taking cues from the men's wardrobes to present a new interpretation of the classic suit, with high necklines and pronounced shoulders. Jean Paul Gautier earned fame for dressing femme fatale Madonna for her worldwide tour and Asian designers such as Issey Miyake, Yohji Yamamoto, and Rei Kawakubo became world-known.

Romeo Gigli showed an extremely poetic take on fashion, Gianfranco Ferré began to work for French couturier Dior, and another Italian, Moschino, stood out for his irreverence toward trends and above all his mockery of the big brands.

---

1. ABBA "Gimme! Gimme! Gimme! (A Man After Midnight), 1979.

1984/1989 The Gold Fever and the "Feminine Revolution"

Modern jewellery had evolved from a traditional concept of fine jewellery using stones into a new industrial era employing technologies drawn from the creative work of goldsmiths, opening up new horizons for chain manufacturing. An emblem of this decade was the Papillon Necklace by Carlo Weingrill, which perfectly interpreted the tradition and dedication involved in jewellery making. This piece denotes refined techniques in its gold work and pays homage to years of industrial evolution, bringing innovation to the product as well as the process.

1   2   3

1. De Lazzari—photography from the original marketing campaign
2. Pasquale Bruni—photography from the original advertising campaign
3. Chiampesan—the original advertising campaign

During the '80s, Italian manufacturers used a careful production process for creating pure gold jewellery. Gold chains, both basic and industrial, were reproduced in refined and sinuous forms. The concept of the classic chain was distorted, enhancing jewellery with warm and sensual dimensions, yet in reasonable, wearable weights.

This renaissance of goldsmith-inspired jewellery was carried out with the technical support of machines for producing gold chains, in combination with skilful designs that expressed deep research and individual style. This period was defined by both product innovation as well as the innovation of manufacturing.

During those years, Pomellato launched the "Rondelle (washers) necklace" wherein circular elements moved freely amongst one another, creating a "harnessed" motion effect. The array of chains and mesh utilizing new techniques offered some very interesting, distinguishable lines, such as the pure, simple tubular chain in gold and gourmette characteristic of the company Carlo Weingrill, or the work of Chiampesan.

1

042

2

3

1. Pomellato "Rondelle" necklace made of gold and
   featuring the characteristic hidden clasp
2. Roberto Coin—the typical drawn tubing
3. Parure by Buccellati
4. Flat, tubular necklace available in the three colours
   of gold by Carlo Weingrill

4

Collections by Roberto Coin were distinctive for its twisted wire. The signature "tubogas" proposed by Bulgari was further evolved and presented by Carlo Weingrill. De Lazzari, thanks to a strong marketing campaign, reinforced this concept of the new wave of gold jewellery by launching its "Oro Addosso" line and campaign which immediately experienced strong recognition and visibility. The horizons of simple gold jewellery thus evolved into an extremely innovative play of colors and combinations of materials.

'90s General Scenario

Trends '90s

The '90s were marked by the return of minimalism as a response to the excess of the glamorous '80s. A desire for security, truth, and new values gained ground. Major global events such as the Persian Gulf War halted consumption, and people began to understand that the wild, golden '80s had foreshadowed a period of restraint. Consumption decreased, unemployment rate reached a record high, and a trade crisis spread throughout the world: the '90s were the new '20s. The motto "less is more" was widely popularized. American designers such as Ralph Lauren, Calvin Klein and Donna Karan became well-known for their minimalistic and clean-lined fashion, celebrating a style rooted in sensuality and simplicity. In 1992, Karl Lagerfeld declared to magazine *Contemporaine* that "the real luxury lies in the lining," a clue that behind the simplicity hides an understated richness.

In the second half of the decade, fashion's iconic top models reigned supreme: sexy, fun-loving, and spirited muses of their time, they conveyed desire and joie di vivre. Gianni Versace was the first designer who realized their power: animating his catwalks with only the top models declared a return to celebrating glamour and sensuality, personifying it though the beauty of these catwalk stars.

1990/1994 Jewellery is Contrasting the "Less is More" in Fashion

During the early '90s, jewellery brands felt the need to create new forms in an effort to further enhance their identity. Designers presented elegant gestural expressiveness, offering new ways to wear a classic ring in the hope of creating future iconic symbolism. The Mille Fedi ring by Pomellato was the perfect incarnation of the aesthetic philosophy of time: precious materials and a bold design manifested in an unparalleled piece of jewellery.

Thanks to its movement, this ring is extremely playful, as the careful threading of multiple rings creates a fascinating volume. The stylistic evolution of those years also leads to new experiments in stone cutting, both precious and semi-precious, which have become inseparable companions of gold jewellery production.

During that time, Pomellato launched its Byzantium line and later Mosaic line, wherein cabochon cut semi-precious stones were set with claws of generous dimensions, perhaps as a challenge against the canons of traditional jewellery. Henceforth a great success, these lines created and influenced a new concept of combining gold jewellery and stones.

Color inspires the design aesthetics during those years. It was precisely the pursuit of new chromatic interpretations that gave birth to Nouvelle Bague, a Florentine company noted for bringing back the use of a cold enamel technique initiated by its own research, pushing the company to invent new forms of expression, accompanied by a message of delicate transgression.

1995/1999 Platinum, a New Challenge and the Minimal Looks

Platinum, the world's most precious metal due to its inalterable resistance and difficulty to manipulate, became a new challenge and the latest style application of second half of the 1990s. Many companies joined the trend and began working with this challenging metal to create new shapes, new hues, and intangible refinement. The "Luci e Ombre" set created by Aldo Arata, founder of Monile, won the International Press Award in 1996. The set was comprised of a string of modules in techno-silk and polished platinum, each embedded a diamond, forming an ellipse.

1

2

3

4

5

1. *Mille Fedi Ring by Pomellato*
2. *Indian Collection by Nouvelle Bague*
3. *Metropolitan Collection by Nouvelle Bague*
4. *Cross by Pomellato, Bisanzio collection, gold and garnets*
5. *Pomellato—"Mosaico" earrings in yellow gold and tourmaline in "cabochon" cut*

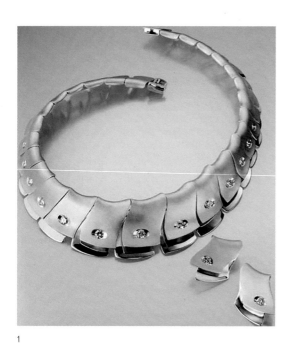

1. *"Luci e Ombre" set Aldo Arata*
2. *Recarlo—choker*
3. *Pomellato DoDo—Lucky Charm*
4. *Flli Menegatti Sterling Silver and Enamel Statement Rings*
5. *Flli Menegatti Solid 925 Sterling Silver*

1

2

3

4

5

The popularity of this "white" metal also sparked interesting developments for jewellery in 925 sterling silver. In fact, silver has enormous cosmetic potential, with fewer weight constraints compared to gold and offers more room for creativity due to its lower price. Fratelli Menegatti created new collections using silver that played with volumes and challenged new boundaries of shape.

The end of the 1990s also marked a moment of reaction to and objection of the extreme opulence of fashion jewellery in the past. Word spread about minimalism in fashion and accessories and designers followed. Recarlo's choker necklace was the essence of elegant simplicity: a semi-rigid cable with a row of sparkling diamonds. This minimal trend further manifested itself with the launch of the DODO line by Pomellato, consisting of small pendants in a single gram of gold with an added value: a message. Cute Adornments also included collectable cute baby animal charms as well as 925 silver pendants in new proportions and surface treatments.

New Millennium General Scenario

Trends in the
New Millennium

The world rejoiced at the start of the new millennium for the fact that the Y2K "bug" did not destroy the planet. However, the 2001 terrorist attack on the Twin Towers and Pentagon sent shock waves throughout the world, leaving permanent scars on a generation and inviting a series of global terrorist attacks that persisted into current times. Combined troops invaded Iraq, commencing

Brooch Caterpillar by The House of Vhernier

the first stage of the Iraq War. In addition, the worst global financial crisis since the Great Depression impacted nearly every country and thrust the world economy into decline.

When Barak Obama became the first African American President in U.S. history, it re-opened the dialogue about racial equality, and soon gender equality followed: the LGBT movement gained strength as members and supporters of the community demanded the right to marriage and non-discrimination.

The cultural icons of this decade were four independent single women: the glamourous, passionate fashionistas on *Sex & The City* who taught a generation of women to revel in life even without a partner. Careful wardrobe placement played an important role in raising awareness about high fashion in the everyday lives of modern women and promoted many brands that continued to dominate customer mindshare, from magazines to catwalks, and on TV screens and beyond. While the film *The Devil Wears Prada* revealed both the attractive and the dark sides of the fashion industry, it further emphasised the importance of the sector and the power that magazine editors had at that time.

2000/2004 The Soft Stone Surface

During the early years of the new millennium, jewellery became more sculptural, while settings were extremely refined, as if stones were suspended airlessly without any metal framework. An iconic piece from that time is the Caterpillar Brooch in white gold, diamonds, mother-of-pearl, and rock crystal by Vhernier.

An inarguable work of art, this piece was the result of laborious, meticulous goldsmithing techniques. Thanks to this method, the stone, carved from a single piece, created a smooth, transparent color effect and undulating shape that lend volume and radiance to the brooch.

However, the new century ushered in radical changes as consumers gradually shifted their perception and approach to jewellery: instead of shopping for

1

2

050

3

4

5

1. Chantecler's Necklace from the Fireworks Collection

2. Iconic Pomellato Nudo, 2001

3. Fantasia Collection by Roberto Coin

4. The First Collections by Franco Pianegonda-made of 925 silver and semi—precious stones

5. Collection of Animalier brooches by The House of Vhernier—each carved from a single ston

timeless pieces, customers desired accessories in the name of self-expression, that enhanced their personality and fashion look. With the launch of Franco Pianegonda's first creations in 925 sterling silver, the artist strongly and dramatically revolutionized the concept of jewellery. "We produce philosophy," Franco enjoys saying, when asked about the essence of the collection.

The years 2001 and 2002 welcomed an array of new hues and introduced a style of using colored stone pavé that referenced the work of Fauvist painters of the beginning of the previous century. Chantecler presented the Fireworks collection and Roberto Coin the Fantasia collection. The house of Vhernier innovated stone cutting and introduced a collection of curvy and voluptuous animals, carved entirely in stone. The main trend at that time was a great chromatic creativity, and furthermore, a huge push in research and new technologies.

2005/2009 Be Jewelled

From 2005 to 2009, jewellery flirted with fashion. Full of good humor, jewellery emerged as a stand-out with a special twist in new plating hues, like rose gold, and pushed boundaries of bold color combinations of stones. Shapes became softer, chains turned thin, briolette-cut stones were reintroduced, and gems were often attached on one side only, sometimes on a metal mesh to allow for fluidity. Along this new path, jewellery became less rigid and more adaptable to the movement of the body.

Exclusive techniques passed down from the previous generation were also implemented, such as the burin technique, and the "guitar string" technique. Ancient methods found a contemporary home in Marco Bicego's creations. Shapes and styles winked at the fashion world, almost as if they wanted to break through the invisible wall that divided the two categories in order to create new combinations and wear-ability.

The iconic bracelet from the Siviglia collection by Marco Bicego embodies all these elements. The brand prides itself on the "Made in Italy" concept, creating precious jewellery that is tangibly lightweight and soft-hued, with elegantly

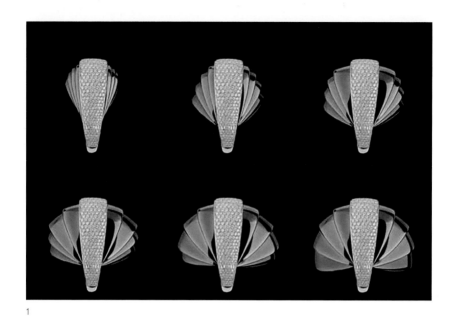

1

2

3

4

5

1. The Armadillo Bracelet by Mattia Cielo
2/3. The Timeless "Paradise" by Marco Bicego
4.Bracelet from the Siviglia Collection by Marco Bicego
5. Pasquale Bruni's Ghirlanda Necklace

cut semi-precious stones. Following tradition, the brand employs a technique that dates back to the early fifteenth century, a derivative of methods used by goldsmiths during the Middle Ages.

Metal processing during this decade underwent a further stylistic leap where surfaces were "treated" using new techniques in order to give metals a more textural, detailed appearance. Working with new technologies in metal, Mattia Cielo launched collections Bruco (Caterpillar) and Armadillo. Both collections featured a "spring" within each piece that played on ergonomics: the jewellery pieces changed and mutated with movement.

The logical evolution of this trend in research, innovation, and technology was the introduction on the jewellery scene of materials formerly used only in other sectors, such as ebony in the Calla necklace by Vhernier and Victoria by Pomellato or jet (lignite) in the Tango collection by Pomellato. These "new" materials were the early signs of a shifted path for the jewellery industry in the years that followed.

1

2

3

4

1/2. Tango Collection by Pomelatto
3. The Calla—necklace made of ebony and gold by Vhernier
4. Pomellato—the Victoria necklace featuring ebony

Current Decade General Scenario

Trends in current decade

The current decade opened with the Arab Spring, a series of anti-government protests and aggression across the Middle East and North Africa in 2010, eventually leading to terrorist attacks and demonstrations around Europe, marking a time of uncertainty and economic turmoil.

In the U.S.A., a great political shift disrupted the country when Donald Trump was elected president, as his governing philosophy "America First" is in sharp contrast to the goals of the World Economic Forum. China's increasing economic prosperity and enormous consumer market dominates in retail, and the wealthy Chinese population continues to migrate globally.

A technology-immersed generation of consumers now moves seamlessly from the real world to the virtual one, as AR and VR permeate all spheres of contemporary society. The internet is king, and online shopping is increasing. Fast fashion companies urge customers to buy continuously, yet it is met with global awareness of environmental destruction (with China in on the environmental clean-up), as brands emphasize transparency, sustainability, and circular production.

The world is becoming more globally connected as countries and consumers once distant are now united by shared social media platforms and online shopping, opening emerging customer markets.

Outspoken, liberated young Muslim women—"M Generation"—are raising their voices for equality and with it, bringing financial buying power as well as their customs and taste. Despite continuing global racism against Muslims and immigrants, fashion is now becoming more inclusive (plus-sized and disabled models have campaigned tirelessly for their place in the industry). For the first time in the history of the catwalks, Anniesa Hasibuan hosted an all-hijab catwalk show last year, one more example of how fashion mirrors modern cultural shifts.

2010/2018 New Horizons for Design

When Ghiaccio, the titanium bracelet by Mattia Cielo, won the Best Diamond Jewel at the Couture Design Awards in Las Vegas in 2010, it marked a moment when technology, new discoveries, and innovation merged to create unique shapes and a refreshed way of looking at jewellery.

The Ghiaccio bracelet was made in laser-cut titanium using a special cold fusion process, with the central element showcasing pavé diamonds. The use of titanium—renowned for its application in aerospace and car technology—combined the possibility of eccentric shape with the comfort of lightness. The concept of contemporary luxury inherent in all of Mattia Cielo's collections is exhibited in the object's ability to become an expression of the wearer's body and personality and not in terms of the quantity of precious materials whithin.

This current decade holds a great deal yet to discover. In terms of trends, it is a contrasting period, following the lines of personal of taste rather than general consensus. Numerous offerings embrace the various stages of a woman's life, aligning the stylistic choices with lifestyle and apparel.

There is certainly a return to romanticism, filled with florals, fruit, and the "animalier" concept, yet in a very soft interpretation. Elements of each piece are small, rich in detail, with sophisticated workmanship.

Where white pavé is showcased, the dimensions are generous and reference classic motifs, as in the pavé cross by Recarlo. Weights are re-thought and hollow workings dominate in order to restore lightness as well as reconcile for the increased value of gold, now at a historically high price. Damiani launched

1

2

3

4

1. Titanium bracelet Ghiaccio by Mattia Cielo
2. Damiani-s necklaces from the Damianissima Collection
3. Gold Earrings with a Perforated Logo by Chantecler
4.The Lucrezia Cross Made of White Gold and Diamonds by Recarlo

the Damianissima collection dedicated to celebrating the Maison's logo in celebration of its 90th anniversary. Chantecler offers a range of iconic earrings with perforated lettering, synonymous with elegance and sophistication.

One challenge was the achievement of movement within a jewellery piece, and the line Rugiada by Mattia Cielo sets the standard for this artistic approach. Starting in 2009, a climate of stylistic contrasts emerges, ever stronger. Bold transgression and the return of aggressive forms, rock influences seem to celebrate the style of the warrior woman in society, fashion magazines, and on the catwalks. In a more transgressive trend, Repossi launches the Berbère collection of phalange rings and piercings.

Roberto Coin, in other-worldly opulence, designs a line of rings and bracelets of generous forms in the "animalier" theme, studded with precious stones.

The recent years welcome the emergence of new designers with an energy of innovation, using technology and avant-garde research within a philosophy of hybridisation—the mixture of irregular and geometric, artificial and genuine, real and virtual—which is changing the very essence of jewellery today.

Modern jewellery can be conceived with advanced of artisanal technologies, with traditional or hyper-technological raw materials, either expensive or low cost, with unique and increasingly surprising results. For example, Paola Volpi's work uses galvanic electroforming to design one-of-a-kind jewellery pieces. "The fascination that traditional jewellers had with precious stones, she has with trying out new industrial materials. 'Going to an electric cable producer,' she says, 'is a marvellous experience for me.' In addition to transformation, representative of her vocational ethics, she has an approach based solidly in arts and culture, especially the Arte Povera movement, and an almost magical manual capacity."[2] Manuganda's creations are fully achieved thanks to 3D technology, laser sintering, and manual finishing. The artist uses alternative materials such as rubber, stainless steel, titanium and nylon in an eclectic path toward unconventional jewellery. Her collections are explorations of shape and are distinguished for their contemporary style and polished combination of materials.

2. Cristina Morozzi for Interni

1

2

3

1. Lion Limited Edition Ring by Roberto Coin
2. Roberto Coin's Scorpione Bracelets
3. Berbère Collection by Repossi
4.Rugiada Collection by Mattia Cielo

4

1

2

3

1. *Fiamma Collection by Manuganda—a gold or silver ring with pearl that resembles a hug*
2. *Manuganda Contemporary Treasure# Tube collection*
3. *Paola Volpi's Wind Collection Created in 3D Printing*
4. *Collection Sponges by Paola Volpi—obtained through galvanic electroforming*

4

1

2

1/2. Jewelshape

Jewelshape was born from the common goal of founding designers Olimpia Aveta and Beatriz Biagi, to advance jewellery-making and bring it further into the contemporary.

A customizable design, based on their study of wearable shapes, offers the vast potential of a new wave of craftsmanship that combines manufacturing traditions with avant-garde digital technologies. The pieces are mainly created from metal and nylon components: silver galvanised with contrasting colors or sintered nylon decorated with customisable prints.

Jewellery has always been at the crucial crossroad point between art, design, fashion, and manufacturing technology. On the one hand, it is an art with its majestic transcendence, on the other hand, it is a form of fashion with the ever-changing flow of seasonality. The panorama of jewellery finds novelty and strength in its capacity to challenge material concepts and to adopt new technology. As Roland Barthes stated about fashion jewellery: "It doesn't share the power of gold anymore" (Barthes, 2006, "Chapter 5"). Further enhancing the appeal of jewellery creation is the intriguing fact that most of the workmanship of its beautiful pieces originates in ancient techniques and skilled hand craftsmanship.

Jewellery has always evolved hand-in-hand with apparel trends specific to each era. It plays an increasingly important role in the fashion landscape as an economic growth factor and a vehicle of brand identity. No longer a mere accessory, jewellery carries its own weight and lives in symbiotic bond with contemporary fashion.

Reference

Bain & Company. 2018. *Worldwide Luxury Market Monitor*. Milan: Fondazione Altagamma.

Barthes, R. 2006. *The Language of Fashion*, 1st ed. New York and Oxford: Berg Publishers.

From Architecture to Fashion...
Design Is All about Ideas

Guillermo GARCIA-BADELL

*Professor, Dean of Centro Superior de Diseño de Moda de Madrid(CSDMM-UPM),
Universidad Politécnica de Madrid*

Mercedes RODRIGUEZ

*Academic Vice-Dean of CSDMM-UPM, Universidad Politécnica de Madrid,
Universidad Politécnica de Madrid*

We are used to distinguishing different disciplines of design (industrial design, architecture, object design, jewellery design, fashion design) as we distinguish periods of art (gothic, renaissance, baroque, classic, modern). Moreover, we are used to distinguishing conceptual and figurative art at the time that we confuse craft and design. The main objective of this paper is to clarify how important concepts and ideas are in any form of creative activity and to explain the difference between crafters and designers. Actually, designers work not only with technique issues, but with conceptual expositions (which leads to innovation). In that sense, the Centro Superior de Diseño de Moda de Madrid (CSDMM-UPM)—the fashion center of the Universidad Politécnica de Madrid—tries to teach their students to focus on design as a holistic discipline, which requires technical, technological, scientific, and a humanistic approach.

63

Introduction

In conceptual art the idea or concept is the most important aspect of the work. When an artist uses a conceptual form of art, it means that all of the planning and decisions are made beforehand and the execution is a perfunctory affair. The idea becomes a machine that makes the art.

According to this definition from Wikipedia, it is only in "conceptual art" where ideas are the prominent element of the piece of art. However, even in the most primitive forms of art, when our antecessor started drawing in the caverns, the idea of communicating thoughts was more important even than the result itself.

It is, therefore, the purpose of this paper to explain how important ideas are in any kind of creative discipline in order to explain some of the present works carried out in the Centro Superior de Diseño de Moda of the Universidad Politécnica de Madrid (CSDMM-UPM) as an example of how concepts can lead design process and its communication and exhibition. Therefore, in this paper we will start reviewing some classic references about the process of art in order to show the importance of concepts, ideas, and innovation in design. Finally, some examples of student work will illustrate how this postulate can help creative teaching and learning.

Does "Non-conceptual" Art Ever Exist?

It is easy to identify concepts in the contemporary forms of art. Thinking about some of the better-known artists today, they always focus on the ideas that are behind each piece. Damin Hirst, for example, links his work to the concept of life and death, and how human beings face it. Hirst titled one of his most famous pieces, "The Physical Impossibility of Death in the Mind of Someone Living" (1991), which consists of a tiger shark preserved in formaldehyde in a vitrine. Later, in 2007, he created "For the love of God" (see right), a sculpture consisting of a platinum cast of an 18th-century human skull encrusted with 8,601 flawless diamonds. And recently he inaugurated "The Miraculous Journey," 14 bronze sculptures that depict in vivid detail the gestation period, ending with a newborn.

Looking back at art history, we should quote "When Attitudes Become Form," the exhibition organized by Harald Szeemann in 1969 at the Kunsthalle Bern. Forms issue was definitely overcome, then concepts and attitudes started being more explicit in any form of art. However, any previous form of art did not lack for a conceptual background either. In that sense, Kandinsky (1912) pointed out that art pieces should be understood connected to the period when they were conceived. "Every work of art is the child of its age and, in many cases, the mother of our emotions." Moreover, according to Kandinsky, art is always linked to a specific sensibility, to some "internal truths" that depends on the artist and his context. "Like ourselves, these artists sought to express in their work only internal truths, renouncing in consequence all consideration of external form."

Kandinsky realized already in this treaty "Concerning the Spiritual in Art," that there is something above forms, something that he calls "spiritual," something conceptual. From there, we can try to analyze art looking to these concepts behind the pieces more than looking to the meaning of the scene itself: the problem is definitely more abstract than figurative.

Moreover, we can find similarities and differences, not only according to formal aspects, but especially regarding the ideas that led artists of different historic periods. For example, when in the Renaissance we finally dominated space with drawing techniques, the perfection of the perspective was secondary face to the importance of transmitting the idea of the perfection of human beings, created by God as an image of himself. In that sense, Kandinsky distinguish between "melodic compositions" and "symphonic composition." A melodic composition seems simple and obvious, so it can be used to express unity and order, it is why it

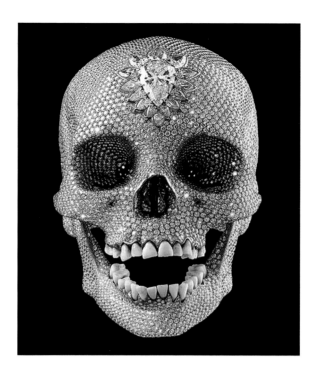

For the love of God. Damien Hirst, 2007

was mainly used during Renaissance period. Moreover, according to Kandinsky, that kind of harmony was sought after by Renaissance artists Raphael and also by other period artists such as Cézanne. Obviously there are differences (Raphael sought to reach Renaissance perfection, and Cézanne wanted to preserve some classic unity in impressionist paintings), but both used identical composition models for expressing a similar idea of harmony (see p. 66).

It is not casual that Cézanne looked back to Renaissance in order to find unity. In that sense he was greatly impressed by other painters, such as Piero della Francesca. Della Francesca not only knew the mathematical laws of geometry, but also had a strong sense of forms, colors, and composition in general that was important for Cézanne's research of harmony, as pointed out Kenneth Clark (1969).

The idea is, therefore, that forms without concepts are useless in any period of art. Actually, composition is not a question of cuteness, it is a way for expressing ideas. As another example, lighting, as composition, has been another perpetual source of inspiration and research for artists. James Turrell's work has an explicitly conceptual way of facing this issue: "In working with light, what is

1

2

1. The Canigiani Madonna. Raphael, 1507
2. Les Grandes Baigneuses. Cézanne, 1898–1905

really important to me is to create an experience of wordless thought, to make the quality and sensation of light itself something really tactile" (James Turrell, 1990). Even if we recognize a really contemporary point of view in Turrell's approach, it is not so different than other period's way of facing light as an artistic issue. Actually, theoreticians of the early 20th century already pointed out how light became a material itself once space laws were definitely controlled:

Since the discovery of perspective, painters began to represent the optical image of light moulded and bent by the various mediums of the environment. They developed progressive skill first in delineating the three-dimensional sculptural appearance of the object-world, later in mastering light and shadow as space articulating forces, and finally in representing space as luminous by dissolving solidity into light substance (Kepes, 1994).

When talking about some artistic universal issues as composition or lighting we tend to distinguish conceptual art from other artistic trends, generally confining it to figurative forms of art. However, as we see, art is always about ideas. Can design be conceptual then as well?

"Firmitas, Utilitas, and Venustas," Architecture Concepts for Any Discipline of Design

Architecture is the masterly, correct, and magnificent play of masses brought together in light" (Le Corbusier, 1923). Talking about light as a concept, and talking about art and design, it is mandatory to talk a little bit about architecture.

Since Vitruvius (1st century BCE), we distinguish three aspects of the discipline, *firmitas* (related with construction itself and structures), *utilitas* (related with functionality), and venustas (related with beauty). Thinking about design, we can also distinguish those same three elements. For example, in aerospace engineering, designing a plan requires also to face technical and physical issues, functional problems, and, of course, aesthetic decisions. Thinking about jewellery or fashion in general, technique is also important, usability is necessary, and nobody dresses or puts on a jewel so as not to look more handsome.

Vitruvius postulates that we are tempted to isolate the artistic aspect of architecture, in the same way that we can think that a design can be beautiful without being useful (or the other way round). Moreover, thinking about Vitruvius's ideas, we are also temptated to confuse crafters and artists in the sense that both of them can use techniques in order to produce beautiful and useful objects. However, can we distinguish them? What is the difference between workers and architects? Is there any clue for identifying an artist versus a simple painter?

Efforts to revive the art-principles of the past will at best produce an art that is still-born. It is impossible for us to live and feel, as did the ancient Greeks. In the same way those who strive to follow the Greek methods in sculpture achieve only a similarity of form, the work remaining soulless for all time. Such imitation is mere aping. Externally the monkey completely resembles a human being; he will sit holding a book in front of his nose, and turn over the pages with a thoughtful aspect, but his actions have for him no real meaning (Kandinsky, 1912).

Historically it has never been easy to identify an artist, even less to recognize a genius. Looking back on Impressionism, even Monet painting "Impression, Sunrise" (1872), was despised by art critics. Vincent Van Gogh himself was not considered a "real artist" during his lifetime. It is true that distinguishing art is a complex issue, however, a purpose of this text is trying to find some clues, looking back to Art History and identifying how important ideas and concepts can be.

Kandinsky tries to capture the difference between copying and creating. If we try to paint as Raphael, Cézanne, or Velázquez we can maybe reproduce their style and technique, but we will never achieve or reach their spirit. Art is based on concepts that are indivisible of a period and of a certain artist. Art must be innovative.

In the same way, concerning design, crafters can of course reproduce any piece (even those that are more complicated from a technical point of view). However, crafters only replicate ideas, for becoming good designers they have to innovate: working through concepts becomes essential.

As in any kind of design, we can also distinguish crafters from designers in fashion. Any designer has to be surrounded by the better technicians, but he has to lead the process as the one who works with new tendencies and concepts. Consider some of the best fashion designers ever, Yves Saint Laurent, for example. We have beautiful pictures in mind of the period when he started work as the main designer of the Maison Dior in 1957. There, we can see Yves Saint Laurent controlling the process helped by some chefs d'atelier, that is, specialized crafters that know even better than he did how details and techniques have to be used in the company. This same figure, the *chef d'atelier*, is also there in every picture of John Galliano— working for Dior (1996–2011)—and now with Raf Simons as shown in the recent documentary film Dior et moi (Tcheng, 2015).

06:

It is not uncommon then that crafters have even more technical skill than designers, and moreover, as at Dior, some of these technicians can be more important than designers in order to maintain the spirit of a brand. However, innovation is the work of designers, who need, unquestionably, to work with concepts and ideas.

Some CSDMM-UPM Examples

The Centro Superior de Diseño de Moda de Madrid of the Universidad Politécnica de Madrid (CSDMM-UPM) has taught fashion as a discipline since 1986. It is the pioneering fashion institution in Spain. The CSDMM-UP leads the most prestigious internal rankings (as BBVA-IVIE), and it has been awarded with the latest National Fashion Award for Academy and Culture. In the CSDMM-UPM the approach to fashion design is kind of professional and holistic. That means that, on the one hand, it relies on professional designers to teach future designers, and on the other hand it thinks that designers have to have a general cultural background.

Therefore, three kind of teachers work in the CSDMM-UPM. First, professionals working in the fashion industry. Some of the better Spanish fashion designers (Ana Locking, Juan Vidal, Miguel Becer, Maya Hansen, or Daniel Rabaneda), jewellery designers (BIIS, Sara Lasry, and Rubén Gómez), costume designers (Ana López Cobos and Clara Bilbao), and professionals of the retail industry (TENDAM professionals) are part of the CSDMM-UPM teaching team. Second, CSDMM-UPM professors are also expert technicians. Third, the CSDMM-UPM has academicians, PhD professors, and researchers in the field of fashion.

According to this, CSDMM-UPM students face different design challenges with a same *leitmotiv*, design process has to be led by ideas. Looking back to some of the designs shown in the last World Symposium for Fashion (WoSoF), we can easily see how design approach, technical solutions, and even the marketing decisions are led by the same original idea.

This is true in any kind of design. In jewellery, for example, Cristina Arredondo launched a jewellery line called "Balances" (see p. 70), where pieces are made in two kinds of gold (white and yellow). The technical problem of course, is how to combine the two different materials, but the aesthetic issue and the

1

Balances

2

070

1. *Balances. Cristina Arredondo, CSDMM-UPM 2017*
2. *Horse Riding Bags. Jorge Fernández, CSDMM-UPM 2017*
3. *CSDMMAG, The CSDMM-UPM Fashion Magazine, 2018*

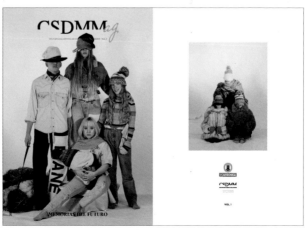

3

communication decisions depend also on this "balance" between white and yellow gold.

CSDMM-UPM students work in jewellery as they do in fashion and complement design. Looking to another example, Jorge Fernández bags (see left) are inspired by horseback riding. Every detail of his bags have to have their inspiration from horseback riding. This theme also carries through into the communication and marketing campaign for the products.

Ideas are therefore basic for designers, only through concepts can we reach innovation. Moreover, as we see, ideas are fundamental nowadays in fashion communication: we do not buy products, we buy aspirations: fashion buyers buy ideas. In that sense, the CSDMM-UPM has launched a new fashion magazine, CSDMMag (see left), made by students with their own designs, their own photography, and their own fashion approach. Working, as professional editors, is the only way to understand how ideas are also important in fashion communication.

Conclusion

We are used to distinguishing figurative and abstract art. Moreover, we are used to thinking that only contemporary art is based on concepts. However, as we see, artists and designers have always worked with ideas. Only through concepts and ideas we can reach innovation. For the CSDMM-UPM, this holistic approach to the creative disciplines is vital: only teaching how to deal with ideas in order to make design decision will permit future designers to face a contemporary global context completely flexible and unpredictable.

Reference

Adcock, C. E., and J. Turrell. 1990. *James Turrell: The Art of Light and Space*. California: University of California Press.

Clark, K. 1969. *Piero della Francesca: Complete Edition*. London: Phaidon Press.

Kandinsky, V. 1912. *Über das geistige in der Kunst*. Munich: R. Piper & Co.

Kepes, G. 1944. *Language of Vision*. Chicago: Paul Theobald and Company.

Le Corbusier. 1923. *Vers une Architecture*. París: Esprit Nouveau.

Tcheng, F. 2015. *Dior et moi [Motion Picture]*. The Orchard.

The Enduring Links between Jewellery and Fashion
From Craft to Design

Elizabeth FISCHER

Professor, Dean of Fashion and Jewellery Design, Head—Genève School of
Art and Design, HES-SO Geneva, Switzerland

Jewellery and clothing enjoy different life spans—jewellery is made of hard and enduring materials whereas clothing is made of perishable ones. However, both are necessary elements in the play of social appearances. For centuries precious jewels, intimately linked to dress, were the preserve of the elite, worn as patrimonial symbols of rank, prestige, and antiquity of lineage. The major social and industrial shifts of the 19th century deeply changed the manufacturing, materials, and market of jewellery. The trappings of the new wealth of business persons and industrialists increasingly rivalled the prized ornaments of the long-standing aristocracy, while a growing affluent middle class aspired to new kinds of jewellery (Fischer, 2010). To meet this demand, jewellers used cheaper materials, like steel and colored paste, which influenced the design of jewellery and ushered in the costume jewellery of the following century.

The gradual simplification of dress and democratization of fashion during the 20th century marked the rise of costume jewellery and all types of non-precious ornamentation for dress. Gabrielle Chanel's 1926 little black dress is considered one of the starting points of modern fashion and the instigation for new ways of using jewellery. Chanel boldly mixed precious and costume jewellery, thus putting the focus on aesthetic function as signifier of taste rather than indicator of rank, fortune, and status (Banta, 2011). In combining fake and real jewels she consciously charted the way for women to appropriate jewellery as a personal and chosen expression of taste and statement of identity, just like any other accessory, heralded modern consumer practices. Ornament and beauty weren't equated with preciousness anymore. Jewellery, more especially costume jewellery (which started as the imitation of high jewellery), entered the category of accessories that includes shoes, gloves, hats, scarves, bags, etc., which followed the fashion trends. As the main adornment of pared-down modern dress, jewellery, far from being accessory, was deemed an absolute necessity. Furthermore, Chanel freed jewellery from its centuries-old bond with a woman's dependence on a man, as either legitimate spouse or kept woman. Wealth was equated with masculinity and fashion with femininity. High jewellery is now bought by women themselves as adornment and investment whereas for centuries this was the preserve of men. Precious gems, usually worn on formal occasions only, are now even paired with everyday wear such as jeans and sneakers, blurring the boundaries between high and mainstream attire.

The hippie revolution brought two major changes in Western dress. The body of both men and women was suddenly much more revealed and men adopted

Lisa Defago, Capillophilia—hair, silver © Head-Geneva

Lisa Defago, Capillophilie—porté, hair, silver © Head-Geneva

some traits of feminine fashion, among them the wearing of necklaces, bracelets (often in leather and other non-precious materials), and a single earring. The masculine adoption of jewellery further confirmed its transfer to the category of fashionable accessory. Pop singers of the 1970s–1980s such as Elton John were instrumental in popularizing the masculine adoption of jewellery and glamorous accessories. The rap singers who followed used oversized jewellery with unusual ornaments (pendants in the shape of car emblems for example) as symbols their achievement as black men in the Western world, because white role models of male success did not apply to them. Jewellery and fashion for men have become a rich area for design development and constitute a rapidly growing market. Fashion's impact extended to entry-level watch design with the appearance of the revolutionary Swatch in the 1980s, a watch made out of plastic, with fun designs, accessible to the general consumer for less than $60. In this case, the cultures of fashion and jewellery design were successfully applied to the very traditional field of watch design, hand in hand with engineering, to produce a completely novel way of creating a watch and launch it as a fashion accessory—following trends—rather than a time-piece.

The contemporary body isn't so much clothed as adorned with accessories. This has ushered in new types of ornaments, applied directly to the skin. Tattooing and piercing have existed since antiquity, used as discriminating signs, for specific groups living at the margins of society. These ornaments became particularly visible with the punk movement, as signs of rebellion against the establishment, before being taken up by the mainstream. The fashion industry used this type of skin decoration to create shock waves on the catwalk and in advertisements. With its adoption as an ornament by younger generations, piercing no longer has rebellious connotations. It's used to enhance specific parts of the body and add a kinetic dimension to the human figure (MacKendrick, 1998). The studs and other items used for piercing exactly fit the definition of jewellery. However, they aren't considered as such yet even though they have largely inspired new ways of wearing traditional jewellery, yet another instance of blurring boundaries between high and low.

Gold is now a color that has migrated from immutable precious metal to sequins and spangles glittering on T-shirts and bags, or on wash-away tattoos, and highlights the bling paraphernalia of rap and other musical and street cultures. The generalization of sparkling ornamentation high and low has blurred the ancient boundaries between the preciousness of a status-defining gem and the flashiness of a passing fad.

In the 1990s, jewellery was used in spectacular ways to highlight fashion in catwalk shows. The visual impact created by stunning jewellery brought the focus on the body and was often used to summarize the style of the designer in a kind of pictorial shorthand (Evans, 2007, 231–33). In shows and advertisements, jewellery has become a way of expanding the brand's message. As Suzy Menkes wrote:

When you come out of shows by three powerful, creative designers and remember first the shoes, or perhaps Chanel's fab new bangles and icon-scattered purses, or Lacroix's cute animal-shaped wicker baskets, you have to ask this question: Have accessories become more important than the clothes? (Menkes, 2002)

For the past 30 years, accessories have brought in the most income for high and low brands. In the hierarchical relationship between clothing, considered essential, and accessories, considered secondary, sales have tipped in favor of accessories. Designing accessories can now mean big business.

Jewellery is now in the fore, indispensable in the performance of fashion (dress and accessories) on the catwalk and in the street. Today, both young men and women have wholly adopted this culture of the accessory, wearing caps, earrings, chains, bracelets, sporting and indispensable electronic devices, and wearables decorated with trinkets, i.e., jewellery as ornament for accessories. These items often embody what is most precious to the contemporary individual. With wearables, preciousness may be in the immaterial and not the material, and longevity in the age of obsolescence has taken on new meanings. However, their function as indicators of status, social relationships, and taste remain paramount in our society.

The bodies of today engage us in our social life, are the standard bearers of our identity, and are still the main seat of emotions, sensations, actions. The bionic bodies so often imagined for the future should retain the same capacities, augmented by extensions made of materials. Fashion, accessory, and jewellery designers are now free to explore much wider avenues than practicality and social rituals. Using the body as a catalyst rather than a location, they question our relationship to materials and to artifacts and can challenge the traditional narrative of body, product, and identity.

The skills and processes used in fashion and jewellery design can be instrumental in redesigning objects outside the usual scope of these fields. Eyewear, more specifically sunglasses, entered the realm of fashion as a statement of status and taste as of the 1950s, having come a long way from its function as medical prosthesis (Pullin, 2009). This revolution came about through embracing the design culture of the fashion industry. The same process could benefit the development of prosthetics, which is usually oriented by medical considerations and developed by engineers intent on performance, out of touch with the needs of a normal existence. Aesthetics, comfort, ease of use, and everyday wearability are key for the acceptance of a prosthetic device, and are elements designers are used to take into account (Sobchak, 2004; Fischer, 2013). In 2018, one of the prize-winning projects at the Hyères international fashion festival focused on designing hearing aids as desirable jewellery.

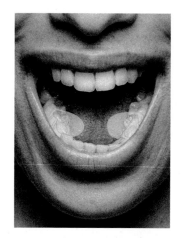

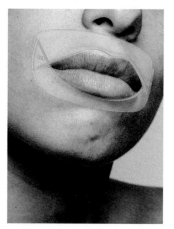

078

Suzanne Craviari, Augmented Mouth—virtual jewellery,
2020 © Head-Geneva Jewellery
To change the facial expression by playing with the shape of the mouth and
teeth with the help of made to measure Instagram filters.

Fittingly, the Swarovski Fashion Accessories Grand Prize of the Jury went to product designers Flora Fixy and Julia Dessirier who were approached by photographer Kate Fichard to re-think the crude, perfunctory design of domestic hearing devices. The resulting project H(Earring) sits at the junction between medicine and fashion. The judges were impressed with how the aid had been emphasized and exaggerated using wax casting and 3D modelling – its sculptural qualities rendered in precious metals. "Fashion is an amplifier for socio-political issues. Our jewellery is first an answer to the user's needs, but it is a political tool too," the winners said.[1]

These examples speak in favor of a more cross-disciplinary, collaborative approach and testify to the fact that fashion and jewellery design have embraced a wider shift in attitudes to creation. Craft and engineering can work hand in hand to bring innovation in the creation of equipment for the body. As long as objects are meaningful vectors in our relationships with others and our environment, and the more materials are intricately incorporated to the body and the person, fashion and accessory design will have a part to play in society and in individuals' lives and can bring about innovative pathways in the conception and production of highly complex contemporary artifacts.

79

Reference

Banta, M. 2011. "Coco, Zelda, Sara, Daisy, and Nicole: Accessories for New Ways of Being a Woman." In *Accessorizing the Body, Habits of Being I*, edited by Christina Giorcelli and Paula Rabinowitz, 82–107. Minneapolis and London: University of Minnesota Press.

Evans, C. 2007. *Fashion at the Edge: Spectacle, Modernity, and Deathliness*, 2nd ed. New Haven, CT and London: Yale University Press.

Fischer, E. 2010. "Jewellery and Fashion in the Nineteenth Century." In *The Fashion History Reader: Global Perspectives*, edited by Giorgio Riello, Peter McNeil, 311–13. London and New York: Routledge.

Fischer, E. 2013. "The Accessorized Ape." In *Contemporary Jewellery in Perspective*, edited by D. Skinner, 202–08. New York: Lark Books.MacKendrick, K. 1998. "Technoflesh or, 'Didn't that Hurt?'" *Fashion Theory* 2(1): 3–24.

Menkes, S. 2002. "Baubles, Bangles and Bags: Who Cares about the Clothes?" In *International Herald Tribune*, 6.

Pullin, G. 2009. *Design Meets Disability*. Cambridge: MIT Press.

Sobchak, V. 2004. *Carnal Thoughts: Embodiment and Moving Image Culture*. Berkeley: University of California Press.

---

1. https://www.wallpaper.com/fashion/hyeres-2018

In Terrā Mediā
The Hybrid Territory of Les Métissages

Nichka MAROBIN

Historian, Researcher, Curator

*"Often fashion is considered as an interest or a silly
or superficial practice,*

tendentially associated with youth and stupid individuals,

*rather than art, design or society
and consequently dismissed as irrelevant."*

–Tim Edwards (2011, 19)

Before entering the theme of this text, I thought it could be useful to introduce my work, so one can easily approach the project of the life and dialogues of forms in this hybrid territory that I call "Terrā Mediā," a middle earth between fashion and contemporary jewellery.

I was a curious eleven-year-old when I approached, for the first time, the Flemish masters: while I was reading an interesting mystery novel, I bumped into the precious detail of the crown, standing at the feet of the almighty God in the Ghent Altarpiece of the Holy Lamb, painted between 1426 and 1432 by Jan and Hubert van Eyck and commissioned by Josse Vijd who is depicted, together with his wife on the external wings, in the chapel of St. Bavo's Cathedral in Ghent.[1] Subsequently, it was always another detail painted by Jan van Eyck, always a crown, taken from another panel and now at Musée du Louvre in Paris: "The Madonna of Chancellor Rolin,"[2] a work commissioned to the painter by Nicolas Rolin, chancellor of the Dukes of Burgundy, which definitively led me to the study of the Flemish art history. This is to say that, from the very beginning, jewels have peeped into what would have become, over the years, my field of study, that of the history of Flemish and Dutch art.

And even years later, when the theme of my dissertation was consolidated with the study of zoomorphism, hybrids, and fantastic creatures in Renaissance ornament prints beyond the Alps, the jewel was able to sneak in. Among the sharpened tendrils and the grotesques arrived from Italy as flatteries from the south of Europe as a new ornamental feeling, what was previously relegated to the frames, all that

1. http://closertovaneyck.kikirpa.be/
2. https://www.louvre.fr/en/oeuvre-notices/virgin-chancellor-rolin

vegetation populated with tiny licentious creatures that made life swarming at the margins, came to the fore. Here, then, all this patrimony had begun to assume a real autonomy, becoming an inexhaustible source of themes and models for the goldsmiths' shops of imperial cities such as Nuremberg and Augsburg.

The taste for the hybrid, for the study of the life of the forms and their migration in the field of ornamentation gave the start, in 2014, to the research project of "Les Métissages," a series of combinations taken from the world of fashion combined with those of contemporary jewellery that highlight the idea that it is possible to achieve the same aesthetic result through different means of expression, which are, in this case, fashion and jewellery.

This "associative game" that, at the very beginning, was a different path aimed at proving and reading the different references and the sources used by contemporary jewellery, turned out to be much more than a simple "hunt" to the stylistic appeal, but a real "system" of shapes, ideas, ornamental stylistic elements, patterns, and motifs that, by recurring from a *coutourier* to a goldsmith artist and vice versa, have unveiled—and unveil—both the fixity and the variation of forms as well as the migration of ideas and have opened up a changing landscape where these two forms of arts have a constant dialogue.

Fashion and jewellery (and in this case what we call contemporary jewellery, or studio jewellery in the Anglo-Saxon field) (Besten, 2012, 9–10) have always been considered and relegated to the role of art forms subordinate to fine arts, especially paintings, since from them—as well as from Nature—they have drawn inspiration and mimetical forms (Leach, 2012).

As an example of direct interpretation from the arts and of a continuous flow of exchange and circularity we can think it to the "Mondriaan collection" created in 1965 by Yves Saint-Laurent[3] or, as a great example of artistic marriage on all levels, a Mila Schön's dress inspired by Lucio Fontana's "Concetto Spaziale" and photographed by Ugo Mulas, dating from 1969.[4]

---

3. https://museeyslparis.com/en/biography/lhommage-a-piet-mondrian
4. BELLISSIMA. Italy and High Fashion 1945–1968. exhibition catalogue curated by Maria Luisa Frisa, Gabriele Monti and Stefano Tonchi, NSU Art Museum Fort Lauderdale (February 7–June 5, 2016) and MAXXI: National Museum of the XXI Century Arts in Rome (2016), 19.

This circularity, this "simultaneous relationship between past and present" as clearly states M. L. Frisa in her book *Le forme della Moda* (Frisa, 2015, 20) creates that constant game of looks and references that is the same variety of fashion. Looking back and all around, it gives the idea of how fashion is a seismograph of time, just like contemporary jewellery is.

It becomes clear, then, that "talking about fashion does not mean talking about clothes" (Frisa, 2015, 7) and talking about contemporary jewellery does not mean talking about disparate materials and abstruseness.

Talking about these areas means talking about complex systems that touch on themes such as art, design, sociology, anthropology, economics, education, culture, and aesthetics. Talking about contemporary fashion and jewellery means talking about complex systems, seismographs of time, taste, of the visible and the invisible and of a complex system of forms.

Forms: Anticipations and Collisions

In his book *The Life of Forms* in 1934, Henri Focillon stated:

History is usually a conflict of precociousness, of actuality and of delays. ...The history of art shows us, juxtaposed at the same time, survivals and anticipations: slow, delayed forms, simultaneous of inventive and rapid ones (Focillon, 1943).

The forms, as presented in the studies by Henri Focillon, have the ability to recognize themselves through time and space and, as he demonstrated in the series of studies on Roman art—then continued by his student Jurgis Baltrušaitis (1972; 1986; 1988) along the gothic phases—they find a fertile territory precisely in the applied arts since it is in the field of decoration and ornament where the forms demonstrate their own vitality.

This restless life that emerges from the hybrid territory of the Métissages highlights how two art forms such as fashion and jewellery interact with each other equally. It is no longer a matter of a jewel created as a function of a garment, nor of a garment and an object having a specific derivation from other

Catherine O'Leary, "Ephemeral," Sculptural Dress—wool and silk layered dress, handcrafted with traditional felting method, 2011

forms of art; it is neither a direct reference nor a re-proposal nor a meditation, but rather the testimony of a clear, definite life.

About the migration, the proliferation and the repetition of the ornamental motifs, I quoted Henri Focillon and Jurgis Baltrušaitis: both have concentrated their research on Romanesque and Gothic art, looking and carefully studying the origin of some ornamental elements and the way in which they have moved and reproduced over the centuries. But if for the life of the forms studied by Focillon and Baltrušaitis it was a process of "continuity," "Les Métissages" is a process of study by "contiguity," and this concept is as fascinating as it is complex.

And since in these processes of contiguity coexist—at the same time—as fixed (the shapes are repeated) but with variation (each material gives to the forms a different vitality), as anticipation and collision, we can see how a similar investigation and interpretation of empty and full spaces have been achieved both by the Australian textile artist Catherine O'Leary and by the Japanese metal-maker Keiko Kume,[5] both exhibited in 2015 during the JOYA Barcelona Art Jewellery Fair.

The two artists didn't know each other and yet, the similar investigation on the same subject gave life to an unpredictable and visual conversation of forms, sizes, and colors.

So, a life that is constantly changing and perpetuating itself, in continuous development and in constant renewal, since, making our own a famous phrase by Italo Calvino, creativity "is a place where it rains" (Calvino, 2012, 91).

Conclusion

I was often asked for a definition about my "métissages" and I have to admit that I still find it difficult to define them. But, if I want to trace a perimeter (geographically imprecise) and a "possible" working method, I could say that, "Les Métissages" are nothing more than the result of archives of my memory.

5. Métissage n. 4: The distant Rhymes from the exhibition "Les Métissages" at JOYA Barcelona 2015; see also JOYA Barcelona Exhbition catalog, page 99. http://www.catherineoleary.com.au/ ; http://kume-keiko. wixsite.com/works ; http://www.joyabarcelona.com/index.php/en/

Keiko Kume, "Wonders 034," Art Object—hammering, open work, brazing,
brass, silver—50mmx80mmx60mm from the exhibition "Les Métissages"
at Joya Barcelona, 2015, curated by Nichka Marobin

Assisted by a constant search online on web platforms and stored in files clearly organized in my memory and in my personal computer.

How does a Métissage come to life? There is no rule in this regard: sometimes it all starts from the search for a specific object in the field of jewellery research; sometimes it is the reverse path, looking for a specific fashion creation; other times the forms themselves are revealed: memory begins to work and they bloom before my eyes.

Moreover, this project has a lot to do with another key concept: that of "sister arts,"[6] which is "the close kinship or family air that is found between the expressions of the various arts in every age of the past" (Praz, 2018, 35).

All the combinations published until today [almost one thousand] offer a dialogue between two forms of art, banning all the hierarchies that Western art history has taught us about artistic disciplines, which relegated fashion creations and

6. See the wroks of Mario Praz in the book references

jewellery to "sub-categories" of applied arts. The juxtapositions witness and reveal two different, yet complex systems of forms always recurring through time and space: receptive affinities as selected affinities.

And finally, the most interesting aspect of this project is that none of the makers, artists, and fashion designers knows each other: this is truly surprising. According to Focillon, talking about the life of forms implies a concept of continuity, but this is not the same case of the "métissages," in which anticipations, conflicts, and collisions coexist freely. The only contact between the fashion designer/coutourier and the jeweller/maker is given by the forms and their restless, constant exchange between these two forms of art: contemporary jewellery and fashion, and photographing, all making up that hybrid territory that I call "Terrā Mediā."

#LesMétissages is project born on the web: to see all the combinations published and posted since 2014, please see the website www.themorningbark.com and the Instagram and Facebook feeds #LesMétissages.

Reference

Baltrušaitis, J. 1972. *Le Moyen Âge fantastique. Antiquités et exotismes dans l'art gothique.* Paris: Editions Flammarion. Translated from Italian, Il medioevo Fantastico. Antichità ed esotismi dell'arte gotica, Milano: Adelphi, 1973.

Baltrušaitis, J. 1986. *Formations, Deformations, Paris: Editions Flammarion.* Translated from Italian, Formazioni, deformazioni. *La stilistica ornamentale nella scultura romanica.* Milano: Adelphi, 2005.

Baltrušaitis, J. 1988. *Réveils et prodiges.* Paris: Editions Flammarion. Translated from Italian, *Risvegli e prodigi. La metamorfosi del gotico.* Milano, Adelphi, 1999.

Besten, L. D. 2012. *On Jewellery: A Compendium of International Contempray Jewellery.* Stuttgart: Arnoldsche Verlagsanstalt.

Calvino, I. 2012. *Lezioni Americane: Sei proposte per prossimo millennio,* 14th edition. Milano: Mondadori.

Edwards, T. 2011. *Fashion in Focus: Concepts, Practices and Politics.* London and New York: Routledge.

Focillon, H. 1943. *Vie des Fomes suivi de l'éloge de la main.* Paris: PUF. Translated from Italian, *Vita delle Forme seguito da Elogio della mano.* Torino: Einaudi, 1972.

Frisa, M. L. 2015. *Le forme della Moda,* Società editrice il Mulino.

Leach, R. 2012. *The Fashion Resource Book: Research for Design.* London: Thames & Hudson.

Praz, M. 2018. "La stretta parentela o aria di famiglia che si riscontra tra le espressioni delle varie arti in ogni epoca del passato." In *Menemosyne. Parallelo tra lal letteratura e le arti visive.* Milano: Abscondita.

Fashion Artifact, and Design as a Social Facilitator

Naomi FILMER

Senior Lecturer, on MA Fashion Artifact, London College of Fashion, University of the Arts, London, UK

I am a designer, maker, and teacher located within fashion as a creative context. My training was positioned within the traditions of contemporary craft and jewellery, yet since graduating from the Royal College of Art in 1993 I have worked in and out of fashion, developing my skills through collaborations, exhibitions, and commissions that have influenced and directed the further development of my practice. My focus has been on the body as both site and means through which to confront ideas of wearing, adorning, alluding to, and abstracting from objects in relation to it.

I consider jewellery and accessories as agency in this critical reflection of the body, in particular their role in the act and idea of wearing and adorning, although I describe my work not as jewellery, but as artifact for display, as exhibition props and a prelude to sculpture. This reflection provides the existential basis and central themes of my work but also has informed my teaching over 25 years in design schools in London, across Europe, and internationally to undergraduates and postgraduates. Since 2010 I have been a senior tutor of the MA Fashion Artifact course at London College of Fashion, which I consider close to my practise, as I will explain.

In this article, I offer an overview of the development of my work by looking at a series of projects. Collectively these works describe a pathway from jewellery as fashion catwalk accessory, as installation for fashion exhibitions, and finally as sculpture/contemporary objects for exhibition. The shifts in dialogue and idea that lie between categories of jewellery, adornment, and object has become a legitimate discursive place in which to locate what I consider to be the identity of my work. This sense of an in-between space in which work explores and engages with transitions between media and context is where I want to introduce what we do at the MA Fashion Artifact at London College of Fashion. We present an educational platform that enables students to develop thought, evolve design methodologies, and explore possibilities for placing their work in contexts that reach beyond fashion. To best illustrate this I will present selected works by MA Fashion Artifact graduates who, from a place of discussion and reflection, have made works that offer critical influence on contemporary culture in the form of accessories, jewellery, and products.

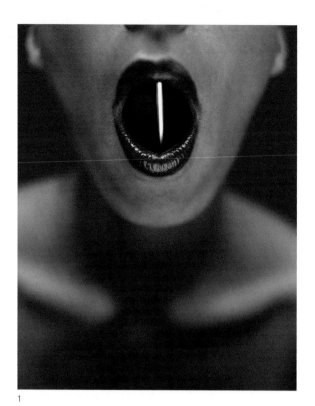

1

2

1/2. Naomi Filmer for Hussein Chalayan, 1996
   Mouth and Ear-behind Light/ Mouth Bar
   Materials—LED lights, resin capsule, silver rod, dental wire
   Photography © Gavin Fernandes

Colliding with Fashion

An important part of my work as a designer/maker since the 1990s has involved catwalk collaborations with fashion designers in London and Paris, including Hussein Chalayan, Alexander McQueen, and Anne Valerie Hash. These have provided opportunities to showcase my work worn by live models, on stage, before an audience, where the work was illustrative and indicative of the themes that defined the catwalk collections. Far from any commercial context these projects gave me space to explore the tension between the wearer and the object, looking at placement, scale, and material as relative to and interactive with the body. In these investigations I looked into the role and impact of the body and the accessory, questioning which was the dominant factor: when the work commands space and a physical pose, does the body wear the object, or the object wear the body?

Mouth jewellery made for Chalayan (see left, above) was made based on the theme of human alarm: one work forces the mouth open for us to see into the internal cavity, while the other work illuminates the inside space. Both bring focus to the mouth of the model rather than the jewellery, yet the work dictates facial position.

The Ball in The Small of My Back for McQueen (see left, below), made to reference a flamenco dancer, commands the model to position her arms behind her back, poised, restricted, with hands on display only from behind.

Working at the fast rhythm of fashion permitted me a sense of freedom that I hadn't experienced on the contemporary jewellery scene. There I had paid greater attention to the crafted output of my work at a slower pace, whereas in the fashion industry production was more urgent, with the pressure to produce two collections a year plus special projects for editorials. This sense of freedom of pace, plus the reality of working on low budgets, required me to reconsider my approach to materials.

I made work for fashion editorials and exhibitions using the ephemeral and temporary qualities of materials such as ice for jewellery and chocolate for a mask and gloves. These works necessitated a focus on the value of material, sensation, and experience as significant aspects of my work. There were limitations, however, since making work for the catwalk required me to illustrate and display themes dictated by the fashion designers, which subsequently led me away, into other less constraining directions.

Intimacy of Material and Flesh

Wishing to explore a more intimate dialogue with both wearer and material, I made a collection of ice jewellery for a solo exhibition in 1999 at the Judith Clark Costume Gallery, London (see right, above). In this work the question of dominance between the body and my work returns. The temperature of the human flesh that wears the ice dominates its frozen state, yet for a little while, the ice overbears the wearer. Direct contact with ice chills the skin and slightly stings, shortly followed by a reaction of goose bumps that decorate the skin's surface. As the ice melts water drops run along the contours of the body that wears it. The ice thaws, the body is left wet. The water evaporates and what remains is the memory of the sensation and experience. Ultimately the ice jewellery brings attention to the value of water, to experience, and to memory.

Display: Mannequin Prosthetics

Working with curator Judith Clark on the exhibition Behind Before Beyond, 1999, initiated collaborations that have focused recurrently on the theme of display, resulting in the development of display props that we describe as Mannequin Prosthetics.

These are cast synthetic accessories made for mannequins and tailor's dummies that bring details from the human body to adorn the artificial bodies, normally used to exhibit dress in a museum and exhibition context (see right, below). Clavicles, the jaw line, earlobes, and hands are cast as prosthetic decoration subverting traditions of jewellery as adornment on the body. Instead they offer human details as decoration to embellish the artificial body that makes the artificial more familiar, closer to ourselves. These works perform equally as props and as artifacts that challenge traditional ideas of adornment and wearing.

Judith Clark and I have returned to this concept in four projects over 15 years, changing details in material, framing, and placement:

- *Malign Muses; when fashion turns back—MOMU, Antwerp, 2004*
- *Simonetta: La Prima Donna della Moda Italiana—Palazzo Pitti, Florence, 2008*
- *Galerie Privée: Museum of Louis Vuitton Archive—Vuitton Villa, Paris, 2015*
- *Cristóbal Balenciaga Fashion and Heritage archive exhibition—Balenciaga Museum, Getaria, 2018*

1. Naomi Filmer, Ice Hand Disk,
  Behind Before Beyond 1999, Material—Ice
  Photographer © Nicola Schwartz

2/3. Naomi Filmer for Judith Clark,
  Mannequin Prosthetic, Spectres
  When Fashion Turns Back, 2005

1

2

3

Accessories Inform Sculpture

As the thinking behind my work developed further in the direction of non-wearable adornment, I moved away from making work to be worn, giving attention instead to the body as an informant for sculptural objects designed to be illustrative of the physical aspects and actions of our bodies.

To demonstrate this, I will discuss some commissions in more detail to define my thinking through adornment and display as idea.

"Out of the Ordinary; Spectacular Craft" the V&A, London 2007

In 2007 I was commissioned by the British Crafts Council to make new work for the group exhibition "Out of the Ordinary; Spectacular Craft" at the V&A, London.

Responding to the theme "out of the ordinary," I made an installation of work to illustrate my perspective on the human body as unique and extraordinary. A significant part of my installation was 10 glass spheres, entitled "Ball Lenses." Each of these 10 ball lenses focussed on a body part which is set into the ball. The ten body parts are hollow castings taken from a live model, then electro-formed, silver plated, and lined with a layer of flesh-colored flocking. They featured an eye, ear lobe, one clavicle, shoulder, armpit, elbow, a hand on hip, the back of a knee, heel, and toes. Collectively the ball lenses describe a body in its absence. As individual objects they command attention to each of the extracted body parts and further develop my idea of human physiology as both decorative and precious.

"The Art of Fashion; Installing Allusions" the Museum Boijmans Van Beuningen, Rotterdam, 2009

Casting these and other prosthetics led to a shift in my practice, moving away from wearables to making objects that, while adopting the surface language of mannequin prosthetics, are presented as sculpture, as artifacts made for exhibition to allude to the body.

In 2009, I was commissioned by curators Judith Clark and José Teunissen, on behalf of the Han Nefkens Foundation, to make work for the exhibition "Installing Allusions: The Art of Fashion" at the Museum Boijmans Van Beuningen, Rotterdam. I created a series of four sculptures entitled "Breathing Volumes," through which I sought to explore and illustrate the act of breathing. I describe them as three-dimensional sketches depicting a sculptural play on the idea of a definable space through which a person passes, as they breathe in and breathe out. To identify that point of collision between the body and the object, each piece features a chin cast. Three out of the four works are made from a synthetic compound painted white, adopting the surface aesthetic of mannequins (see below). Both the chin and the surface reference previous exhibition props, yet they are now objects developed as sculpture that alludes to the body and displayed in a fashion exhibition. These works are now part of the Han Nefkens private fashion collection.

1

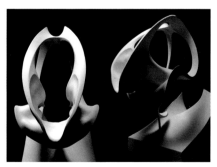

2

1. *Naomi Filmer,Heel and Toe Ball Lense,*
   Out of the Ordinary, 2007

2. *Naomi Filmer,Breathing Volumes, The Art of Fashion;*
   Installing Allusions, 2009
   Material—Synthetic polymers
   Photographer © Jeremy Forster

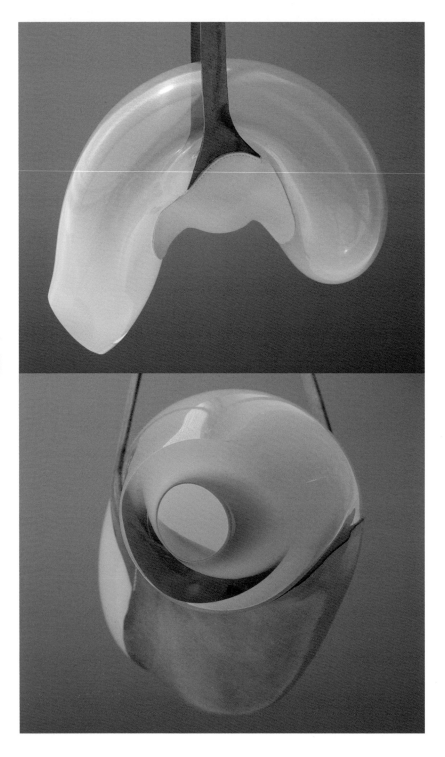

Naomi Filmer, Suspended Bodyscapes, 2010 Material—Glass, leather Photographer © Jeremy Forster

Suspended Body-Scapes, 2010

Working with breath as a theme developed the conceptual aspect of my work, shifting attention beyond the physical form of the body to its physiological processes and actions. It also results from collaborations with other craftspeople. I am not always the physical maker of my work, as I enjoy a combining materials and techniques to materialise my ideas. I do not aspire to be a master of all the techniques required to realize my work, preferring to engage with the expertise of other makers and craftspeople. Working alongside and watching master glass blowers in particular has influenced my thematic work on breath. In the craft of glass blowing, breath is critical to facilitating and directing the processes of making.

In 2010 I worked on a short residency with master blowers at the National Glass Centre in Leerdam, the Netherlands, who worked with moulds and body casts that I retrieved from my archive (originally made for "Ball Lenses," 2007, for the "Out of the Ordinary" exhibition). Glass bubbles were blown into and over the negative spaces of the moulds of a shoulder, an armpit, and an elbow. Following and directing the shapes that evolved, while surrendering to the pace and control of the blowers, I constituted the resulting blown bubbles into a series of works entitled "Suspended Body-Scapes." The final glass objects are suspended by leather straps, which are stitched to leather harnesses, previously formed against the glass at precisely the points where the plaster mould had originally taken form from a live model. There is a sense that the leather wears the glass, and the glass has worn the mould that was formed upon the model for the original plaster cast—a reflexive engagement with the body that makes the work an essential act of craft as design and making. These glass pieces allude to the body, yet transform the parts once recognizable (in "Ball Lenses") into abstracted passive, languid forms, presented in fleshy hues suggestive of inner human organs and phalluses—as seen in the image here.

Reflecting on this sequence of projects and the works that have resulted from them shows clearly my consistent and recurrent focus on the body as a means through which to confront ideas of wearing, adorning, alluding, and abstracting objects in relation to it. The experiential creative and expressive pathway that began in jewellery, passed through fashion, and now hangs as sculpture constitutes an informative approach that continues to inform both my making and my teaching.

MA Fashion Artifact;
London College of Fashion, UAL

For the past 10 years I have been teaching at London College of Fashion on the MA Fashion Artifact program. The objective of the 15-month course is to develop fashion accessories as an independent platform for creative practise. Now in its twelfth year, it is recognized internationally as an incubator of artisan designer makers, where traditional craftsmanship and industrial technologies are studied and facilitated for the making of contemporary fashion products. It defines its position within education and for the wider creative industries by offering provocative design possibilities and speculation in a changing spectrum of arenas and audiences. As designers, students are encouraged to build comprehensive and independent perspectives on the role and importance of the body and objects within fashion. As makers, they are directed to develop sound methodologies for thinking through the practise of making and to develop excellent craft skills.

Students' ideas and philosophies have culminated in both wearable and non-wearable objects that assert new meanings to challenge, critique, and redefine accessories, reflecting and influencing the world in which we live. The spectrum of works produced by graduates of the program is exemplified by the following selection, identified within four specific directions that introduce some of the trajectories they pursue. These show pathways that graduates have taken, developed from their graduating collections and evolving into further work for production as well as providing a basis for establishing independent practice in research, teaching, consultancy, and performance. They show how fashion education offers a platform for the creative conception of products as critical agency in both socio-cultural and personal terms. These works live beyond fashion, displaying ways of thinking and expression that can facilitate contemporary social life.

Heritage and Craftsmanship

For her Masters collection Sarah made travel trunks and luggage cases designed for new spaces and places, referring to the multi-faceted metropolitan cities and lifestyles in which we live and travel. The cases fold over chair backs, wrap around corners, and tuck against desk edges. They claim and dominate the space where they are placed, defining the architecture details at locations travelled to and through.

For the fabrication of this collection Sarah worked closely with a manufacturer specializing in the production of travel goods to make the metal frames onto which she built obscure bespoke leather cases. By employing traditional leather skills with frame-making production techniques she applies the history and legacy of craftsmanship to a speculative design proposal, which offer new perspectives on luggage to identify a shift in contemporary work and travel.

Sarah produces her own brand of small leather goods, selling in selective stores across the UK and online. Additionally, she offers private handmade bespoke leatherwork courses from her studio in Herefordshire, UK.

Product and Manufacture

With a focus on production and material as a design framework Bei created a set of beauty grooming tools. Six products were made using a compound Bei developed by casting human hair into a bio-resin. By wrapping human hair around transparent acrylic rods, then casting them into bio-resin, Bei follows a sequence of cutting and sanding to achieve a pattern within the compound that mimics leopard skin and tortoise shell. The material evokes an impression of luxury products from last century made with exotic animal skins, horn, and shell—materials now forbidden and classified as ethically wrong to source. Bei works resourcefully instead with human hair to create a compound that imitates exotic skins, yet is clearly something else, thereby using a by-product to create elegant tools that groom our bodies which in turn provide the material to decorate the tools: an interesting connection between user, material, and function. Since graduating Bei Zhang has worked with the footwear company United Nude and is currently teaching at BIFT University, Beijing.

Fashion Artifact as Political Voice

Francesca's work outlines the socio-political issue of gender inequality. In her works she illustrates a narrative of particular historical and autobiographical events that document gender inequality in both the workplace and wider society. Her objects, accessories, and garments are metaphor and representation of the case studies she worked from. Dumbbells, a factory work jacket, book cover, belt, and wallet are adorned with sketches and hand-written diary extracts stitched into

1

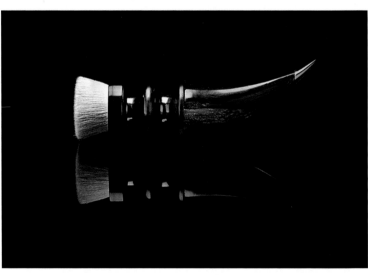

2

1. Sarah Jane Williams (UK, graduated in 2009), Arched Case, Crafted Collection, 2009
   Material—Vegetable tanned leather, brass trim, and wood fittings
   Photographer © Jimmy Beltran

2. Bei Zhang (China, graduated in 2017), Face Brush, Grooming, 2016
   Material—Badger hair, walnut wood, bio-resin, human hair
   Photographer © Eks Oliver

3

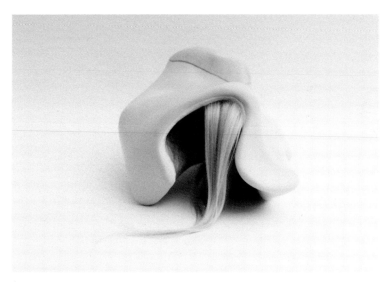

4

3. *Francesca Smith (UK, graduated in 2017), Dumbbells, The Power of Her, 2016*
   Material—Vegetable tanned leather, linen thread, plywood, cast iron
   Photographer © Joe Josland

4. *Anne Fleur van der Vloed (the Netherlands, graduated in 2017), Bodily, 2016*
   Material—Bio resin, fiber glass, silicon rubber, human hair
   Photographer © Eks Oliver

Ana Rajcevic (Serbia, graduated in 2012), The Other Side of Evolution, 2012
Material—Jesmonite, latex rubber strap
Photographer © Nicole Vizioli

and etched onto wood and leather panels embedded in the works. The illustrations and text carry the political voice as a narrative to embellish symbolic artifacts.

Some works from her final collection are now on display at the Museum of London to mark the 100-year celebration of the suffragettes. These contemporary additions support the data and artifacts that document the events and impact of the suffragettes in London over 100 years ago. Currently Francesca is currently working as a designer of jewellery and accessories for High Street retail.

Anne Fleur has a medical condition that results in her living with acute pain. Refusing to appear as victim to the condition, she seeks to embody a physical experience of pain in her work. For her graduating collection she made a series of cast polymer works suggestive of abstract self-portraits; sculpted as contorted, painted in a color to match her skin tone, featuring human hair dyed to the exact shades she colors her hair, and leather covering to further reference her flesh tones. The awkward, distorted and abstracted mannequin-like works Anne-Fleur made represent both personal appearance and physical experience.

For Anne-Fleur health is a political issue. She seeks to locate her work as public art in medical institutions, acting thereby to challenge taboos on discussion of shared experiences of ill health in wider social settings. She is currently negotiating to install an exhibition of her graduating works in the hospital in Rotterdam, the Netherlands, where she herself has received long term treatment.

The Performative Body and Prosthetics

Ana made a series of abstracted anatomical accessories titled "The Other Side of Evolution" that extend, morph, and sculpt the body. They transform the wearer into new profiles, animalistic and ergonomic, which Ana proposes to be hypothetical evolutionary reconfigurations, based on the human obsession with speed. The collection was intended for catwalk display and as performance props.

Since graduating Ana has developed her work in two directions. First, by collaborating with the British contemporary dance group Neon Dance, making props that explore the role of objects in the context of dance and movement. No

Jo Cope (UK, graduated in 2017), *Looking for Love, 2017*
Material—Calf leather, wood and brass heels
Photographer © Nigel Essex

longer accessories or costume, her works act as critical agents of choreography and performance. Second, Ana's research explores new technologies and contexts for making prosthetics, collaborating with artists and scientists at the Neurorobotics Research Laboratory in Berlin.

For her Masters collection Jo used traditional shoe-making skills to develop a series of reconfigured shoes: exaggerated, extruded, twisted, and surreal. "Love Triangle" shows three abstracted pairs of shoes composed into a triangular formation, presented as installation and/or apparatus for performance. Other shoes remain as objects for display. Jo describes her artifacts as a metaphor for human relationship dynamics and personalities. As wearable objects for performance, Jo's work provides content for choreographers exploring similar themes of inter-relationships. As installation the absence of the body requires her audience to imagine the persons involved in the personality dynamics her works suggest.

Since graduation Jo has regularly collaborated with artists, choreographers, and performers practicing in areas where fashion overlaps with performance. Exhibitions of her work bring performance into the art gallery, rather than placing it on stage. She gives workshops and teaches in the fashion department at De Montfort University, Leicester.

As outlined by the selection of graduate works, the pathways for exploring the complex of relations between artist craftwork and design, the body and adornment, jewellery and sculpture, that have developed through my own practice and in the work of students on the Fashion Artifact MA at LCF share common preoccupations and themes. We are all engaged with changing contexts in which work is placed for both use and exhibition, particularly in areas where related industries of art, craft, design, and performance overlap one another.

The graduates I have discussed exemplify how the course enables students to develop from a design and creative basis in fashion education to making and displaying work beyond that original framework. This makes clear that the categories in which they may have been educated and trained need not constrain the form, substance, and character of the works they produce. What directs the professional pathways of makers are the artifacts they produce. The works themselves, together with the evolving dialogue that accompanies them, become agents in facilitating change in the sites and contexts in which they come to be displayed and used. The platform we have developed on the MA in Fashion Artifact at LCF provides space for the evolving dialogue and focused making. The graduate results provide significant contribution to the evolution of fashion accessories beyond adornment, as key to expressing ways of thinking for design and living. It is in this way that I see fashion artefacts as social and cultural facilitators.

Can Professional Jewellery Designers Using Consensual Assessment Technique (CAT) Achieve an Appropriate Level of Interrated Agreement When Judging a Specific Jewellery Design Creativity Task?

Mala SIAMPTANI

Designer and Researcher

The consensual assessment technique (CAT) (Amabile, 1982) is a commonly used technique for the assessment of creativity, according to which the best judges of creativity are experts of the specific domain in question. This paper will review existing research on the use of CAT within the design domain. The research strategy used is a reflection of the theories being investigated and in extending such research this study has been designed to explore whether CAT can be used as a measure of jewellery design creativity.

As required when applying CAT, 30 artworks in the form of ring designs were collected and accessed by seven professional jewellery designers for their level of creativity, technical execution, and aesthetic appeal. Once the judgments were obtained, ratings on each dimension were then analyzed for inter-rated agreement in addition to their relationship with creativity and the two other design attributes (technical execution and aesthetic appeal).

The findings are especially significant given the fact that CAT procedure had never before been employed as a means of measuring creativity within jewellery design. Hence due to the lack of research in the area, a benchmark should be established for further studies.

Introduction

The jewellery designer's pallet is one without limits, informed by an endless stream of ideas, themes, motifs, as well as historical references. Jewellery design can be considered as subjective self-expression, which has evolved through the centuries according to the social as well as the economic factors of the time. When considering how much the field of jewellery design has expanded over the years, one might contemplate on the growing number of academies and universities providing courses where the techniques of designing and making of jewellery are taught.

Through the years, jewellers have attempted to test the boundaries of the field by breaking new ground either by inventing new techniques, exploring different materials, or simply by investigating whether something is possible. Thus, jewellery is a domain that can be divided to a few subcategories, with the primary ones being fine, fashion, contemporary, and art jewellery. Fine jewellery can be considered as the leading category of the field since designs within this category are created with precious materials and can be used as an investment, or desirable objects worth collecting and passing down to new generations. On the contrary, the term fashion/costume jewellery refers to more affordable, nonprecious pieces fabricated with plated metal, used to embellish one's outfit. Contemporary jewellery in an attempt to expand the entire concept of jewellery (in terms of making and wearing it); it is perhaps the most undefinable category as many different kinds of objects and practices can be considered part of it. Like contemporary and fashion jewellery, art jewellery breaks away from the limiting idea in which jewellery is valued according to the precious materials that it is made out of. Art jewellery is very much related to contemporary jewellery as an unrestricted jewellery category since it values innovative thinking and creative expression, forming a blurry boundary between art and jewellery.

The starting point of the process of developing a piece of jewellery is, like most design subjects, the initial concept thought which can be communicated in visual terms and then becomes concrete when taking form through the employment of various systems of fabrication.

In the competitive and at times commercial world of jewellery, the creative and novel designs can occasionally stand out and be acclaimed purely for that reason. Nonetheless, being creative in this field may not necessarily be a matter of originality, especially when it comes to fine jewellery. Repetition is fairly common in jewellery design since, for manufacturing purposes, it saves time. Where as fine and fashion jewellery are often mass produced, contemporary and art jewellery are mostly one of a kind. Kneller (1965) argues that one of the paradoxes of creativity is that in order to think originally we must familiarize ourselves with the ideas of others. This case can be supported in jewellery as each creator views ideas from fellow designers in order to produce a more original or desirable wearable object.

Philosophers and psychologists interested in the study of creativity have for a long time been questioning the relationship between process and product. Rhodes (1961), in an attempt to organize creative research, has developed the "four P's of creativity." This model segregates the creative person, product, process, and press (environment) where Rhodes states that:

The word creativity is a noun naming the phenomenon in which a person communicates a new concept (which is the product). Mental activity (or mental process) is implicit in the definition, and of course no one could conceive of a person living or operating in a vacuum, so the term press is also implicit (Rhodes, 1961).

Throughout the years, many researchers have attempted to define creativity, however, for the purposes of this paper the definitions of Amabile and Stein are of importance. In 1953 Stein introduced the terms "useful" and "novel" in his definition of creativity:

Creativity is a process that results in novelty which is accepted as useful, tenable, or satisfying by a significant group of others at some point in time. While Amabile in 1983 stated: "A product or response is creative to the extent that appropriate observers independently agree it is creative. ...and it can also be regarded as the process by which something so judged is produced (Stein, 1953).

Although Stenberg (1991) questioned such precise definitions and suggested that assessments of creativity need be broaden and reassessed.

As there seems to be a great interest, for researchers, to assess creativity, many methods have been constructed and implemented, such as divergent thinking tests, self-assessment inventories, or judgments of products. Much of this research was focused on measuring divergent thinking (Wallach and Kogan, 1965; Getzel and Jackson, 1962; Torrance, 1966), with Torrance been the most common tests used in recent years (Davis, 1997). Although the Torrance Test of Creative Thinking (TTCT) focuses on understanding and nurturing qualities that help people express their creativity, it does not necessarily assess creativity. Some of the uses of TTCT, as suggested by Torrance, is to understand the mind, its development and functions, to discover effective bases for individualizing instruction, in addition to examining the effects of educational programs and teaching procedures. The majority of these methods have a lot of similarities with IQ tests and have been constructed in order to maximize individual differences. Hennessey et al. (2011) identifies that existing subjective assessment methods relied on products that depend heavily on the participants' level of expertise. Nonetheless, when it comes to evaluating a creative product, there are several approaches using different instruments applied in the education system, asking educators to rate specific aspects of student's creative products. Runco stated that divergent thinking tests have yet to be socially validated, thus in 1984 he created the Teachers' Evaluation of Students' Creativity (TESC) test. This instrument was developed for teachers' conceptions of creativity and was later used to rate creativity in gifted, talented, and non-gifted children, with results suggesting that social validation is related to creativity assessment and divergent thinking tests can be considered socially valid in terms of the teachers' judgments.

Although these instruments have been well used and provide valuable insights in creativity research, for this particular study a different approach was used to measure creativity in jewellery design, which focused on the creative product. The consensual assessment technique (CAT) was chosen as it is based on the idea that the best measure of the creativity of a work of art, a theory, or any other artifact is the combined assessment of experts in that field (Kaufman et al., 2008). Even though this idea of using experts to rate creative products has been around for quite a long time, the consensual assessment technique, as it is used today, was created by Teresa Amabile (1982).

This method has been used extensively in creativity research and has been called the "golden standard" of creativity assessment (Carson, 2006). Its widest use is in research because it is based on judges and comparisons of actual products created by subjects whilst not being tied to any particular theory of creativity and it mimics the way creativity is assessed in the "real world." Unlike divergent thinking tests, were the participants are required to respond to a series of predetermined items or questions, what sets the CAT methodology apart is the fact that subjects simply produce an actual product.

Amabiles (1982) defined creativity as existing only when recognized by others. This in the only theory that CAT may be considered to be based upon; the belief that experts in a given domain can recognize creativity when they see it. Unlike any other measures of creativity, such as divergent-thinking tests, since defined creativity criteria is absent, CAT is made more robust as an instrument, as it does not rely on researchers choosing the right criteria (Dagny and Balder, 2015). When experts in any given domain cannot recognize creativity when they see it in that domain, then no assessment of creativity can have any meaning (Baer, 1994).

Previous researcher (Amabile et al., 2011) using CAT, have demonstrated that although creativity in a product may be difficult to characterize in terms of specific features, it is something that people can recognize and agree upon when they see it. In addition, people familiar with a particular domain can agree with one another on this perception. CAT has been used to measure both individual and group creativity, for the purposes of which a variety of tasks has been used to measure creativity in poems, drawings, T-shirt designs, advertisements, short stories, music, and paper collages to name a few. Baer and McKool, in their paper published in 2009, advocate that CAT can indeed be implemented to judge creativity in just about anything that can be considered imaginative or original work.

Amabile (1983, 1996) used CAT to compare creative performance under different motivational constrains, while other studies investigated gender and ethnicity differences in creativity (Kaufman et al., 2004; Baer, 1994) also looked into the long term stability of creativity in a given domain. Amabile (1996) in a series of studies found that the when participants are offered some sort of reward, creative performance seems generally at a lower level. In later studies conducted in 1997 and 1998, Baer investigated these effects of motivational constraints and how they influence the creativity of boys and girls, with results indicating that boys showed higher creative performance than girls.

In studies conducted in 1994 by Hennessey, 30 undergraduate students served as judges of 20 geometric designs created on Apple computers by 14 upper-level psychology students.

The process and finished product were both stored on the computer via a program that was written specifically for this study. The raters were then split into two groups in order to have half assess the final product and the other half assess not only the finished product but also the steps that went into producing that product. This study concluded that, when using CAT, untrained raters can recognize and agree upon the creativity, technical goodness, and aesthetic appeal of computer designs but also the creativity, technical goodness, and aesthetic appeal of the process that went into producing the designs.

Jeffries (2012) highlights the existence of very few CAT studies within design journals. Reasons for this might be exactly because CAT is not tied to any particular definition of creativity or because of concerns regarding its validity as a measure of creativity in design. In a more resent study, Jeffries (2015) investigated the reliability of CAT as a measure of graphic design creativity. In addition, this study looked into the impact of discarding technical execution in assessing creativity in the field. Results of this study showed acceptable inter-rater reliability for these tasks, with higher levels showing when judges were asked to discount technical execution when assessing creativity.

Valgeirsdottir and Onarheim (2015) were inspired by Hennessey's CAT setup in 1994, and asked their judges to assess creativity, technical advancement, aesthetic appeal, and the added field of purchasability. The researchers concluded that CAT is not an appropriate method to use when determining attributes such as purchasability and potentially other attributes could relate to consumer behaviors better.

Pilot Study

Untracht (1985) stated that a jeweller's knowledge increases not only with one's hands on experience in the field but also by observation. "The ability to recognize and understand concepts and process makes possible a profound 'conversation' between the jeweler and any finished work." Thus, jewellers should be able to assess products designed in this field. Nevertheless, as CAT has not been applied in jewellery before, a pilot for this methodology had to take place prior to the main study.

The focus of this pilot study was on the judges' consensus and not the participants, the influence of teaching, or environment factors that may impact creativity. Thus, following Kaufman et al. (2008) indications that CAT is based on the idea that the best measure of creativity of a work of art, a theory, or any other artifact is the combined assessment of experts in the field, five professionals were recruited to rate 30 designs.

For many CAT studies, participants—under experimental conditions—are required to carry out a task in order to create a piece of work. Baer et al. (2004) state that the standard format for CAT is to have experts' judge creativity in artworks produced under identical conditions (all subjects receiving identical instructions and time limitations). Although recent studies show that CAT may also work when products are created under different conditions. Therefore, for the purpose of this pilot, a range of 30 ring design images of already existing pieces of jewellery, designed by professionals during 2009–2013 were selected. These pieces were images of ¾ views of the designs on a plane white background.

Kaufman and Baer's (2012) suggestions on who would be an appropriate expert to judge the creativity of a specific product were taken into consideration, setting the perameters for the five designers chosen who had: a minimum three years of professional experience in the field of either contemporary jewellery, fine jewellery, or art jewellery. Individual meetings with these judges were set and these 30 pieces were presented to them. Judges were instructed to look

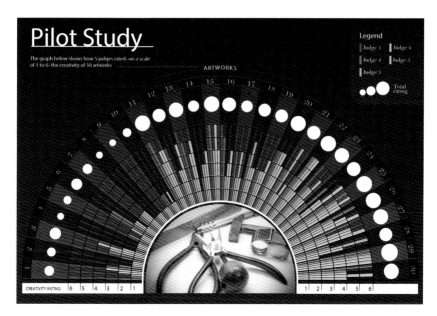

Graph 1

13

through the jewellery pieces, and rate them for creativity, with no need to explain or defend their ratings in any way; they were asked only to use their own sense of which is more or less creative (relative to the other jewellery pieces provided). The judges were also asked to use their own subjective definitions of creativity when rating these designs, then to group the artworks into low, medium, or high rating categories. Lastly, they were asked to assign a numerical rating between 1 and 6 (1 being the least creative and 6 being the most creative). The ratings of the five judges are reported in Graph 1 (see above).

Hennessey et al. (2011) state that although creativity in a product is difficult to characterize in terms of specific features it is something that people can recognize and agree upon when they see it. Interestingly, this was the case with the pilot: once the judges' ratings were obtained, they were then analyzed for reliability. As it is the standard procedure when applying the Consensual Assessment Technique (Valgeirsdottir and Onarheim, 2015; Kaufman et al., 2008), in order to estimate the reliability of the pilot, a Cronbach's alpha calculation had to be performed.

If according to Hennessey et al. (2011), the acceptable correlation coefficient level is 0.7, the results of this pilot were highly acceptable, as the Cronbach's alpha calculation was 0.899.

Main Study

Key to this project was to discover how creativity can be measured when it comes to jewellery design. Creativity, for the purposes of this study, is defined as existing only when recognized by others. Results of this pilot show that when using CAT, the judges can agree on what is creative when it comes to jewellery design.

This study utilizes the consensual assessment technique for the reason that it is a subjective assessment tool and, therefore, the requirements set by Amabile (1982) were followed. The judges were all familiar with the domain in question, made their assessments independently, and were instructed to rate the artworks in relation to one another. In addition, to prevent bias, all judges viewed the works in a different randomized order. As CAT is applied to jewellery for the first time, the judging panel were asked to assess not only creativity, as it was the case with the pilot, but also technical execution and aesthetic appeal. This was set in place in order to access how these other features relate to the creative judgments, if at all.

Hennessey et al. (2011) provided recommendations for mirror real-life assessments, in which researchers would be better served if they allowed the judges to apply their own definitions of creativity rather than imposing specific definitions to them. Hence no definition of creativity was presented to the judges in this study. Baer and McKool (2009) state that since CAT is the only method not tied to any specific theory of creativity, it is therefore unbiased to the ongoing debate on domain specificity.

In continuing with assessing the impact of varying constrains on a creative performance, studies such as Kaufman, Baer, and Gentile's (2004) seemed very useful as they concluded that regarding gender, race, and ethnicity, CAT scores show very little evidence of differences. Therefore, the use of participants coming from 12 different countries should not be considered a limitation.

Task Selection

After careful consideration of the pilot findings, a task was set for the main study, requiring the participants to design a ring. This task took into account the comments judges were making while rating the art works for the pilot. Therefore, the participants were asked to create technical drawings showing plan, front elevation and ¾ view on an A4 paper.

Materials used:
-Silver
-Red gemstone

Sketch Example

Even though historically jewellery has been made from a diverse range of materials, from textiles to glass, wood, plastics, or precious metals and stones, the participants taking part in this study were asked to design a piece using a minimum of 80% silver while the remaining 20% could be any material or their choice. In addition, they were asked to give a short explanation of the materials and colors used on the lower right-hand side of the A4 sheet. They were asked to be as creative as they could be and an example of how this task should have been presented was also given to them.

Participants

When collecting the brief responses from university students their similarity was apparent and therefore the use of other participants such as professionals and novices was essential. Judges might find it challenging to rate designs too similar in quality and thus a range of diverse artworks should be presented to them (Jeffries, 2015). Thus, 14 students took part, of which nine were second- and third-year undergraduates and five were postgraduates; these were in addition to seven jewellery design professionals and nine novices making up the 30 participants with a range of work that could be presented to the judges.

While in Hennessey (1994), subjects received course credit for their participation, later on in a series of studies, Amabile (1996) found that leading participants to expect some sort of evaluation or even a reward after completing a required task lead to generally lower creative performances. Thus, no such promises were given to the participants in this study. In previous studies, Baer and Oldham (2006) suggest that time pressure can influence people's creative performance, while

Mueller and Kamdar (2011) concluded that social constrains, such as seeking help from teammates, can aid creativity in addition to enabling a relationship between motivation and creativity. Thus, when dealing with a brief, some resources or social constrains may influence peoples' creative problem solving and performance. Hence, all 30 participants for this study were given the same exact instructions and a week to finalize their design, however, some of the novices were not able to draw their design and therefore were given a week to think about their design, leading to a 20-minute support session with me to assist them in creating a 2D drawing as the brief required.

Participants

When collecting the brief responses from university students their similarity was apparent and therefore the use of other participants such as professionals and novices was essential. Judges might find it challenging to rate designs too similar in quality and thus a range of diverse artworks should be presented to them (Jeffries, 2015). Thus, 14 students took part, of which nine were second- and third-year undergraduates and five were postgraduates; these were in addition to seven jewellery design professionals and nine novices making up the 30 participants with a range of work that could be presented to the judges.

While in Hennessey (1994), subjects received course credit for their participation, later on in a series of studies, Amabile (1996) found that leading participants to expect some sort of evaluation or even a reward after completing a required task lead to generally lower creative performances. Thus, no such promises were given to the participants in this study. In previous studies, Baer and Oldham (2006) suggest that time pressure can influence people's creative performance, while Mueller and Kamdar (2011) concluded that social constrains, such as seeking help from teammates, can aid creativity in addition to enabling a relationship between motivation and creativity. Thus, when dealing with a brief, some resources or social constrains may influence peoples' creative problem solving and performance. Hence, all 30 participants for this study were given the same exact instructions and a week to finalize their design, however, some of the novices were not able to draw their design and therefore were given a week to think about their design, leading to a 20-minute support session with me to assist them in creating a 2D drawing as the brief required.

Suitable Judges

Kaufman et al. (2008) state that CAT is based on the idea that the best measure of creativity of an artwork, a theory, or any other artifact is the combined assessment of experts in the field.

Amabile (1996) suggests that the average of expert judges used to rate artworks in CAT can be just over ten with a minimum of two. That is because the greater the number of judges, the higher the overall inter-rated reliability correlation (Kaufman et al., 2008). On the other hand, using fewer than five experts runs the serious risk of having an unacceptable low level of inter-rated reliability. Five to ten experts represents a sufficiently large group, although the level of expertise within the domain for all judges need not be identical. Thus, following the suggestions of Kaufman and Baer (2012) on who would be an appropriate expert to judge the creativity of a specific product, seven jewellery experts with a minimum of three years' experience in the field were selected.

This group of independent experts were selected to rate the 30 ring designs produced for this study, since they were familiar with the domain in which the designs were created for and the response articulated by the participants. These judges are practicing in two different subcategories of jewellery; three are fine jewellers and four contemporary jewellers with enough experience in the field to be able to have some implicit criteria for creativity, technical execution, and aesthetic appeal.

Following Amabile (1982, 1996, and 2011) recommendations on who would be the best panel to make such judgments, raters—for his study—did not exchange views with each other so as to avoid influencing one another's judgments in any way; they were not trained in any way by the researcher either. The instructions given to them were to use their own subjective definition of creativity, technical execution, and aesthetic appeal to rate the designs in comparison to one another.

Instructions to Judges

In recent studies, focused on graphic design (Jeffries, 2015), results showed that aggregated scores are more likely to appear when using a caveat on technical execution, which enabled distinctions within a group on creativity levels. Thus, this study asked judges to discard technical execution when rating for creativity, in addition to aesthetic appeal, cost, or even profit potential. When assessing creativity, technical execution, and aesthetic appeal the judges were asked to rate the rings solely on the basis of each of these attributes. The reason for this was to see if the judges could differentiate each attribute from creativity and detect if any positive correlations would appear between them.

Following the footsteps of Jeffries (2015), the set of instructions given to the judging panel was an adopted version of Kaufman, Baer, Cole and Sexton's 2008 study, and inserted was a sentence adapted by Baer's 1993 CAT instruction.

> *Please look through these art works and rate them for creativity. There is no need to explain or defend your ratings in any way; we ask only that you use your own sense of which is more or less creative (relative to the other jewellery pieces provided).*

> *We realize that creativity probably overlaps other criteria one might consider (for example: aesthetic appeal, or technical execution, cost, or even profit potential), but we ask you to rate the artworks solely on the basis of their creativity.*

> *Please look through these artworks three times, and rate them for creativity.*
> * *The first time familiarize yourself with all the artworks provided.*
> * *The second time, group the artworks into low, medium, or high ratings.*
> * *The third time, assign a numerical rating between 1 and 6 (1s being the least creative and 6s being the most creative).*
> *There should be a roughly even number of artworks at each of the six levels. It is very important that you use the full 1-6 scale.*

For this study, when meeting with the judges, the same procedures were followed for all seven.

Results

This study used participants that came from 12 different countries and judges from six. The 30 participants who gave their consent to take part in this study were 27 females and three males, with a mean age just over of 27 years (SD: 7.85, median: 26). The judges were four females and three males with ages ranging from 32 to 63 and a mean age just under 42 (SD: 11.04, median: 39). All seven judges were professional jewellery designers with experience in the field ranging from six to 35 years and a mean just over 15 years.

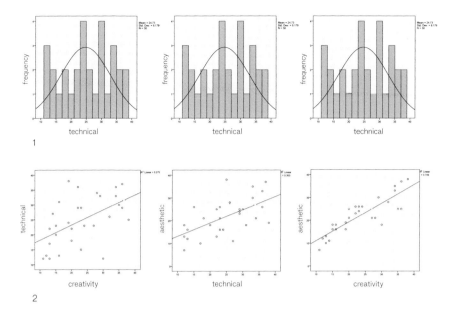

1

2

1. *Graph 2*
2. *Graph 3*

Cronbach's Alpha calculation was performed for each of the rated attributes, as it is a standard procedure when utilizing CAT. This calculation helps to determine whether it is justifiable to interpret scores that have been aggregated together as well as to enhance the validity and accuracy to the interpretation of this study's data. For this ring task, ratings of all seven judges were found to be highly consistent for creativity with an alpha of 0.86. Even though results showed slightly less consistency for technical execution (a = 0.84), and aesthetic appeal (a = 0.80), reliability is highly acceptable for all three attributes.

The distribution of the creativity ratings is shown in Graph 2 (skewness = 0.73), the technical execution ratings (skewness = -0.26), and the aesthetic appeal distribution (skewness = 0.66). We can see that, especially for the creativity ratings, the scores are positively skewed with more scores concentrated around the lower values.

A sum over all of the judges' ratings was calculated for all 30 ring designs and correlation analysis was performed with Pearson's r being calculated to measure the degree of linear relationship between these variables. The strength of the correlation between creativity and technical execution is shown in Graph 3, with Pearson's r at 0.52, suggesting a strong positive correlation between the scores,

Main study

Key to this project was to discover how creativity can be measured when it comes to jewellery design. This graph exhibits the ratings taken from all 7 judges on creativity, technical execution and aesthetic appeal of the 30 ring designs presented to them. The results demonstrate that the inter-rated reliability was acceptable for all attributes, as Alpha for all was above 0.7, with the highest being the creativity rating results at 0.86. This calculation is helping to determine whether it is justifiable to interpret scores which have been aggregated together as well as to enhance the validity and accuracy to the interpretation of this study's data

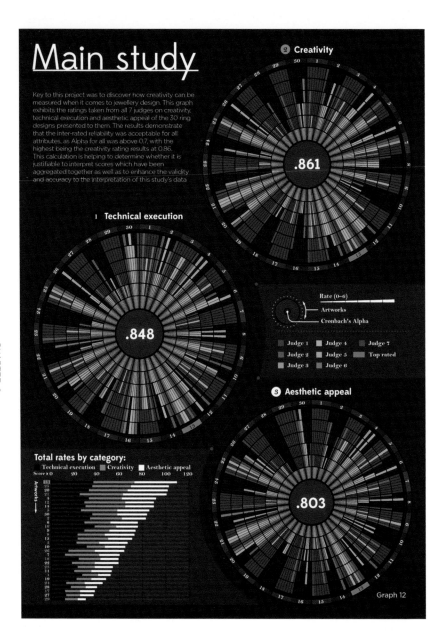

② Creativity

.861

Ⅰ Technical execution

.848

Rate (0–6)

Artworks

Cronbach's Alpha

Judge 1   Judge 4   Judge 7
Judge 2   Judge 5   Top rated
Judge 3   Judge 6

③ Aesthetic appeal

.803

Total rates by category:

Technical execution   Creativity   Aesthetic appeal

Score ▶ 0   20   40   60   80   100   120

Artworks ⟶

Graph 12

Graph 4

in addition to a significant correlation at the 0.001 level (1-tailed test). Graph 3 was used to help us understand the relationship between these variables. The strength of the correlation between creativity and aesthetic appeal is shown with Pearson r at 0.86, suggesting a very strong positive correlation and a null hypothesis of no correlation between the two attributes is rejected at the 0.00 level. The strength of the correlation between technical execution and aesthetic appeal is with an r of 0.59, suggesting a strong correlation, while a null hypothesis of no correlation between the two attributes is rejected at the 0.00 level. The ratings of the five judges are reported on the main study graph.

This study was designed to examine these three questions: (1) Are professional jewellery designers able to reliably assess the creativity of a given ring design task?(2) Is it possible for these judges to separate creativity from technical execution and aesthetic appeal? And, (3) if so, what is the relationship between these ratings?

Although CAT is acknowledged by some researchers as a prominent method of assessing creativity (Kaufman et al., 2008), very few studies can be found in design journals (Jeffries, 2012). One reason for this might be the fact that the use of CAT can be very resource intensive. CAT requires more time (Kaufman et al., 2008), particularly time for expert judges, than most other methods of creativity assessment. The a ssembly of the judging panel is not a simple task, and one cannot replace experts with novices (Kaufman et al., 2008) for this particular project.

Since CAT has not previously been used with the purpose of investigating the relationship between creativity and jewellery design, the findings of this study can be considered a benchmark for future studies. Thus, there was a need for a pilot to evaluate whether a group of professionals could agree on what is creative in the field of jewellery design.

The results of the pilot, and main study, demonstrate that the inter-rated reliability was acceptable for all attributes, as they were all above 0.7, with the highest being the pilot results at 0.89. Like the small amount of studies found to be directly related to design, the CAT in this study has shown sufficient levels of consensus within the jewellery domain.

When questioning what task could potentially measure creativity, the answer was not so clear prior to this study. Creativity in artworks that have been created under different conditions can still be used in CAT, as there seem to be no limitations to prevent judges from comparing these art works (Baer, Kaufman, and Gentile, 2004). However, Kaufman et al. (2008) advise that the artworks have to be of the same kind, as one cannot expect judges to produce meaningful comparative ratings of creativity with a mix of different artworks. In line with these results and suggestions, for the pilot and main study, there was only one style of jewellery piece presented to the judges. A ring was selected as it could be considered as a style that presents fewer difficulties for the participants to design and most appropriate for the judges to rate instead of presenting them with a variation of pieces, such as necklaces, bracelets, and rings.

For the pilot, the lack of different viewpoints for each design was resolved in the main study by adding the requirement of three views for the technical drawing showing plan, front elevation and view on an A4 paper. This was introduced to the brief in order to give judges a better understanding of how a piece looks in addition to the materials used. The constraint of using 80% silver was set in place to attain some sort of uniformity, as well as having a material that all judges were familiar with. There were no limitations on what colors or media to use on the A4 sheet, as long as all three design views were clearly displayed. The participants were also free to use CAD (Computer Aided Design) if they felt more comfortable with it than producing a hand drawing. The notes provided by the participants about the work, on the lower right hand side of the A4 sheet, were also introduced to the brief, in order to give the judges a clearer idea about each of the designs.

According to Hennessey (1994), if all judgments were made in the same order by all raters, there would have been high levels of agreement reflecting methodological artifacts and therefore the results would not have been reliable. For that reason the rings were shown in a different order to each judge. Reliability is important because in the absence of reliability it is impossible to have any validity associated with the scores of this scale.

Various other published documents have provided recommendations for requesting from the judges to rate, in addition to creativity, technical execution and aesthetic appeal. This requirement was met by retrieving these additional evaluations in this study, it was possible to examine the degree of relatedness or independence of these dimensions in subjective judgments of the 30 ring designs in question. In Amabile's paper (1996) the researcher identified that judges were able to differentiate creativity from these other aspects. Nevertheless, in an earlier

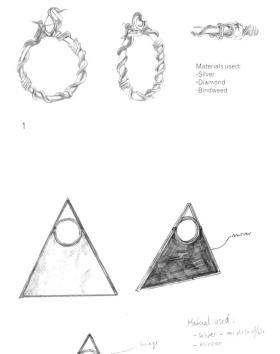

Materials used:
-Silver
•Diamond
-Bindweed

1

mirror

Material used:
- silver - oxidised/blc
- mirror

hinge

2

1. Example 1
2. Example 2

study, Hennessey (1994) indicates that, within some domains, it may be difficult to obtain ratings of product creativity that are not highly positively correlated with judges' assessments of a product's technical goodness or aesthetic appeal. This was the case with the main study, as the results showed that while the experts agreed in their judgments of creativity, there were significant positive correlations with the technical execution (r .52), and aesthetic appeal (r .86) judgments. As these correlations seem quite high, such result can be intrepid in terms of judges failing to discriminate between these three attributes. Another possible interpretation might be the fact that in the domain of jewellery design, creative pieces must be well executed as well as aesthetically pleasing. A jewellery piece may be valued more for its aesthetic content than the preciousness of the materials it is made out of. Since jewellery is linked with the wearer's individual external physical appearance, aesthetic awareness is present. On the contrary, the message of some pieces might go in the exact opposite direction against established aesthetic attitudes and demand a different type of attention when worn.

The brief set out to design a ring has been verified to be a suitable task, however, more revealing were the correlations between creativity, aesthetic appeal, and technical execution. The main point to consider is the fact that this study has demonstrated that CAT is a favorable method when assessing creativity in jewellery design. This study adds to the already existing research supporting the idea that at any point in time there is no more valid or objective measure of creativity of an artwork/design than the collective opinions of a group of professionals in the field. However, it is unquestionably true that experts might not always agree with each other, and their opinions may change over time, especially for a field like jewellery design were fashion trends play such an important part.

Limitations and Suggestions

This study has a few limitations. First, the use of professionals who practice in two different areas (contemporary jewellery and fine jewellery) within jewellery design may or may not have had an influence on the results. Future studies could investigate any possible individual differences between different groups of judges. As we break away from the traditional concept of jewellery in terms of using different materials, there is perhaps a difference on what can be considered creative in fine jewellery and what can be considered creative in contemporary or art jewellery. Thus, the correlations between these fields should be further investigated.

When it comes to contemporary art, one might argue that creativity may be highly dependent on the story of the creative process. In Valgeirsdottir, Onarheim, and Gabrielsen (2015), the researchers investigated if information about the process behind developing a product plays a role in the assessment of the creative process, with results showing small but not significant effect. Nonetheless, is this the case when it comes to jewellery? Will perceptions of creativity levels increase if information on the concept of a design is presented to the judges in jewellery design assessment?

With the rapid technological advancements in the past decade, Computer Aided Design (CAD) played an important role in design, in terms of its capabilities, in general. CAD has pushed the boundaries, particularly in jewellery design, as it is used in order to save manufacturing time, in addition to making complicated pieces, which we were not possible in the past, achievable.

If the birth of contemporary jewellery is the result of designers attempt to rebel against the restrictive boundaries of the field, then what should be put in place to assess the work of the new generation of jewellers? Future studies could explore to what extend does CAD influence creativity within the design domain.

Conclusion

Previous researchers work in developing and validating the Consensual Assessment Technique for quantifying creativity, as well as other aspects of diverse creative products, has made possible a variety of experimental studies in creativity research. Even though, for over three decades, researchers have employed CAT in their investigations of creativity, there seemed to be a lack of research in the area of jewellery design. This study could be considered as an established benchmark for further studies.

For this study we were not looking for a measure of skills or traits that are hypothesized to be part of creative thinking or performance, but instead we were assessing actual creative products and therefore CAT was an appropriate method. It has many potential applications, especially within the creative industries but it is not without limitations, such as crafting an appropriate brief for the participants, as well as being very resource intensive when it comes down to assembling participants and groups of expert judges.

The research question is concerned with whether a group of experts can reach a consensus on what they identify as creative, technically executed well, and aesthetically appealing in jewellery without being provided precise definitions of these three attributes.

One might conclude from the results of the current study that CAT is an appropriate method when determining attributes such as creativity, technical execution, and aesthetic appeal in jewellery design. When looking at the statistical results, it is revealed that technical execution and aesthetic appeal display a significant relationship with creativity, thus further research is needed in order to investigate the overlap between these three attributes and a possible effect on the use of CAT when measuring creativity in the domain of jewellery design.

Reference

Amabile, T. M. 1982. "Social Psychology of Creativity: A Consensual Assessment Technique." In *Journal of Personality and Social Psychology*, 43 (5): 997–1,013.

Amabile. T. M. 1983. *The Social Phycology of Creativity*. New York: Springer-Verlag.

Amabile. T. M. 1996. *Creativity in Context: Update to the Social Psychology of Creativity*. Boulder, CO: Westview.

Baer. M., and G. R. Oldham. 2006. "The Curvilinear Relation between Experienced Creative Time Pressure and Creativity: Moderating Effects of Openness to Experience and Support for Creativity." In *Journal of Applied Phycology*, 91(4): 963–70.

Baer,J., and S. S. McKool. 2009. "Assessing Creativity Using the Consensual Assessment Technique." In *Handbook of Assessment Technologies, Methods, and Applications in Higher Education*, edited by C.Schreiner, 65–77, Hersey, PA: IGI Global.

Baer, J. 1994a. "Divergment Thinking is not a General Traid: A Multi-domain Training Experiment." In *Creativity Research Journal*, 7: 35–46.

Baer, J. 1994b. "Performance Assessments of Creativity: Do They Have Long-term Stability?" In *Roeper Review*, 7(1): 7–11.

Baer, J. 1997. "Gender Differences in the Effects of Anticipated Evaluation on Creativity." In *Creativity Research Journal*, 10: 25–31.

Baer, J. 1998b. "Gender Differences in the Effects of Extrinsic Motivation on Creativity." In *Journal of Creative Behavior*, 32: 297–300.

Carson, S. 2006. Creativity and Mental Illness. Invitational Panel Discussion Hosted by Yale's Mind Matters Consortium, New Haven, CT.

Davis, G. A. 1997. "Identifying creative students and measuring creativity." In *Handbook of Gifted Education*, edited by N. Colangelo and G. A. Davis, 269–81. Needham Heights, MA: Viacom.

Getzels, J. W. and P. W. Jackson, 1962. *Creativity and intelligence: Explorations with Gifted Students*. New York: Wiley.

Hennessey, B. A. 1994. "The Consensual Assessment Technique: An Examination of the Relationship between Ratings of Product and Process Creativity." In *Creativity Research Journal*, 7(2): 193–208.

Hennessey, B. A., T. M. Amabile, and J. S. Mueller. 2011. "Consensual Assessment." In *Encyclopedia of Creativity*, edited by M. Runco and S. R. Pritzker. Boston: Academic Press.

Jeffries, K. K. 2015. A CAT with Caveats: Is the Consensual Assessment Technique a Reliable. The Third International Conference on Design Creativity (3rd ICDC), Bangalore, India.

Jeffries, K. K, 2012. "Amabile's Consensual Assessment Technique: Why has It not been Used More in Design Creativity Research?" In *Proceedings of the 2nd International Conference on Design Creativity (ICDC 2012)*, Vol.1, 211–20.

Kaufman, J. C., J. Baer, and C. A. Gentile. 2004. "Differences in Gender and Ethnicity as Measured by Ratings of Three Writing Tasks." In *Journal of Creative Behavior*, 39: 56–69.

Kaufman, J. C., J. Baer, J. C. Cole, and J. D. Sexton. 2008. "A Comparison of Expert and Nonexpert Raters Using the Consensual Assessment Technique." In *Creativity Research Journal*, 20: 171–78.

Kaufman, J. C., J. A. Plucker, and J. Baer. 2008. *Essentials of Creativity Assessment*. New Jersey: John Wiley & Sons.

Kaufman, J. C., and J. Baer. 2012. "Beyond New and Appropriate: Who Decides What Is Creative?" In *Creativity Research Journal*, 24(1): 83–91.

Kneller, G. F. 1965. *The Art and Science of Creativity*. New York: Holt, Rinehart & Winston, Inc.

Mueller, J. S., and D. Kamdar. 2011. "Why Seeking Help from Teammates Is a Blessing and a Curse: A Theory of Help Seeking and Individual Creativity in Team Contexts." *Journal of Applied Psychology*, 96(2): 263–76.

Untracht, O. 1985. *Jewellery, Concepts and Technology*. New York: Doubleday Dell Publishing Group Inc.

Runco, M. A. 1984. "Teachers' Judgments of Creativity and Social Validation of Divergent Thinking Tests." *Perceptual and Motor Skills*, 59: 711–17.

Rhodes, M. 1961. "An Analysis of Creativity." In *The Phi Delta Kappan*. 42(7): 305–10.

Stein, M. I. 1953. "Creativity and Culture." In *The Journal of Psychology*, 36: 311–22.

Sternberg, R. S. 1991. "Three Facet Model of Creativity." In *The Nature of Creativity: Contemporary Psychological Perspectives*, edited by R. S. Sternberg, 125–48. Cambridge, N.Y.: Cambridge University Press.

Torrance, E. P. 1966. *The Torrance Tests of Creative Thinking—Norms-technical Manual Research Edition – Verbal Tests, Forms A and B – Figural Tests, Forms A and B*. Princeton, NJ: Personnel Press.

Valgeirsdottir, D., B. Onarheim, and G. Gabrielsen. 2015. "Product Creativity Assessment of Inovations: Considering the Creative Process."In *International Journal of Design Creativity and Innovation*, 3(2): 95–106.

Valgeirsdottir, D., and B. Onarheim. 2015. Beyond Creativity Assessment: Comparing Methods and Identifying Consequences of Recognized Creativity. The Third International Conference on Design Creativity (3rd ICDC), Bangalore, India.

Wallach, M. A., and N. Kogan. 1965. *Modes of Thinking in Young Children: A Study of the Creativity: Intelligence Distinction.* New York: Holt, Rinehart & Winston, Inc.

27

Sustainability through Materials
An Approach by SILENT GOODS

Volker KOCH
Founder of SILENT GOODS, Leather Craft Artisan and Consultancy.
Visiting Lecturer at Central Saint Martins, UK

At SILENT GOODS we believe that not everything you wear needs to shout for attention. It crafts luxury goods shaped by a silent aesthetic that prioritizes neutral yet beautiful product over the brand that is behind it. As a counterbalance to the constant shifts of fashion, it offers a permanent range of archetypal bags: resolutely designed for a single purpose, and hand-made by our passionate team who has dedicated their lives to their craft. Sustainability and transparency permeate the choices we make as a company. We want to make a positive social and environmental impact by selecting the most incredible yet sustainable materials available, offered directly to the consumer without the retail mark-up.

This article outlines our principles, highlights how we select sustainable materials, and addresses the emotional aspect of materials and its significant impact on sustainability.

Photography © Andy Malone

SILENT GOODS Founding Principles

1. No Logos
By completely removing all labels, logos, and meaningless detail, we create pieces of real quality that remain understated, quietly accentuating your natural personal style, not "hijacking" it.

2. Sustainable Materials
We are aware that making things will inevitably leave a footprint. Our

commitment is to step lightly and pay attention to even the smallest steps. The use of suitable materials stands at the forefront of our perspective on sustainability and we have put in a lot of care into making good choices.

3. Repairability

Discarding a product when it breaks should not be the only option. A well-looked-after bag, carefully made from good materials, and mended when in need of repair should have a life expectancy of many years, if not decades.

4. Transparency

We choose to be completely open about everything we do. There is a digital tag embedded in each bag. Simply by scanning it with your phone, you can access information about your bag, documented to the last detail. You can trace the full supply chain, track the journey each material takes right from its source, and see exactly how these elements make up the price you pay.

Selecting Appropriate Materials

At the beginning of the selection process for SILENT GOODS materials, we find it vital to have a thorough understanding of our supply and value chains. This also means finding out, scrutinizing, and assessing each step taken by our suppliers to create the components that we require.

Only then can we set and communicate the criteria to which the components are chosen. Hereby it may seem easier to communicate our choices as a company through familiar labels, like "recycled" or "organic," and such labels are easy to understand as either good or bad, cheap or expensive, sustainable or polluting. In reality, however, this approach does not always represent the true nature of things. Organic does not always mean eco-friendly and synthetic does not always mean bad for the environment. Once the criteria are set, we then evaluate and consider each component for suitability, environmental impact, and longevity.

When examining the typical "ingredients" for one of our leather bags, we can identify the following component groups: leather, textile, metal fittings and zips, reinforcements, adhesive, stitching thread, and packaging materials.

Leather

We only use one kind of leather from a single manufacturer. The naturally tanned, certified organic cow leather, tested and certified free of harmful substances, gets produced by the 140-year-old Tärnsjö House of Leather in Sweden. The raw material is exclusively locally sourced and comes from just three selected farms in the region.

Textile

For the lining we have chosen the hard wearing, gold certified Cradle to Cradle™ fabric Cycle 245 by the reputable German textile mill Lauffenmühle.

Metal Fittings and Zips

All our metal fittings are custom made from uncoated, hand-finished stainless steel by the Kin Lik Metal Manufactory in China. The end result is several times as costly as the most premium bag components currently on the market. It is worth it for us because it offers two distinctive benefits: first, because of the high quality base material it does not need to be coated in a precious metal; and second, because it is not coated or lacquered, there are no layers to wear off—something that happens to standard fittings through wear with different materials layers are revealed underneath. Plating and lacquering are highly toxic processes, so by omitting these we are also lessening our environmental footprint.

Even though the well-known zip manufacturer YKK offers a basic metal zip range with recycled tape (the fabric part of the zip), we were not fully satisfied with the handling of this product and opted for their top of the range Excella zip. We are hopeful and encourage zip manufacturers will invest into developing premium sustainably oriented products, something that is currently lacking in the market.

Reinforcements

A good quality leather bag uses a number of different supplementary materials in its construction, which are hidden to the eye. This is how bases are stiffened and stitching is reinforced. We use natural and recycled reinforcements as much as possible, such as leather fiber board, which is made from 90% recycled leather shavings, and natural fats and latex made by Salamander GmbH in Germany.

Adhesive

Most leather goods are made with a neoprene contact adhesive, which is a highly toxic solvent-based glue that needs specialist equipment to protect the maker's lungs. Our choice is the non-hazardous contact adhesive, Aquilim 315 produced by Renia in Germany—a water-based adhesive that is significantly less harmful to the makers and the environment.

Sewing Thread

For our seams we selected Mara rPET, a sewing thread produced by Gütermann in Germany and made of 100% recycled polyester. The raw material for this thread is mostly provided by recycling beverage bottles. The collected bottles are washed, shredded into flakes and melted. The microfilaments obtained from this are the basis for the Mara rPET thread range.

Packaging

While the product's materials are the main focus, we have made considerate choices for the packaging as well. To ship our bags, we source used and redundant cardboard, the kind that would normally be thrown away by big stores. The box might not look so impressive when it arrives at your door, but we believe there is a certain beauty to it, safely wrapped and closed with our white paper tape baring the phrase "It's what's inside that counts."

For our dust bags we partnered with an innovative Finnish start-up to create them. Made of their award-winning sustainable material "PAPTIC," it replaces what would traditionally be a plastic based product with a material that is light and durable, yet as easily biodegradable as cardboard.

Product—Wearer Relationship

While the material choices have a significant affect on the environment, we are aware that the biggest impact that we as a designer-manufacturer have, is dependent on the relationship formed between the product and the wearer. If for any reason, emotional or practical, the wearer discards the product before the end of its life expectancy, the resources and the footprint of the manipulation of those resources, that have gone into the creation of that product do not fulfil their potential and are effectively wasted.

1

2

1/2. Photography © Andy Malone

At SILENT GOODS we believe that cultivating this bond between the wearer and the product will have by far the biggest impact on the product's sustainability. This insight has evoked questions in us that have informed our perspective as well as the design of our products:

1. How do we create a product that does not become defunct emotionally?

2. How do we competently and easily fix a product that becomes defunct physically?

3. How do we create a company that is able to provide a service to the customer that does not end at the point of sale, but only begins?

In response to this, and with the help of the Sustainable Design Cards© formulated by the Designskolen Kolding, we have developed four building blocks that support and propagate an emotional product—wearer bond:

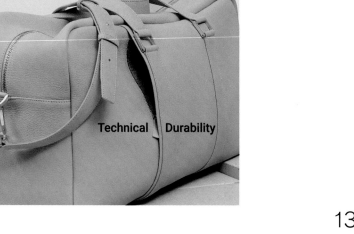

Technical Durability

1

134

2

1/2. Photography © Andy Malone

Design for Disassembly

We design our bags and our metal components in a modular construction. This way, should a component be damaged or broken from wear and tear, it makes it easier to remove product elements and replace them with new parts.

Technical Durability

During the product development phase, we conduct a risk assessment in which we aim to align our various materials' durabilities with the product's intended lifespan with respect to functional influences, such as abrasion, tearing strength, and aging. For example, in our handbag manufacturing, this insight could translate into identifying and eliminating potential weak spots or strengthening areas under constant tension (such as handles and their attachment points) by reinforcing these or by stitching them with a double seam. This way, over the lifetime of the product, breakage can be delayed, maximizing on the already used resources and minimizing the environmental footprint.

35

Maintenance and Repair

We offer a permanent warranty for the lifetime of a product, promoting and facilitating reparability and free product care. We invest in allowing our customers to form a bond with their product and at the same time build a sense of trust in our company.

Aesthetic Lifetime

We consciously use full grain vegetable tanned, unsealed leather for our bags, with the development of personal patina adding a unique aesthetic value that only increases over time. In every product this patina will be developing differently over time, depending on the environment it is used in and determined by the habits of its wearer. This shapes a sense of history and results in an emotional bond with the owner.

The last but extremely important aspect of the aesthetic lifetime of our products is our choice to keep the collection limited and not offer seasonal styles continuously from a design perspective. Instead, we deliberately choose not to follow the cyclic nature of the fashion industry and have just one core range of products, with a monofunctional design approach.

Contemporary Jewellery Design in South Korea
Historical Development and Current Status

Yong-il JEON
Professor, Kookmin University, South Korea

Contemporary jewellery from Korea has recently been enjoying increased visibility in global arenas. A large number of Korean jewellery artists have been recognized in international competitions, and young artists are being frequently invited by leading museums, galleries, and art fairs. With the aim of examining this increase in Korean artists' worldwide participation since the mid-2000s, this article explores the external influences, transformation process, and social dynamics of the past three decades of the development of Korean contemporary jewellery. Moreover, it seeks to better understand the backdrop to this achievement through a survey of the environment and conditions in which present-day jewellers are working.

Previous Generations and Their Influence

The development of contemporary jewellery can be said to have begun in the mid-1980s. Korean craft, which encompasses the field of jewellery, boasts an extensive history tracing back more than 1,500 years. Nevertheless, the correlation between this tradition and contemporary jewellery is weak. Only after the first half of the twentieth century, marked by the Japanese occupation (1910–1945) and the Korean War (1950–1953), and then the 1960s and '70s, which witnessed the establishment of modern Korean art, could the realm of contemporary jewellery rise to prominence.

Until the 1980s, the term "jewellery" conjured up among Koreans the tradition of *yemul*, or wedding gifts offered by the bridegroom's family to the bride, which normally included a set of jewellery comprising a ring, earrings, and necklace made with precious metals and stones. It was only after this point that jewellery designed and made by professionals who studied at fine art colleges began to emerge under the name of "contemporary jewellery" and "art jewellery." People known as "jewellers" eventually emerged, and exhibitions showcasing jewellery were organized by galleries that had previously focused on paintings.

This initial period for contemporary jewellery was ushered in mainly by metalsmiths who returned home after studying abroad. Many of these craftspeople had studied both metalwork and jewellery and then assumed professorships at prominent universities in Korea. They subsequently educated students in both fields.[1] Among those who studied metalwork for the first time at graduate schools abroad and came back to Korea in the early 1980s, key figures of the period include Seung-hee Kim and Lizzy Yoo, who studied in the United States; Sung-Won Martha Lee and Yae-Kyung Choo, who studied in Germany; and Jin-soon Woo, who studied in Sweden. These individuals exerted a substantial influence. In fact, despite the presence of other artists of the same age or older who had been educated entirely in Korea,[2] the early days of Korean contemporary jewellery was under a firm international influence.

The Korean-American Metal Arts Workshop, 1986.
This four-day grand-scale workshop at which seven American artists
visited Korea was well-received by Korean artists and students,
particularly the live demonstrations of techniques.

This period also witnessed the initiation of active international exchanges. American metalsmith Jack da Silva offered lectures in Korea for two years starting in 1982, and British goldsmith Stephen Bort did so for six years from 1983. A large-scale exhibition showcasing the work of 57 American jewellers was held at the Walker Hill Art Museum in 1986. In the same year, prominent American figures in the fields of metalwork and jewellery, including Robert Ebendorf, visited Korea for an international workshop.[3] During this four-day workshop they offered live demonstrations of various techniques, which was met with great enthusiasm among the Korean metalsmiths and jewellers who had been feeling a powerful thirst for new techniques. Komeila Hongja Okim, professor of Metal Art at Montgomery College in the United States, also served

1. These craftspeople were preceded by what could be considered the first generation of contemporary metalwork (or metalcraft) in Korea, which was led by figures active as both artists and educators. These include Kwon-hee Shin, Yoon-woo Chang, Chan-kyun Kang, and Hyun-chil Choi. These pioneers of contemporary metalwork established the foundation for the education in jewellery that took place in the following generation.

2. There are also artist/educators such as Jung-sil Hong, Jae-young Kim, and Kyung-hee Hong, who are of the same generation as those who studied abroad.

3. The Korean-American Metal Arts Workshop, 1986, held in Kookmin University, Seoul.

as a bridge by introducing American metalwork and jewellery education in Korea and facilitating exchanges between the two nations.

Many students continued to pursue overseas study. In the 1980s, the United States was the most popular destination for study abroad, whereas in the 1990s, the destinations expanded to include Japan, Germany, and the United Kingdom. Consequently, bilateral exchange with these countries increased. After the turn of the new millennium, the German influence on the metalwork and jewellery in Korea became prominent. The overseas study and international exchange experiences of this first generation of metalsmiths and jewellers laid a foundation for the active participation in global venues today enjoyed by contemporary Korean jewellers.

A New Generation of Jewellers and Education

From the 1990s onward, jewellery education in Korea grew more specialized, and jewellery emerged as an independent field. Unlike in the previous generation, which pursued both metalwork and jewellery, new artists concentrated on the sole professional production of jewellery. This gave rise to "studio jewellers," most of whom had completed an in-depth study of jewellery-making at an overseas graduate program after pursuing both metalwork and jewellery as an undergraduate in Korea. They mainly studied in the United States and Germany, and, therefore, the influence of these two countries on the Korean education system increased significantly.

Jeweller Jung-kyu Lee. In Korea, studio jewellers rose to prominence in the early 1990s

Korean contemporary jewellers, including Jung-hoo Kim, who received her Bachelor's degree from Seoul National University in Korea and her Master's from the State University of New York at New Paltz in the United States; Jung-kyu Lee, who studied at Fachhochschule Pforzheim in Germany and École Nationale Supérieure des Arts Appliqués et des Métiers d'Art (National School of Art and Design) in France; Myung-joo Lee, who studied at Hongik University in Korea and University of Georgia in the U.S.; Kwangsun Lee, who studied at Seoul National University and Fachhochschule Pforzheim; Dongchun Lee, who studied at Kookmin University in Korea and Fachhochschule Pforzheim; and Yeon-mi Kang, who studied at Seoul National University and Southern Illinois University in the U.S., comprised the first generation of contemporary jewellers to become university instructors.[4] They pioneered an education program specifically for jewellery that differed from the metalwork-focused scheme of the past, and actively introduced to the students globally recognized works of contemporary jewellery. It is during this period that the world of contemporary jewellery, which had established itself as an independent form of art in Europe since the 1970s, began to be introduced in Korea. Owing to the role and influence of these figures, jewellery making in Korea came to occupy a more significant position than metalsmithing after the new millennium.

In the curriculum, the teaching of techniques was of the greatest importance. Despite the change in the perception of jewellery in the context of "art jewellery," craftsmanship and completeness remained the central criteria in evaluating work. The techniques that were taught had been sourced from diverse areas. First, the metalworking techniques acquired in the U.S., Europe, and Japan by first-generation metalsmiths after the 1980s accounted for part of this education. This generation of early-period metalsmiths had studied overseas and taught the techniques they picked up abroad. They also consulted a wide range of reference books on technique, most of which had been published in English-speaking countries and Japan. Around 1990, books referencing these texts were published by authors in Korea.[5] In jewellery-making, metalsmithing techniques were later taught together with techniques for non-metal materials.

4. Other first-generation jewellers who served as educators include Meeyeon Jang, who received her Bachelor's degree from Ewha Womans University and Master's from Hongik University in Korea; Jin-Hwan Suh, who studied at Hongik University in Korea and the State University of New York at New Paltz; and Jung-lim Lee, who studied at Seoul National University in Korea and Florida State University in the U.S.
5. Some examples include Metal Craft (Hollym, 1985) by Soon-hwa Kwak, Metalwork and Jewellery Making (Design House, 1994) by Yong-il Jeon, and Goldsmithing & Jewellery Making (Jewellery Woman, 1999) by Kyeong-a Kim and Jung-lim Lee.

Jewellery design and making, which had been taught as part of metalwork courses within the university curriculum, emerged as the central subject starting in the late 1990s.

Secondly, the curriculum also included time-honored Korean craft techniques. Traditional jewellery and ornaments in Korea trace all the way back to the sixth century, but their connection with contemporary jewellery is quite insignificant. However, some traditional craft techniques, mainly transmitted by successors of traditional craft, have attracted the attention of contemporary jewellers. Traditional methods such as silver inlay, *Keumboo* (a gilding technique for applying thin sheets of gold to silver), and *ottchil* (lacquering) have been incorporated into contemporary Korean jewellery.

Thirdly, techniques from the realm of commercial jewellery are also included. Commercial jewellery, also called "fine jewellery," which established a solid foothold as an autonomous industrial area in the mid-twentieth century, was produced in workshops, staffed with a skilled labor force supplemented by apprentices. The techniques involved largely concerned the working of precious metals and stones incorporated into the university curriculum. This inclusion of techniques from commercial jewellery into the curriculum was partially driven by the large number of artisans with commercial jewellery experience among the studio assistants hired by the first generation of metalsmiths. In this light, jewellery education in Korea and the curriculum built around a broad spectrum of techniques was carried out with a focus on the practice of "making." Studio courses both in undergraduate and graduate programs in Korea required students to produce a greater number of works compared to those at overseas institutions, and strongly emphasized the completeness of objects by craftsmanship.

Within the context of contemporary jewellery, a dependence on technique may count as a weakness. A reliance on hand-based techniques from beginning to completion is likely to constrain the work within a fixed form or process and result in an outcome blind to the use of machine tools. However, Korean practitioners counterbalanced or overcame this challenge through the use of diverse hand skills demonstrating a mastery of the material. The importance of the "well-madeness" of a work, a standard that jewellers established during this period, continues to this day.

The greatest transformation in the field of jewellery since the start of the twenty-first century is the explosive expansion of the range of materials involved. The use of varied constituents beyond metals in the production of contemporary jewellery has become a worldwide phenomenon. The daring innovations using non-metal materials that began in Europe in the 1970s spread rapidly almost in an identical manner in Korea starting in the 2000s. Jewellery witnessed an expansion from metals into non-metals, including artificial materials such as plastic, synthetic resin, and silicone to existing natural materials such as stone, wood, and bone. From the mid-2000s onward, young jewellers concentrated their efforts on the discovery of their own unique materials. It was often the case that the material used determined the characteristics of a work.

This expansion in materials also led to an extension of the boundaries and diversity of contemporary jewellery, accompanied by increased resonance with and enthusiasm from global audiences. This change in turn fueled the production of more studio jewellers in Korea. One person in particular—jeweller and educator Dongchun Lee—played a crucial role in this process. Lee received a diploma from Fachhochschule Pforzheim in Germany. He began teaching at Kookmin University in Korea in 2003. He applied the contents and methods of the European jewellery education of the time to the Korean curriculum, with a particular focus on the study of materials. Large numbers of the students whom Lee educated and fostered are currently leading active careers as global artists. Many of them show similarities in having developed their own design language based on particular materials. To name just a few, there is Seulgi Kwon, who works with silicone; a specialist in ramie fabric, Mina Kang; Choonsun Moon, who uses plastic and wood; Ye-jee Lee and Hea-lim Shin, focused on leather; Yeseul Seo, who concentrates on felt; and Yo-jae Lee, who uses frog skin in combination with an assemblage of various other media.

Moreover, Dongchun Lee demonstrated to gallerists as well as to the general public how a wide range of other materials besides metals could be used for jewellery. This took place through a series of key special exhibitions curated by

1

2

1. Shin-lyoung Kim, Upside Down, bracelet, 925silver, 999silver, nickle silver, 65 mm x 20 mm, 2012 Craftsmanship was the core of Korean jewellery education, and the completeness of a work became the most important standard of evaluation.

2. Sang-hee Yun, Red Wens— Necklaces, ottchil, wood, 925silver, 250 mm x 65 mm, 2009
   Lacquering, known as ottchil in Korean, is a traditional technique that is still being successfully utilized in contemporary jewellery.

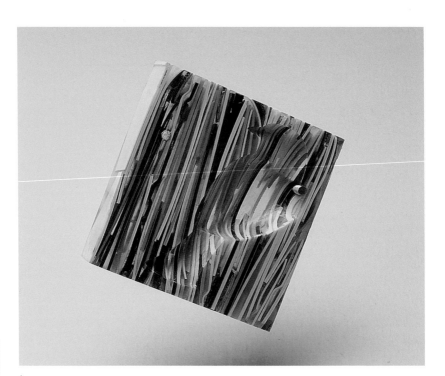

1

2

1. Dongchun Lee, Rainy Season#Brooch, detergent bottle (HDPE), resin,
   75 mm x 75 mm x 15 mm, 2017

2. Poster of "Plastic, Pastic, Pastic", 2002
   Through both curating the exhibitions and his professorship at Kookmin University, Dongchun Lee, played a
   crucial role in expanding the use of diverse materials in Korean contemporary jewellery.

Lee held in Seoul, including *"Plastic, Plastic, Plastic"* (2004, 2017), *"Mythology of Material"* (2012), and *"Wood-Extended Life"* (2016). This shift in the perception of materials had a gradual influence on other Korean jewellery artists of the era. From the mid-2000s, the expansion in materials was accepted as a natural phenomenon in Korean contemporary jewellery and led to the rise of a new group of artists applying novel materials, a group younger in age than the established jewellers who worked mainly with metal.

The reliance of jewellery on the characteristics of a given material means that it is comparatively limited in embedding symbolism or narrative within a work. Nevertheless, Korean jewellery artists are generally capable of extracting visual force from the properties of the material through craftsmanship. In fact, the work of many Korean jewellers entails an abstract form that is closely related to the material's properties, therefore intuitively producing a powerful image.

Contemporary jewellery education in Korea, which has undergone specialization since 1990, has produced many jewellery artists since the mid-2000s. This has led to the establishment of a community of studio jewellers for the first time in the country.

Present Status

Among the approximately 200 four-year colleges and universities in Korea, roughly 50 provide courses on crafts, and 25 of these offer undergraduate and graduate programs in metalworking and jewellery. Every year introduces almost one hundred students who have obtained a degree in the fields of metalwork and jewellery. In fact, this number includes only those with postgraduate degrees, not even those with bachelor's degrees, who are more likely to take a designer-oriented rather than an artist-oriented path. More than half of these students have launched careers as jewellery artists. Of course, not all manage to survive as jewellers, but it is a fact that larger numbers of young artists are jumping into the field in Korea compared to European countries and U.S. Given the considerable body of jewellers, a correspondingly large number of diverse and frequent exhibitions showcasing contemporary jewellery are being held. In terms of the frequency of jewellery exhibitions, Seoul is the leading city in the world. This tally includes many highly sophisticated international exhibitions.

However, the number of jewellery artists or exhibitions certainly does not translate to the amount of jewellery being sold. The understanding of contemporary jewellery remains poor. Let alone among the general public, even in the art world there is a lack of understanding of contemporary jewellery. The primary reason underlying this is likely the strict and conservative hierarchy in Korean art circles, which remain firmly centered on the fine arts. As a result, craftworks, including jewellery, are neither properly evaluated nor appropriately compensated. In fact, more than half of the small-scale jewellery exhibitions in Korea are not organized by galleries. Instead, individual artists rent out venues and fees to showcase their works. Since these exhibitions lack the support of professional curators or gallerists, it becomes even more difficult to make sales.

Gallery O, managed by jewellery artist Miwha Oh,
is the only gallery in Korea specializing in the sale of contemporary
jewellery created by jewellers from both Korea and abroad.

Craft Ahwon in Seoul, which serves as both an art shop and gallery.
There are a number of art shops and museum shops in Korea that sell a selection
of crafts together with souvenirs. However, there is only a few that
sell contemporary jewellery.

At present, there are few places specializing in contemporary jewellery and its sale. In fact, Gallery O, a space in Seoul managed by the jeweller Mihwa Oh, is the only venue that sells selected contemporary jewellery works by both Korean and international artists on a regular basis. Gallery Baum on the outskirts of Seoul also focuses on contemporary jewellery. The gallery mainly sells the works of jeweller Jung-kyu Lee, who runs the space, but also presents a few international exhibitions scattered across the year. Also in Seoul are Craft Ahwon, Space Duru, and Sanwoolim Art & Craft, which showcase and sell contemporary jewellery alongside other works of craft. These few galleries are pioneers working to expand the customer base for contemporary jewellery in Korea.[6] Apart from these operations, contemporary jewellery is sold in shops together with other crafts or commercial jewellery, as well as in museums alongside souvenirs. In Korea, ceramics remains the leading category in terms of sales, and wood working has become highly popular as a pastime. In comparison, the markets for metalwork and contemporary jewellery are extremely small.

International Activities

The domestic lack of understanding and limited sales of contemporary jewellery has caused young jewellery artists to turn their eyes to foreign markets since mid-2000 's . Proficient in the use of the internet, this new generation of jewellers has more actively worked to participate in overseas exhibitions and competitions compared to previous generations. Shortfalls in domestic sales notwithstanding, a favorable reception from abroad and the competition between artists have helped to lift Korean contemporary jewellery up to international standards. This sort of enthusiastic international engagement was also largely influenced by their teachers' generation, many of whom studied abroad and were actively involved in international exchanges.

The annual Craft Trend Fair organized by the Korea Craft & Design Foundation. Over the past decade, this Fair has established itself as the largest showcase and market in Korea for contemporary craft, including jewellery.

6. In regard to contemporary jewellery in Korea, there is a stark difference between Seoul and other locations. The only venue that sells contemporary jewellery outside of Seoul is in the city of Busan.

In addition to these internal reasons, various projects by the Korea Craft and Design Foundation (KCDF), which was established in 2003, have provided assistance in the overseas expansion of young jewellery artists. The KCDF is the sole national institution providing comprehensive support for both traditional and contemporary crafts, craft artists, and production enterprises. For the past 12 years it has organized the nation's largest annual craft fair. In doing so, it has provided an important platform to jewellery artists and an opportunity for a set number of artists to participate every year in exhibitions or art fairs overseas. Contemporary Korean craft artists have consequently been able to take part in globally renowned art fairs such as the Sculpture Objects Functional Art and Design Fair (SOFA) in the United States, COLLECT: The International Art Fair for Contemporary Objects in the United Kingdom, and Maison & Objet Paris in France, which would otherwise have been difficult to attend. Moreover, the KCDF annual craft fair has served as an important venue for contemporary jewellery artists to meet with galleries and clients from abroad. Recently, overseas exhibitions of contemporary Korean craft have been presented on a grand scale under the sponsorship of the Korean government in cities including Paris, Milan, Munich, and Philadelphia. Each time an exhibition was held, contemporary jewellery was included as one of the major categories. In addition, it has become possible for young Korean jewellers with their ever-increasing international experience to organize their own exhibitions and participate in various fairs around the world, including in Japan and Europe.

Mina Kang, recipient of the BKV-Prize for Young Applied Arts in 2012.
Since the mid-2000s, many young Korean jewellery artists have moved into
the global arena and are being increasingly recognized
in international competitions.

Mina Kang, Necklace, ramie fabric, thread,
stainless steel,
250 mm x 250 mm x 65 mm, 2012

Meanwhile, young Korean contemporary jewellers have been receiving recognition at international competitions. For example, the names of Korean contemporary jewellers have been steadily appearing in the lists of prize winners in various competitions and invitational exhibitions in Germany, including at the BKV-Prize where Mina Kang and Ye-jee Lee were selected as the winners in 2012 and 2015. The Art Jewellery Forum in the United States boasts a global network and presents its AJF Prize recognizing a single jeweler every year. Much to the surprise of many in the field, it went to Koreans in both 2013 and 2014 (Sooyeon Kim and Seulgi Kwon, respectively). In addition to award recognitions, Korean contemporary jewellers have been more frequently inking distribution agreements with overseas galleries, and growing numbers of their works are being acquired for the collections of public institutions. Many mass media features, including in the internationally-recognized Metalsmith magazine published in the United States, ran articles on Korean jewellery, enhancing interest in the activities of Korean artists within the global arena.

The National Museum of Modern and Contemporary Art, Korea, one of the leading museums in the country, organized a large-scale exhibition showcasing contemporary jewellery for the first time in 2013.[7] At this point there was no curator specializing in craft among the more than 50 curators employed at the

---

7. Ornamentation and Illusion, National Museum of Modern and Contemporary Art, Korea, 2013

1

2

1. *Sooyeon Kim, Chimney of Providence, Brooch,*
   photograph paper, epoxy resin, varnish, fine silver,
   60 mm x 80 mm x 12 mm, 2013

2. *Seulgi Kwon, Blue Breath, Brooch, silicone, pigment, thread, plastic, feather,*
   170 mm x 120 mm x 70 mm, 2017

museum. This was a clear reflection of the attitude of the Korean art world toward craft, including jewellery. For this reason, I was invited to organize the event as a guest curator. I brought together 44 contemporary jewellers active in Korea for the exhibition. Most of these artists contributing to showcasing Korean contemporary jewellery on a grand scale were in their thirties or early forties. This demonstrates that contemporary jewellery in Korea remains a new field in its early stages.

These jewellers who appeared on the scene following the mid-2000s comprise a new category of people who have taken up contemporary jewellery production as their life's work. They can be said to be of the cream the generation of studio jewellers who strove on the one hand to survive in a small Korean domestic market and, on the other, to constantly expand their sphere of activities overseas. The engagement and international resonance that developed under the influence and christening of the previous generation are recorded in the individual stories of Korean contemporary jewellery. These stories are motivating young people at various universities and workshops as they make their attempt at entering the field.

3

4

3. "Ornamentation and Illusion" the first exhibition exclusively showcasing contemporary jewellery organized by the National Museum of Modern and Contemporary Art, Korea in 2013

4. "Ornamentation and Illusion" at the MMCA, Korea, 2013

Beyond Art through the Concept of Jewellery

Contemporary Jewellery in Japan, Its History and Possibilities

Akio SEKI

Art Historian, Chief Curator, Tokyo Metropolitan Teien Art Museum, Japan

In order to think about the present, we should know about the past. Here I attempt to write the history of art jewellery in Japan after WWII through an introduction to three important artists: Yasuhiko Hishida, Yasuki Hiramatsu, and Kazuhiro Ito. I chose these artists because not only did they radically change their mode of expression according to the aesthetics of the era and the generation, they were also leaders who strongly influenced new movements. In addition, I try to find some possibilities for new modes of expression in the future through the works of a five additional artists.

Of course, this text cannot cover the whole history, up to the present, of contemporary jewellery in Japan. In fact, many talented artists have tried diverse approaches until now, with many internationally recognized Japanese artists from each era. For example, starting with Erico Nagai(永井慧悧子), the first Japanese winner of the Herbert Hoffman Prize in 1976, since then 14 Japanese artists have won the award a total of 16 times at the Schmuck in Munich, one of the most famous and important competitions for contemporary jewellery.

In this text, I will hypothesise as to why interests and styles have changed over the course of 60 years in view of the backgrounds and this generations of the artists. However, it is impossible to change everything at one time. In fact, every period embraces contrasting tendencies. Some artists have an interest in form, creating jewellery which could be deemed "small sculpture." Some attempt symbolism. In regard to materials, there are two comparable approaches. One is to choose materials based on their color, texture, plasticity, etc. The other is to choose materials based on conceptual intentions.

Several Japanese artists are active abroad now. The appearance of their international creations inevitably differs from those produced in Japan. Some of them create pieces which express their identity as Japanese or Asians. Some are trying to participate in the international context like Mari Funaki (1950–2010) who was an international artist and a gallery director based in Melbourne.

Meanwhile, I will reference important organizations, institutes, schools, and galleries as much as possible. I hope this text will be an opportunity for readers to get to know them and discover new relationships.

The Discovery of Jewellery—Yasuhiko Hishida: An Artist and an Activist

People in Japan lost their joy in life with the defeat in 1945. Yasuhiko Hishida (菱田安彦, 1927–1981) went to Rome in 1954 and found that jewellery could serve an important function for peace. He returned the following year and soon began to work as a jewellery artist. "UR Accessary Association," the first artist's group for making art jewellery, was started in 1956 under Professor Toshihiko Goto (後藤年彦, 1911–1962), from the metal carving course at Tokyo Fine Art School. Hishida was one of the founding members. In 1964, the Japan Jewellery Designers Association (日本ジュエリーデザイナー協会, JJDA) was established. Hishida became the first chairman. JJDA was very active from the beginning and attracted a lot of attention from artists and jewellery makers.

Hishida was a clear-sighted artist with tactical abilities. He designed jewellery in a modern style to respond to the taste of the era, but also sought new designs to display Japanese aesthetics. He believed that original design mixed with traditional Japanese techniques and motifs was one of the best ways to garner international interest.

Moreover, he was an activist who aimed to enlighten people about the cultural meaning of jewellery. He wrote many books from guides on design and technique to books about historical European jewellery. He played an important role in establishing the Yamanashi Prefectural Government Institute of Gemology and Jewellery Art (山梨県立宝石美術専門学校) and in opening the metalwork course at the Musashino Art University (武蔵野美術大学).

JJDA has continued to grow and remains the only nationwide jewellery artists' association. They started the Japan Jewellery competition in 1965. They continue to hold it biennially and the 30th competition will be held in 2018. They also actively introduce foreign artists and held their first international exhibition, the "International Jewellery Art Exhibition," in 1970. They invited 46 artists from foreign countries include Ronald Pearson from the United States, Bino Bini from Italy, and Herman Jünger from West Germany, amongst others. From the viewpoint of today, their choice of exhibitors displayed great foresight.

There may be instances of craftsmen creating beautiful objects in regards to line and surfaces through effective utilization of gold or silver or platinum without resorting to the use of gems. This is essentially jewellery art.

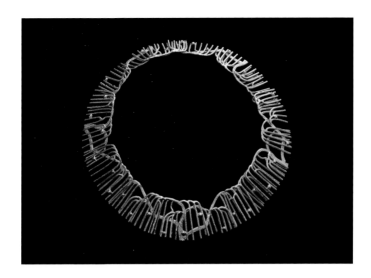

Yasuhiko Hishida, necklace, gold, 1969

55   This was written in the foreword to the catalog of "The International Jewellery Art Exhibition" in 1970—every artist used gold or silver. Many of them used semi-precious stones. In addition, artists who worked with precious stones such as Andrew Grima were also invited. We can find few new approaches to materials except in works by Shojiro Tsuruoka (鶴岡鉦次郎, 1936–2010), who used gold inlaid ebony.

New trials on materials were started vigorously in the latter half of the 1970s. Aya Nakayama (中山あや) is also known for jewellery made from braided cord and lacquer jewellery, while glass artist Kazuko Mitsushima (光島和子) also made jewellery.

Due to the economic growth that began in the 1960s, the public came to want jewellery. The market grew. However, much commercial jewellery was of lesser quality. Moreover, many designs lacked integrity and could verge on tasteless. Department stores immediately paid attention to jewellery artists and gave them venues to hold their exhibitions. Therefore, some of the artists moved in the direction of high-end jewellery with precious stones.

Magazines on commercial jewellery were published such as *Houseki-no-Shiki* (《宝石の四季》, *Four Seasons of Jewellery*) in 1966 and Jewel in 1973. From the beginning both actively took up this new movement of art jewellery.

The Traditional Technique and the Modern Expression: Possibilities of Metals—Tokyo Fine Art School and Yasuki Hiramatsu (1926–2012)

1

Hishida studied at the Tokyo Fine Art School (東京美術学校, presently Tokyo University of the Arts, 東京藝術大学). The school was founded in 1889 to promote traditional arts. The metal carving department was one of the oldest departments. The most famous craftsmen of the era, such as Natsuo Kano (加納夏雄, 1828–1898) and Shomin Unno (海野勝珉, 1844–1915), were invited to become professors. The Meiji government knew the importance of metal carving as art. In fact, traditional metal carving was one of the most important fields of the exportation.

Although the purpose of advancing traditional metal-carving techniques was retained even after World War II, the professors, Kiyoshi Unno (海野清, 1884–1956), Yoji Yamawaki (山脇洋二, 1907–1982), and Toshihiko Goto all had interests in jewellery as an artform suited to modern expressions. The school has produced important artists who are masters of traditional techniques right up until the present day. Some foreign specialists of contemporary jewellery point out that relative to international trends, the Japanese art jewellery scene contains a higher proportion of metal work. A major reason for this is the demands of the market, but it could also be said that many artists who graduated from the university are active in this field.

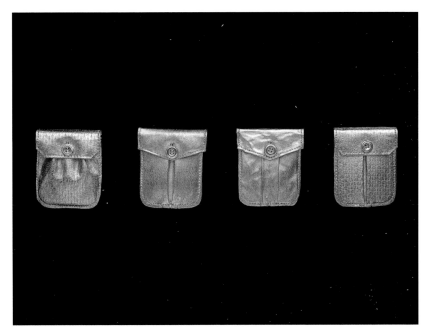

2

3

1. *Yasuki Hiramatsu, Bungle, gold, 1990*
2. *Ichiro Iino, Brooch, silver, 1975*
3. *Fumiki Taguchi, Brooch, silver, 2012*

1. *Mikiko Minewaki, Necklace "Lady Bird," stuffed toy, 2014*
   Minewaki transform many kind of daily use objects into jewellery with unexpected forms

2. *Kazuhiro Ito, Necklace "Wa（輪）," gold wire, hemp wire, photograph and Tung box, 1996*

3. *Hiroyuki Masuko, Necklace, lipsticks, stainless steel, 1994*
   A conceptual work by Hiroyuki Mashiko who studied under Kazuhiro Ito. Ito group tried to use unusual materials to jewellery

1

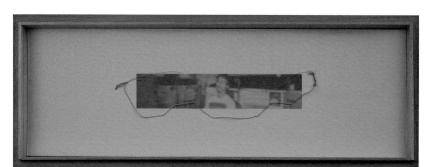

2

3

In Osaka, in the early 1970s, a small group called "Courier" was started by young artists, including Tsubo Fumiko (坪文子, 1937–2017), who would go on to play a leading role there. The group was led by Akinobu Kumagai (熊谷晄之, 1937–2012) who was a professor at Osaka Educational University and had also graduated from the Tokyo University of the Arts.

Yasuki Hiramatsu (平松保城, 1926–2012) taught at Tokyo University of the Arts from 1984 to 1994. He was the first figure to be recognized as one of the leading artists in the international contemporary jewellery scene. He was a strict minimalist from his early days. He made twisted hoop silver rings from the mid-1950s, which are only decorated by his hammer marks. Before 1970, he attempted a method of making wrinkles by rolling a metal sheet by hand. The unique techniques used in his creations surprised his contemporaries. He was given the "Ring of Goldsmiths" from the Society for Goldsmiths (Die Gesellschaft für Goldschmiedekunst) in German in 1994 for his significant contribution to art jewellery.

Hiramatsu's successor Ichiro Iino (飯野一朗) debuted as a new talent with his brooch "Pocket" in 1975. It was praised not only for its cheerful pop feeling but also for his quite new approach to metal. The cotton-like texture was made by pressing metal sheets together with cloth in the roller. He consistently continues to expand the possibility of metal work expression.

Under his guidance, a new generation emerged, such as Fumiki Taguchi (田口史樹) who strips off the metal surface and creates unique facets and Itto Mishima (三島一能) who made decorative traces cutting with a saw. Their attempts to couple contemporary preferences with metal carving techniques have created attractive new styles.

A New Movement of the 1980s—Kazuhiro Ito (1948–1997)

In the latter half of the 1980s, many artists in the European contemporary jewellery scene tried conceptual expression. Kazuhiro Ito (伊藤一廣, 1948–1997) participated in many exhibitions in Europe from 1977. He became one of the chief instructors at the Hiko Mizuno Jewellery College (ヒコ・みづのジュエリーカレッジ) in 1989. He introduced the new European movements to his students.

He never hesitated to consider jewellery as an art. In addition, he retained awareness of avant-garde trends even in his role as an educator. Once he dug a circle, a triangle, and a square geometric depression about three meters wide on the ground with some of his students. He called them "the earth jewellery." Another time, he stacked trees and created pillars of fire. He probably would like to say involvement in the act of decorating something is a type of performance jewellery.

Ito tried a wide range of expressive styles in the course of a 25-year career. The works are simple and fragile, however, they are also sublime in a way. The most characteristic feature of his works is the use of various materials such as scraped trees and waxes, and iron. In one workshop he ordered his students to make jewellery using garbage. He never chose materials to add value or apparent beauty, instead continually trying to ask questions through using various materials. He always thought about how to connect to the public through jewellery. His trials ran parallel with the art world from the 1980s to the 1990s.

The Hiko Mizuno College of Jewellery has been a center for contemporary jewellery. An important exchange exhibition program, the Three Schools Project was started in 1993. Selected students from the Academy of Fine Arts in Munich (*Akademie der Bildenden Künste München*), the Gerrit Rietveld Academie in Amsterdam (replaced by the Royal College of Art, London from 2014), and the Hiko Mizuno College of Jewellery participate in the exhibition, which continues to this day. As a result of this close relationship, several graduates from the Hiko Mizuno College of Jewellery have studied at the Academy of Fine Arts in Munich under Professor Otto Künzli.

The Hiko Mizuno College of Jewellery was founded in 1966 as a jewellery design school by Takahiko Mizuno (水野孝彦) who was another key figure of contemporary jewellery. Not only did he manage the school, he also wrote many books and essays to introduce people to contemporary jewellery.

Is Contemporary Jewellery Expected to Be Art? How Should We Respond to Today's Mentality?

In the past, some customers of art jewellery simply wanted original design. Others were fascinated by the qualities of skillful techniques and the artists' conviction.

However, tragedies such as the big earthquakes in 1995 and 2011 and the limits of economic growth have changed the mentality of Japanese people.

What do people want? Artists try to find new modes of expression to answer this question by using methods taken from other art fields and using the concept of jewellery.

1

2

1. Mari Ishikawa, Necklace "Border," silver
2. Mari Ishikawa, Border, photo

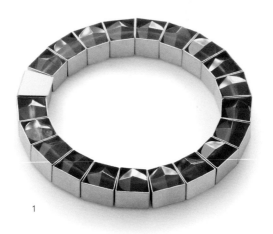

*1/2. Bracelet by Etusuko Tanabe,
picture by Yoshie Watanabe for
the illustrated book Journery, 2012*

2

Mari Ishikawa (石川マリ) studied under Otto Künzli since 1994 and is still active in Munich. She represents a sensitive feeling by depicting the changeableness of nature. She sometimes shows her photographic works, including photogram works, with her jewellery to great effect. It is a favorite media for her from her student period in Japan.

Etsuko Sonobe (薗部悦子) is known for skillfully combining the half-polished texture of natural stones with simple and constructive forms in gold. In recent years, she has collaborated with Yoshie Watanabe (渡邊良重), an illustrator and designer. They made illustrated books together, containing stories related to jewellery.

Ishikawa and Sonobe are trying to find new ways to make the wearer's imagination wider by connecting with other means of expression. We know many artists already show jewellery with other art works both in the Western world and in Japan. However, these two artists' keenness for the expression is unusual and strong.

Other artists are also trying new expressions by using the concept of jewellery. Susan Pietzsch (スーザン・ピーチ) is from Germany. From her early conceptual jewellery such as brooches made of sugar, she seems to have been interested in the fictional nature of jewellery. She started a radical exhibition project "Schmuck 2" in Japan and Germany in 1997. In this project, she invited creators in other fields such as designers and architects to make installations in public space and for publications to explore the themes of "jewellery."

Yuka Oyama (大山由華), who lives in Berlin, creates not only jewellery but also photographs, performance, and video works. In the performance "Schmuck Quickies" (2002–2008) she has a conversation with participants and decorates them extemporaneously using materials from ordinary life to create "jewellery" for them. "Collectors" is a series of photographic works that she made during an artist's residency in the US in 2013. She made masks for various collectors and took photographs of them with their collections. Both works show her strong interests in the identities of others, possibly related to jewellery's ability to unveil the inside of wearers.

Koichi Kurita (栗田宏一) is an international artist living in Yamanashi. He was involved in the contemporary art movement as a jewellery magazine editor and as a jewellery artist during the late 1980s. After that, he started focusing on soil, which is found in various colors depending on the environment. He spent 25 years collecting soil from all 3,233 municipalities in Japan. He creates installations using his collection of various colors of soil. His works seem to inquire about the relationship between the earth and self through the soil. This is deeply tied to his activities in his era as a jewellery artist.

These artists are no longer interested only in making jewellery. However, it is one product of the contemporary jewellery movement and it extends the possibilities of expression in both jewellery and art.

Finally, I would like to write about the platforms for contemporary jewellery. Most Japanese jewellery artists have studied at universities and jewellery school. Besides the Tokyo University of the Arts the Musashino Art University, Tokyo; the Tama Art University, Tokyo; the Nagaoka Institute of Design, Nigata; and

1

2

3

1. *Koichi Kurita, Installation at L'abbaye de Maubuisson, Saint-Ouen-l'Aumône, France, soil, 2014*
   Photography © Koichi Kurita

2. *Yuka Oyama, Collectors "Moonshelf," 2013*
   Photography © Becky Yee

3. *"HOCHsitzen: spring/summer_16 green gold" temporary installation at the HOCHsitz Atelier,*
   Glashagen by Susan Pietzsch &Valentina Seidel, Glashagen, Germany, 2016

the Kobe Design University, Hyogo also have courses in jewellery making. The Yamanashi Prefectural Government Institute of Gemology and Jewellery Art is a public jewellery school in Kofu City, which is a center of commercial jewellery making. Private schools such as the Hiko Mizuno College of Jewellery and the Japan Jewellery Craft School educate not only young students but also adults. The former has a department specializing in contemporary jewellery.

In Japan there is no art museum that has a permanent collection gallery for jewellery. However, the National Museum of Modern Art has over 100 pieces of modern and contemporary jewellery. In addition, they hold exhibitions of Japanese art jewellery, including artists' solo shows such as Yasuki Hiramatsu's exhibition in 2008, and Minato Nakamura's exhibition in 2015. I have curated exhibitions of both historical jewellery and contemporary jewellery at the Tokyo Metropolitan Teien Art Museum and the Museum of Contemporary Art, Tokyo since 1999, including "Catalysis for Life: New Language of Dutch Art & Design" in 2010, which featuring Ted Noten, and "Otto Künzli—the Exhibition" in 2015.

As I wrote above, the Japan Jewellery Designers Association, which is the only nationwide artist-run society, organizes the Japan Jewellery Competition. The Museum of Arts & Crafts, Itami is a public art center, which has both an Art museum and studios open to the public, including for jewellery making. It has held the biennial Itami International Jewellery Exhibition (competition) since 1997.

Since the 1990s some galleries for art jewellery have been opened, such as Arai Atelier Gallery, Tokyo (1997–2018), Gallery Deux Poisons, Tokyo (since 2003), and C.A.J., Kyoto (since 2008). The Hiko Mizuno College of Jewellery has run the gallery Hole in the Wall since 2013.

Critical Approaches to Footwear Design Practice[1]

Eelko MOORER

Visiting Lecturer at HEAD—Geneva in Switzerland; Course Leader MA Footwear at the London College of Fashion; Designer at Eelko Moorer Design Studio

Conceptual design offers a space, free from market pressures, in which design can engage in and explore new areas in order to experiment and develop alternative methodologies related to larger social and cultural issues and anticipate possible futures. Such critical and speculative design methodologies can contribute to different ways of thinking about footwear.

The footwear designers' projects discussed in this article are thought provoking about our current way of life in different ways. Salguero and Cope use associative design, exploring non-functional aspects of shoes to be used as a medium, a vehicle for social-cultural dialogue pointing out critical areas where footwear design can function. The two designers turn footwear into poetic art objects that operate by means of "making the familiar strange" in order to question our modes of thinking.

Ten Boehmer's practice is investigative, experimental, indicative, and open ended in offering critical engagement through deconstruction. She uses a strictly technical vocabulary to question the act of walking in all its technical and cultural aspects, with the anatomical pressure points from which she designs and questions the high-heel as a construct. Salguero, Cope, and Ten Boehmer critically approach footwear through association and negation, raising political and socio-cultural issues through artistic and sculptural expressions.

OurOwnsKIN and Kristina Walsh use both critical and speculative design. They project fictional scenarios, imaginary but believable everyday situations, in which footwear or footwear-related products play a part. By anticipating incorporation of new technologies and sciences in ordinary life, they contribute to a better understanding and critique of the implications of new technological developments before they enter our lives as daily products.

Entire areas of fashion are promoted by capitalism's culture of transition that does not connect to real human issues anymore. All the designers mentioned here are putting human elements at the center of the design experience: Cope by discussing human intimacy, Salguero by referencing objectification, Ten Boehmer with the anatomical pressure points from which she explores

---

1. This paper was originally published at *Fashion Theory Russia* (special edition on decadence), London, July–August 2017.

the high-heel as a construct, OurOwnsKIN with taking inspiration from the workings of human skin and the possibilities this technology might have for producing footwear, and Walsh by questioning real and ideal bodies. Different methodologies and cross-disciplinarity have informed these works involving diverse backgrounds such as jewellery, fashion, biomechanics, kinematics, orthopaedics, and plastic surgery to develop alternative visions, not of style (i.e., superficial and transitional, characteristic of capitalist fashion), but real alternatives—alternative aesthetics, alternative modes of production, and alternative ways of life—i.e. something that is made to endure and to change things in a fundamental way. These critical and speculative approaches are used to counter:

What we are dealing with now (in contemporary society, which) is not the incorporation of materials that previously seemed to possess subversive potentials, but instead, their pre-corporation: the pre-emptive formatting and shaping of desires, aspirations, and hopes by capitalist culture (Fischer, 2012).

And in doing so we reinforce the status quo, the normative. This is why design as critique is so important, because in our capitalist consumer culture it can: "pose questions, encourage thought, expose assumptions, provoke action, spark debate, raise awareness, offer new perspectives, inspire, and entertain in an intellectual way" (Dunne and Raby, 2013). In doing so, the footwear projects in this article use the ideologies and values that are imbedded in the materiality and production of design to contend a form of decadence inherent in current market product culture and ask us to consider what kind of society and future we want to shape.

Footwear in Capitalism's Culture of Transition

Little research has been carried out in identifying areas of critical approaches to Footwear design practice. As in architecture, furniture design, fashion, and industrial design we need to look at the discipline of footwear in order to redefine what it can mean in the 21st century.

Associated with fashion, yet very different from it, footwear as a design discipline and industry embodies all aspects of capitalist reality in every way: landfills contain millions of discarded shoes made of non-biodegradable material; cultural heritage is swept away or commoditized by market forces where child labor as well as underpaid labor is implemented and a marker of social inequality; fast fashion increases demand for cheap quality footwear that is neither sustainable nor healthy for the body; foot health is an overlooked area in medicine with major health consequences. These few examples, raising global issues that are social, cultural, political, technological, and economic, illustrate the need to re-examine footwear's position within fashion footwear, the industry, and the way it is produced, as well as within society and its relationship to the body.

Products are the main exponent of capitalist culture and fashion in that products are capitalism's main driver in providing an illusion of alternative choice. Fashion, caught in an endless cycle of transitions between seasons and shifting hierarchies, is instrumental in achieving this differentiation. Design has become fully integrated into the neoliberal model of capitalism as pointed out by Hal Foster in *Design and Crime* (2002). Fashion is a discipline characterised by "controlled consumption that is based upon automation, accessory features, and inessential differences" (Baudrillard, 1996). "Normal" objects present themselves as reassuring factors of equilibrium as transitional objects, marking an illusionary sense of identity and stability. We see them and are re-affirmed in our being and our self, or our slightly desired difference in the form of a variation from a homogenized automated core.

It is noteworthy that "technically speaking, changes in form and style are signs of immaturity; they mark a period of transition. The error of capitalism as a creed lies in the attempt to make this period of transition a permanent one" (Lewis Mumford quoted in Baudrillard's *The System of Objects).*

What contemporary discussions about the "end of fashion" really are about is that fashion has come to a point of decadence that fashion is not addressing. Footwear, as part of fashion, has been overlooked and so this article deals with how footwear is addressing the issues of this decadent culture.

Decadence as Transition

For this investigation we start from the premise that a period of transition is characteristic of decadence. A term with intensely contradictory meanings, decadence here is perceived as a tendency, a feeling of malaise, rather than a period. "There are no historical contents that can be characterized as decadent in themselves. Decadence is not in statu but in motu." Decadence therefore is not a structure but a direction or tendency.

Although decadence is from all ages, the modern idea of decadence is inherently tied to the idea of progress and includes dissatisfaction with materialism at its root. However, in earlier periods,

The term progress was conceived by analogy with growth and particularly the intellectual development of the human individual. But after centuries of close association with scientific research and technological advance, the concept of progress reached a level of abstraction at which older organic and specifically anthropomorphic connotations could no longer be retained. Progress came to be regarded as a concept more to do with mechanics than with biology (Calinescu, 1987).

This technocratic worldview with advances in biotechnology and computer science has materialized also in our contemporary neoliberal organization of society where an illusion of measurability of life is at odds with that which defines us as human. This results in a feeling that what is human is under threat.

The idea of decadence that we will engage with here is Nietzsche's. Nietzsche described periods of transition as marked by being an area of decadence that is meant to be overcome and saw this neither as positive or negative.

Seeing modernity as a transitional state in itself was not unique at the time. Emile Durkheim for example also saw modern times as a period of transition and moral mediocrity, but to identify this tendency as decadent, and as a period of transformation to happen within the individual and society at large is particular to Nietzsche's theory of decadence.

Nietzsche's theory of decadence is ultimately a theory and critique of ideology. Although the current notion of ideology in the sense of "false consciousness" comes from Marx, it should be observed that Nietzsche's analysis of decadence, and specifically modern decadence, constitutes a first attempt at a comprehensive and radical critique of ideology in general, with a particular emphasis on modern bourgeois ideologies (political, social, cultural) including the ideologies of modernity (Calinescu, 1987).

The works discussed in this article can be perceived as a product of decadence but not as a style of decadence. They are often illustrative and aim to appeal to the imagination. Both aspects were identified with decadence by Nisard when analyzing the work of Victor Hugo in his article "M. Victor Hugo in 1836": "the profuse use of description, the prominence of detail, the elevation of imaginative power to the detriment of reason" (Calinescu, 1987).

Decadence as Critique

Contrary to this conservative view, Gautier, in the introduction to Baudelaire's Fleurs du Mal (1868) and, later, the Decadents used the idea of decadence consciously as a style of critique. The glorification of death and decay as style feature, an extension of romanticism, is not relevant here, and will not be investigated thematically.

What does resonate with decadence is, firstly, that the projects discussed in this article can be seen as decadent in that they embrace different disciplines to inform new works. This coincides with the speculation of Baudelaire in his article *L'art Philosophique* (1859) where he described the characteristic of decadence as the breaking down of the barriers between the diverse arts. And, secondly, the projects described in this article aim to appeal to the imagination and try to seduce the viewer into the works by using everyday objects that we all can relate to. They are purposely thought-provoking objects that address issues linked to capitalism's culture of decadence in a critical way.

I propose to inform this critique by linking footwear not to fashion but to industrial and product design methods, and in particular to critical and speculative design. In line with the idea that fashion footwear design needs to do away with its insularity, new design roles, new contexts, and new methods within footwear design need to be investigated with the help of concepts and methodology drawn from other or related disciplines such as film, science, ethics, politics, and art. Critical and speculative design methodologies investigate just that.

In this article, therefore, we first look at how critical design thinking can be used in footwear through a play with visual references in order to produce awareness. Secondly, we examine how critical design principles can be applied to rethink footwear design and production so as to develop speculative alternatives, not only by offering new products but also in aiming to question social and cultural implications of these products on larger global issues mentioned at the start of this writing.

We do this through investigation of several cross-disciplinary footwear design approaches that might, or might not, consciously apply critical methods. The goal of these alternative methodologies is to approach and investigate footwear by going beyond fashion.

We will ask what cross-disciplinary methodologies they apply, how they can be seen as critical, and in what way they can inform footwear design.

Critical Approaches

Critical design is a form of conceptual design, that is, not the conceptualization process of design but the use of concept as a tool for cultural analysis. "Critical design focuses on present social, cultural, and ethical implications of design objects and practice. It is grounded in critical social theory. Its designers scan the cultural horizon today, offering a critique of what already exists" (Dunne and Raby, 2013).

Jewellery designer Noëllie Salguero's "Trophy" (2012) approaches footwear by the juxtaposition of familiar imagery wherein her high heels have merged with a hunting trophy. The work is associative by referencing both the way women are sexualized through wearing high heels and fur and objectified "as animals" (again with fur), prey to be caught, and boasted about, while at the same time discussing the use of animal products in footwear. The trophy's power lies in the fact that its meaning constantly oscillates between those two areas. Also, it clearly uses design techniques in its making and references wearable shoes, while the finished object enters the realm of art or ornament as a trophy to be hung up on the wall, the shoes having totally lost their usefulness but not their symbolic power.

The technique used here is that of defamiliarization. A method often used in critical design for promoting a heightened sense of perception through attracting and holding attention by stepping away from the functionality and/or familiarity of an object. It is not so much a device but a multitude of devices that make the familiar seem strange. The aim is to produce a unique poetic narrative

Noëllie Salguero, "Trophy," 2012
© HEAD—Genève

73

that attracts the viewer into the designer's thinking.

Salguero's project illustrates how footwear can function as language, a vehicle to communicate a story that deals with contemporary issues through defamiliarization. In critical design this type of work is best characterized by what is called associative design, because "the critical narrative in the works...is embedded into the object form—typically conveyed through familiar archetypes," i.e., by using familiar things to produce new meaning through their unusual association.

This form of conceptual design generally raises questions outside the boundaries of production design, allowing objects to relate to larger socio-cultural issues. This potential use of "the language of design to pose questions, provoke, and inspire is conceptual design's defining feature" (Dunne and Raby, 2013).

Through footwear Joe Cope's "The Language of Feet in the Walk of Life" (2017) makes us question and think about our interpersonal relationships and socio-cultural behaviors. The critical value of this piece lies in the artistic way it is done.

Also essential in Cope's investigation is the use of footwear as language. Psychology of gait and foot positions were researched to see how feet express psychological feeling in order to inform a series of footwear installations.

1

2

3

1. Joe Cope, *"Legs Open Eyes Shut,"* 2016
2. Joe Cope, *"Love Triangle,"* 2016
3. Joe Cope, *"Twisted Stiletto,"* 2016

Defamiliarisation is used by slightly altering familiar shoe stereotypes and then arranging them into symbolic configurations to reach a level of abstraction that is meant to draw the viewer in through a play with presence and absence of the body as is very prominent in "Legs Open Eyes Shut" (2016). Shoes always seem to hold a body when left empty behind because the wearer's character and whereabouts are visibly inscribed in the wear and tear of the shoe.

In "Love Triangle," the shoe is explored as a powerful sexual and gendered object. The stiletto as image and symbol talks of power, desire, and is traditionally equated with feminine seduction. The Oxford shoe embodies classic masculinity and the Chukka boot on the other hand is purposely non-descriptive creating an anonymity that represents a third person who could be either a man or a woman.

The use of stereotypes of gender creates a familiarity through which the viewer is seduced into the work. This, in combination with the arrangement in a circle or triangle or otherwise abstract configurations, resembles the secret mystical symbols found in religious or sectarian cults. This all together creates an installation piece producing an abstract narrative that opens imaginative approaches within the viewer. The color red is essential as it is the key factor for directing the works in an erotic context and it acts as a defamiliarizing device and links the shoes with the realm of legends and fairy tales, wherein shoes with magical powers are often red.

"Twisted Stiletto" (2016) is a frozen act of aggression. Is this act of violence an aggression of male desire against a female? The object is a fossil, a remnant, and turns the work into a psychological questioning of gender relations and erotic engagement.

Cope explores and opens up what footwear can mean and provides us with objects of reflection. She is making us aware of the importance of human contact by touching on the absence of intimacy and real connections in an age of technologies such as internet dating, WhatsApp, Facebook, and the like. Cope brings the body back in, because shoes show body language by pointing in the direction wished for, which is not necessarily in tune with the polite social codes of behavior displayed in social interaction. She shows this by materializing these hidden lines. Furthermore, she investigates foot psychology and shows how this can be used to inform the design of footwear. In this way her project can re-inform the process of footwear design as well as function as a narrative that questions our interpersonal relationships.

All good design is critical. Designers start by identifying shortcomings in the things they are redesigning and offer a better version. Critical design applies this to larger, more complex issues. Critical design is critical thought translated into materiality. It is about thinking through design rather than words and using the language and structure of design to engage people (Dunne and Raby, 2013).

This is what footwear designer Marloes Ten Boehmer establishes in "A Measurable Factor Sets the Conditions of its Operation" (2013). Design is also used here as language, but the language is technical and not referential. It is the language of product design.

Presented as the result of her Stanley Picker Fellowship in the Stanley Picker Gallery at the Faculty of Art, Design & Architecture Kingston University, the piece is set up as an immersive installation.

The result of the installation are investigative pieces, processes, tests, and trials for a new footwear collection informed by engineering principles, as well as a video.

The projected video *Material Compulsion* investigates "the woman in motion" as an engineering problem. Analyzed through filming a high-heeled woman on alternative substrates (ground surfaces) she "dismantles" her as a complex construct:

When placed in alternative settings (through the narrative of a film, for example) or when forced to walk through unique substrates, a woman in heels loses her equilibrium (both physically and culturally) and begins to slip, trip, sink, or stumble, thereby transforming her perceived identity.

In this way, through an exploration of the physics of walking, Boehmer exposes and questions the role high heels play in the cultural construction of female identity in contemporary society.

Rationalised parameters, aesthetic intuition and structural understanding are utilized through deconstructing and reconstructing the process of footwear by applying methodologies used in biomechanics such as measuring gait.

For example, "White Prototypes" displayed on the shelves are test pieces, mapping out specific combinations of foot and ground contact points derived

1

77

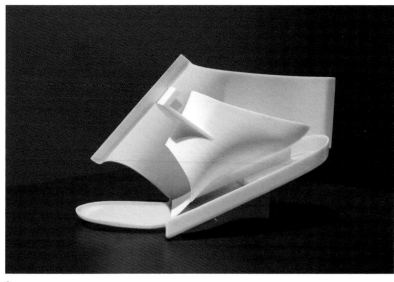

2

1. Marloes Ten Boehmer, "A Measurable Factor Sets the Conditions of its Operation," 2013
   Overview image of the project

2. Marloes ten Boehmer, "White Prototype," 2013
   Photography © Ellie Laycock

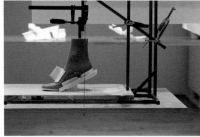

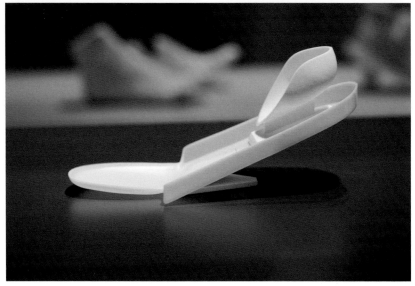

Marloes ten Boehmer, "White Prototypes," 2013
Test pieces displayed on the shelves. Photography © Ellie Laycock

from anatomical and kinematic studies. These have informed a series of design possibilities that challenge conventional culturally defined stereotypes.

"White Prototype" is a case in point, a cross section exposing half the foot. A structure resembling a corrective insole puts the foot in position and is also utilized as closing system to hold the foot. It is in this way that our attention is directed to a narrative that is entirely communicated through shoe-technical references and in construction.

The project's focus on the engineering of a highly charged type of shoe neglects the symbolic issues that this type of footwear is laden with. She also ignores all standard approaches to footwear construction.

This is a purposeful approach because with this method she aims to "shirk fashion trends and styles, (and) is based on research into the structural parameters required to support a foot (in a high-heeled position) while in motion".

It is in this sense that her work should also be seen as critical.

The project offers striking abstract footwear solutions that show new ways of holding the foot in a high heel structure. Here she references the issues evolving around foot health and the body in an unnatural culturally defined position.

Ultimately, a new aesthetic for footwear and the fashion silhouette emerges out of her functional biometrics, kinetic, and kinematic research, as well as a potential alternative approach to footwear design for the industry to function in.

One of the "White Prototypes" has been translated in production— "Bluepanelshoe"—showing how a project developed completely outside the parameters of the marketplace can enter this market after.

Over the past 15 years or so, footwear has seen a huge drive for experimentation in form evidenced in extravagant catwalk designs, as well as in designs exploring the application of 3D printing and how far that can be pushed. Examples are the collaborations between the brand United Nude and product designers and architects such as Ross Lovegrove and Zaha Hadid.

This is an area of conceptual design aimed at producing sculptural and "artistic" objects on the fringes yet remains within the bounds of the commercial world.

Examples of this form-related discipline are concept cars and kitchens. In the area of fashion and fashion footwear this type of conceptual design comes in the form of catwalk shows or shops that promote brands and designers by displaying the latest potential applications of state-of-the-art technologies. In this context, conceptual design is in fact a kind of entertainment. This is not the conceptual design we need.

Many changes are also already happening in fashion footwear, with brands that aim to work sustainably (Veya, Stella McCartney) or to apply technology (notably sportswear companies such as Nike and Adidas).

However interesting and technically innovative these projects are, they don't deal with or discuss social and cultural implications. They function much in the same way as current social and humanitarian design still operates within the limits of reality as it is.

We need to apply another conceptual design approach that offers product proposals and suggestions that do not revolve around adding aesthetic variations or applying new materials and technologies alone; these procedures are in essence solving merely aesthetic problems, answering only the requirements of a culture of transition.

Existing outside the marketplace, new ideas, approaches, and issues can be developed within this conceptual space and inform new possibilities for design itself, new aesthetic possibilities for technology research; or large-scale social and political issues such as democracy, sustainability, and alternatives to our current model of capitalism (Dunne and Raby, 2013).

Critical design uses speculative design proposals to challenge narrow assumptions, preconceptions, and givens about the role products play in everyday life".

OurOwnsKIN (2015–2017) is an on-going project involving artist Rhian Solomon whose practice investigates collaborative practices between medical specialist and designers for exploring the possibilities of skin, and footwear 3D concept development designer Liz Ciokajlo, whose focus is on materials, emerging processes, and design construction.

Supported by Ravensbourne College in London, MV works program (funded by Knowledge Transfer Network, Innovate UK, and the Arts Council), and Innovate

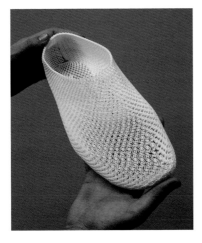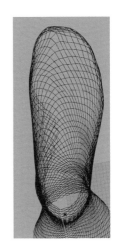

OurOwnsKIN, "OurOwnsKIN," 2016

UK, the project explored whether leather could be replaced as a source and guide to design construction in footwear. Can it be replaced with a material that takes it physical characteristics from human foot skin? Can this approach subsequently be useful to developing designs for growing materials such as artificial leather?

This raises all kinds of questions and potentials: "Can we not grow the whole shoe?" and "What do you grow that shoe on?" If so, it needs a structure. In the medical world scaffolding is created in order to grow things on. Hence inspiration for the design of the scaffolding is taken from medical approaches and methodologies used by plastic reconstructive surgeons.

We used the principles of skin tension lines (Langer Lines) to inspire a computation framework. Springy cells called auxetics were placed into the computation framework to address how the material and design construction can provide fine variations in fit needed in mass produced footwear. The auxetics also seemed to provide a responsive 360-degree structure. From here we pushed the code out to form the sole of the shoe, keeping the code simple. The approach was to design the footwear structure from the inside surface of the foot to the outsole. Our research only scratches the surface of the potential to customise the structure for bespoke performance application (OurOwnsKIN).

Historically, footwear design construction has evolved from the manipulation of the material leather, another animal's skin. Manufacturing machines have evolved to automise how we hand manipulated the material leather to make shoes. "With the introduction of new footwear materials, such as polymers, footwear design constructions evolved under the influence of how to manipulate leather." (OurOwnsKIN)

One area in which shoe design is being reconsidered today is in 3D print which can construct features so fine that the line between a materials' structure and design construction starts to blur, so shoes do not have to be constructed but can actually be grown.

In working with the material skin as an artisan shoemaker, questioning how it behaves and how to cut it, the characteristics and techniques used on human foot skin are explored to rethink how to design for future manufactured 3D-printed and grown shoes.

The result is not a shoe but a design construction and a system conceived for designers to work with in search of new opportunities in the field of shoe design made out of 3D-printed TPU done with laser sintering.

One of the benefits for designers would be the ability to exploit the process with the computer and have an unlimited amount of aesthetic freedom. More importantly, the template allows the creation of design constructions that maximise the benefits of 3D printing for shoemaking. This could have wide-ranging implications both for the manufacturing of shoes and for the final wearer. Not only could it lead to a more efficient production in making shoes, allowing a more sustainable production, reducing significant amounts of waste in shoe manufacturing. It would also lead to more comfortable shoes by utilizing computer technologies for a customized process—measuring for a better "fit" and better performance. Insoles correcting gait for example could be in the shoe already and correcting the way people walk avoiding possible future foot health issues. This has potential in a more human-centred design approach, a new kind of bespoke footwear.

The strength of this project does not lie in the use of footwear as language. The design possibilities remain still un-explored since what is offered as yet is a construction to be designed with. This is innovative, and its critical strength lies in the speculative opportunities and socio-cultural implications offered by this technique.

By putting a product into a future-driven scenario, critical questions about our current way of life are explored. For example, the project raises fundamental

1

2

1/2. OurOwnsKIN, "OurOwnsKIN," Installation shot at the MV Works
   exhibition "Into the Wild at Somerset House," London, 2016

ethical, social, and cultural concerns: how could this help in solving foot health issues, how could it help eradicate the use of animals and polluting products for our shoes. Ultimately, it speculates on growing our own skin and rectifying a body part for optimal function. In this case the shoe becomes second skin, literally, through becoming prosthesis, and raises question about what it means to be human.

Kristina Walsh's project "Footwear beyond the Foot: Extensions of Being" (2017) investigates if footwear design can be used as a tool to improve psychological well-being of lower-limb amputees, and how it can facilitate new empathetic relationships with others as well as with oneself. Amputees and research in this area have spoken about the importance of addressing prosthetics and the multifaceted components of quality of life in conjunction with fashion and design.

In recent years amputees have been used in fashion contexts in order to raise awareness, for example model cum athlete Aimee Mullins in an Alexander McQueen's catwalk show. Walsh takes this further by looking into the practices of the prosthetics industry and the nuanced psychological experiences some amputees face after amputation. This led to a focus on designs that encourage interactions, relating to clinical research finding, interview responses, or techniques employed in cognitive behavioral therapy. The interviews were led with people who weren't public persona such as athletes or models that perform in a superlative way to answer the ideals of our performance-obsessed society. The interviews aimed to collect material about day-to-day basic needs in such mundane activities as going shopping and going to work or getting on the bus, and about how to fit, put on, and wear the prosthesis in a normal daily context, and how the interviewees felt amputees were represented in fashion.

The project is a collection of footwear tools that redefine the parameters of footwear by both proposing new potential products, a more emphatic approach to the revalidation process, as well as offering design tools that are currently not used in behavioral health.

The designs "encourage a positive body image and emphasize social support and questions the limited set of emotional experiences offered through products in the prosthetic industry". The set of products to help the amputee in the rehabilitation process are fully prototyped in appropriate materials.

The "Meditation Station" (see left) is a teaching tool by behavioral therapists. It is a transportable space creating an environment for self-reflection to aid body reconceptualization after amputation. "An essential element since clinical psychology studies have theorized that the first milestone in post-amputation rehabilitation is that one must reconceptualize body image".

This tool is designed as part of the therapy session where the partner is introduced to the process. The objects are to be used between two people—the amputee and a loved one—in order for both to get familiar with the residual limb and thereby restoring intimacy.

The form is abstract yet sensuous, facilitating the foot yet at the same time hoping to tempt the partner into touching; caressing the bottom of the foot

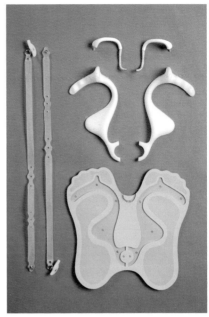

2

1

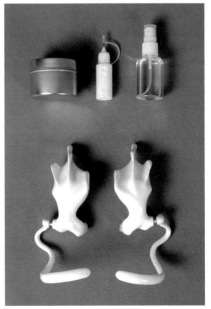

3

1. Kristina Walsh, "The Healing Helix," 2016
2. Kristina Walsh, "Meditation Station," 2016
3. Kristina Walsh, "Foot Feeler," 2016

leaving space for the thumb to move over the amputation. This helps the amputee to build up a renewed positive self-image.

The Healing Helix is an extravagant pair of footwear pieces that aim for the amputee to claim their identity by expressing themselves proudly back into society. This piece is for when the therapy is ending. It aims to showcase the possibilities that could exist for prosthetics to be designed: aesthetic qualities contribute directly to a positive experience of the quality of life and are in this way therapeutic. The Healing Helix redefines fashionable prosthetics and are what Walsh's research has found to be an area of interest both from the point of the manufacturer as well as some amputees.

All these projects focus on re-establishing human connection, either to the person themselves through the Meditative Station, between two people with Foot Feelers, or with the prosthesis reconnecting with the outside world.

In doing so, this project goes beyond merely innovation through inclusivity in that it also aims to enlighten the public perception of prosthetics and support the psychological well-being of amputees. As such, this is a project where product design, footwear design, and fashion merge.

The critical element in Walsh's project is the questions raised about the imperfect body by addressing disability. It does this by creating new images of the human body as well as to provide real product proposals that are imaginative and implementable. The project addresses the issus of social insurance, as an amputee-athlete gets sponsoring for several pairs of prostheses whereas social insurance pays only for more basic prostheses, which don't include state of the art technology or high tech materials (Fischer, 2016).

Conclusion

We have seen that conceptual design is design about ideas and how conceptual space offers design a field to explore free from market pressures. We have distinguished between conceptual design within a market-led context and critical approaches that fully step away from the marketplace and enter the fictional. We have seen that design can engage in and explore new areas in this space in order to experiment and develop alternative methodologies related to larger social and cultural issues and anticipate possible futures.

We have also seen the various opportunities in which these critical and speculative design methodologies can contribute to different ways of thinking about footwear.

The footwear designers' projects discussed in this article are thought provoking about our current way of life in different ways. Salguero and Cope use associative design, exploring non-functional aspects of shoes to function as language. They both explore the potential for footwear to be used as a medium, a vehicle for social-cultural dialogue pointing out critical areas that footwear design can function in.

Here the designer functions as an artist in the sense that they turn footwear into an art object. Both Cope and Salguero have a formalist approach to design where the object is seen to be poetic imagery or have a poetic function. Their approach is informed by art and studio jewellery backgrounds, and in doing so they produce artistic objects that operate by means of "making strange" in order to question our thinking. The habitual way of thinking is to make the unfamiliar as easily digestible as possible. Normally, our perceptions are "automatic," however, "if the whole complex lives of many people go on unconsciously, then such lives are as if they had never been." Art exists that one may recover the sensation of life; it exists to make one feel things, to make the stone stony. The purpose of art is to impart the sensation of things as they are perceived and not as they are known. The technique of art is to make objects 'unfamiliar,' to make forms difficult, to increase the difficulty and length of perception because the process of perception is an aesthetic end in itself and must be prolonged. Art is a way of experiencing the artfulness of an object; the object is not important. Art removes objects from the automatism of perception.

Ten Boehmer's practice on the other hand is investigative, experimental, indicative, and open ended, nevertheless offering critical engagement through deconstruction. She uses a strictly technical vocabulary offering a different form of abstraction than, for example, Cope's work.

The result of Salguero, Cope, and Boehmer are approaches to footwear that are critical through association and negation, however, remaining artistic and sculptural expressions that contain critical ideas, each expressed differently.

The design proposals by OurOwnsKIN and Kristina Walsh can be considered both critical and speculative because they project fictional scenarios in which footwear or footwear-related products could function. Through anticipating incorporation of new technologies and sciences they can help better imagine, critique, and facilitate the effects and possibilities of new technological futures before they enter our daily lives as everyday products. They are "new technological developments within imaginary but believable everyday situations that would allow us to debate the implications of different technological futures before they happen" (Dunne and Raby, 2013).

We established that entire areas of fashion as promoted by capitalism's culture of transition do not connect to real human issues any more. All designers mentioned here are putting human elements at the center of the design experience. Cope by discussing human intimacy, Salguero by referencing objectification, Ten Boehmer with the anatomical pressure points form which she designs and questions the high-heel as a construct, OurOwnsKIN with taking inspiration from the workings of human skin and the possibilities this technology might have for producing footwear, and Walsh by questioning real and ideal bodies.

Different methodologies and cross-disciplinarity have informed these works involving diverse backgrounds, such as jewellery, fashion, biomechanics, kinematics, orthopaedic, and plastic surgery, to develop alternative visions, not of style, but real alternatives—alternative visions, alternative modes of production, alternative ways of life, i.e., something made to endure, to last, to change things in a fundamental way, not just superficial and not to pass—to transition. Styles are always passing and superficial in capitalist fashion.

These approaches are used to counter "what we are dealing with now (in contemporary society, which) is not the incorporation of materials that previously seemed to possess subversive potentials, but instead, their pre-corporation: the pre-emptive formatting and shaping of desires, aspirations, and hopes by capitalist culture" (Fischer, 2012), and in doing so, reinforcing the status quo—the normative.

This is why design as critique is so important, because in our capitalist consumer culture it can: "pose questions, encourage thought, expose assumptions, provoke action, spark debate, raise awareness, offer new perspectives, inspire and entertain in an intellectual way" (Dunne and Raby, 2013). In doing so the projects in this article use the ideologies and values that are imbedded in the materiality and production of design to contend a form of decadence inherent in current market product culture and ask us to consider which society and future we want.

Reference

Baudrillard, J. 1996. *The System of Objects*. New York and London: Verso.

Calinescu, M. 1987. *Five Faces of Modernity: Modernism, Avant-garde, Decadence, Kistch, Post-modernism*. 2nd Rev ed, Durham, NC: Duke University Press.

Dunne, A. 2008. *Hertzian Tales: Electronic Products, Aesthetic Experience, and Critical Design*. Illustrated ed, Mass.: MIT Press.

Dunne, A., and F. Raby. 2013. *Speculative Everything: Design, Fiction, and Social Dreaming*. Mass.: MIT Press.

Fischer, E. 2016. "Au corps du sujet." In *Issue 33. HEAD—Genève*. Geneva.

Fischer, M. 2012. *Capitalist Realism: Is there no Alternative?* London: Zero-Books.

Foster, H. 2002. *Design & Crime (And Other Diatribes)*. New York and London: Verso.

Giorcelli, C. et al., ed. 2011. *Accessorising the Body Habits of Being I*. Minnesota: University of Minnesota Press.

Lemon, Lee T., and Marion J. Reis. 1965. *Russian Formalist Criticism: Four Essays*. Lincoln: University of Nebraska Press.

Malpass, M. 2013. "Between Wit and Reason: Defining Associative, Speculative and Critical Design Paractise." In *Design and Culture: The Journal of the Design Studies Forum*, 5(3): 333–56.

Malpass, M. 2015. "Criticism and Function in Critical Design Practise." In *Design Issues*, 31(2): 59–71.

Malpass, M. 2016. "Critical Design Practise: Theoretical Perspectives and Methods of Engagement." In *The Design Journal*, 19(13): 473–89.

Accessories and Construction of Identities in Fashion
The Case of 19th-Century France

19(

Emilie HAMMEN

Lecturer at Institut Français de la Mode, IFM Paris, France

In a historical perspective, I look back at the emergence of Western consumer culture, as it was forged throughout 19th-century France and when accessories became instrumental in what Roland Barthes describes as "the language of fashion." While this research is based on an exploration of the past, I will argue that our relationship to accessories today, the role they play in the construction of individualities, has remained rather consistent ever since.

Materializing Fashion

In the first decades of the 19th century in France, fashion is gradually entering its industrialized phase: the process leading to the creation of fashionable artifacts is still rather similar to the artisanal context of the Ancien Régime (the time period, spanning centuries and eventually halted by the French Revolution of the late 18th century). A network of various craftsmen is necessary for the fashion consumer to create a new silhouette: one must purchase the raw material (the fabric), embellish it and transform it through embroidery, dyeing, or other types of finishing, and eventually have it transformed into a finished product: a jacket, a dress, or a coat. This strategy, as in the various steps leading to the fabrication of a piece of dress, will more or less last throughout the entire 19th century. Orchestrating these different transformations, from the fabric to the completed garment, the customer is as much—if not more—the creator than the actual maker or artisan.

The early 19th century is also a time when the fashion press develops rapidly— amongst the many titles popular at the time, *Le Journal des Dames et des Modes* to *Le Petit courier des dames*. And if one considers the discourses increasingly produced across these various titles, one phenomenon appears clearly that reveals a profound shift in the understanding of fashion: accessories are coming to be considered as identifiable entities. They are able to claim a certain autonomy from the wearer—they exist as independent objects. Fans from the house of Duvelleroy and gloves from the house of Mayer are amongst the many identifiable pieces and no longer solely depend on their wearer to exist. The comments of fashion journalists in the 1830s or 1840s describe a gathering in a park while emphasizing the cut of a lambskin glove, the opening night of a theatrical play through the delicacy of the shawls spotted on the elegant ladies' shoulders, an evening at a masked ball through the distinctive waist line of a specific corset,...: these are perfect illustrations of the materialization of fashion into an object. In a way, one can assume that accessories, as autonomous artifacts, singularized within a silhouette, offer an early demonstration of a process we can describe as a "fashion recognition," the process of becoming, of materializing fashion.

Why is such an evolution observable in the years before the mid-19th century? What are the changes occurring in the culture of fashion at the time allowing for these objects to gain such recognition?

A first answer lies in the technical transformations profoundly affecting the period: as the Industrial Revolution unfolds, manufacturing processes are radically redefined or simply reinvented. The mechanization of labor, but also the introduction of new tools and materials, leads to an entirely new system of production. In this context, accessories are perhaps the most prominently affected. Patents are taken out by artisans perfecting their craft, providing a legal bind between makers and their products—the official recognition of the inventor's creativity in a commodity encourages this close association between an object and a name.

Both the aesthetics and the mechanics combined in an accessory are therefore acknowledged as the production of an author, more than the result of manufacturer's labor. The "new system invented by Mayer to give glove-making a unique form of perfection" is what consumers visiting his workshop on rue de Choiseul are seduced by. All the elegant ladies who have tried this new system are charmed, and Mayer, who has obtained an exclusive patent, has seen his name marked by success within the Parisian fashion industry.[1] This association between a name and a patent, between a name and the fashionable qualities of a product can be understood as the early stages of what we would today refer as branding strategies. And what is interesting here again, is the fact that accessories—tangible, wholesome, and autonomous objects—as opposed to the still made-to-measure garments, are at the forefront of this new understanding of fashion.

19:

1. Fashion, Petit Courrier des Dames, n°13, t. XXXIV, 19e année, 5 mars 1840, 99–100.

The Language of Fashion

But beyond this technical rhetoric infiltrating the fashion discourse, allowing for observers to recognize an accessory through its unique and innovative materials, components, or constructions, there is another reason why they—the accessories—have such a prominent role in the textual depictions of fashion in 19th-century France. It is connected with fashion's unique ability to take part in the complex semiotics of social representation. This is not a new idea, as shapes of dresses, colors used for coats, shoes, or even jewellery have, throughout the long history of European monarchies, been part of an intricate system of representation of power in court societies. What is new, and interesting for our discussion today, is the political context of post-revolutionary France: the Ancien Régime, and its order of things, having ended with the French Revolution at the end of the 18th century (with the beginning of the 1789 upheaval), the early decades of the following century are shaped by a succession of short-lived political regimes. Democratic republic, constitutional monarchy, empire...French citizens see the very principles of government change throughout the course of a few decades. This rather hectic political context has a direct impact on the understanding of fashion and the role it can play for the modern individual. Hierarchies and clear social differentiations established by centuries of royal power are being redefined, permitting aspiring bourgeois to join the ranks of the new-formed elites, in a society where one is now able to wear what he or she wants.

Having the freedom, both in the legal and material sense, to compose one's own identity, bestows onto fashion a new purpose: choosing a hat, the cut of a glove, the color of an umbrella are not just superficial attempts to display one's personal taste. In a society having abolished aristocratic privileges dictating sartorial laws, these conscious fashion decisions are a way to compose a very visible—and readable—self. The act of self-fashion can no longer be solely connected to a leisurely activity but becomes a way to both establish and affirm an identity.

In 1827 an unknown author, the Baron Emile de l'Empesé, publishes a style manual: *L'art de mettre sa cravate de toutes les manières connues et usitées, enseigné et démontré en seize leçons*. While the author is quite mysterious, the printer and publisher is more notorious—it is the young Honoré de Balzac, which in fact had led scholars to believe he might have written most parts of the book. The manual is meant to show fashionable men how to wear their tie, and more specifically which knot to choose wisely. Thirty-two plates accompany the text to illustrate the many options to work from and the author insists: "the art of wearing a tie is to the society man, what hosting a state dinner is to a politician." Beyond risking to be ridiculed by a bad choice of color or print, the wearer may reveal, through the simple shape of the knot, more profound aspects of his personality. Brave, bold, or curious; coward and narrow-minded; conservative or romantic: as the author suggest "the tie of a genius does not resemble that of an average mind."

No one more than the mid-19th-century dandies will understand and master the act of self-fashioning as an ontological quest: the often referenced legend of Beau Brummel spending hours with his butler to achieve the perfect knot of his tie reflects his aspiration to translate through the materiality of the fabric his ambitious mindset, his quest of absolute elegance and excellence. Becoming what you wear or having your garments reflect your individuality— these issues dominated the purchase of every handkerchief, watch, jewellery, or hat. "Dandyism is almost as difficult a thing to describe as to define. Those who see things only from a narrow point of view have imagined it to be especially the art of dress, a bold and felicitous dictatorship in the matter of clothes and exterior elegance. That it most certainly is, but much more besides," famously writes Jules Barbey d'Aurevilly in his seminal essay "Of Dandyism and of George Brummell" (1845), clearly hinting at this more metaphysical exploration that the construction of one's individual identity entails.

The complex semantical system that the articulation of different accessories represents, on the body of the dandy—but more generally on any given individual from 19th century French society—will quite logically fascinate one the most iconic theorists of linguistics. In 1962, Roland Barthes publishes an article entitled "Dandyism and Fashion." In it he reflects on this specific moment, pertaining as much to fashion history as to France's political and cultural history. Barthes starts by assessing how, the originality in menswear, in men's suits, in the post-revolutionary era was aiming for a more "neutral" and "democratic" appeal. "It is here that we see the appearance of a new aesthetic category in clothing, destined for a long future," Barthes writes "Since it was no longer possible to change the basic type of clothing for men without affecting the democratic and work ethos, it was the detail (the 'next-to-nothing,' the *'je ne sais quoi*,' the 'manner,' etc.), which started to play the distinguishing role in clothing." Here Barthes goes on to describe the various accessories that are the material embodiment of his idea of the "distinctive detail": the knot on a cravat, the buttons on a waistcoat, the buckle on a shoe—almost all exclusively accessories.

The Modern Accessory: Global Distinction and the Luxury Market

This non-verbal linguistic system at play in an autonomous manufactured good, this language of fashion that so efficiently functions through the accessories combined with our more modern and neutral clothes is arguably still relevant today. The context in which these issues were first raised, the first part of the 19th century, is almost 200 years old. However, it appears the fundamental laws of fashion, as they were forged in early industrial and capitalist societies, are somewhat unchanged in Western consumer cultures. And as the players of these early stages of the modern fashion industry have expanded their customer base beyond the circles of Parisian dandyism to embrace a more global market, it appears the distinctive aura of their products continues to serve the same purpose. If the glove-maker Mayer, or the corset-maker Josselin are long gone, the house of Duvelleroy is still operating in Paris today. And while fans are yet to be re-discovered for the fashionable potential, other houses which belong to this cultural context are much more present and active in today's luxury market. Let's remind ourselves that the house of Hermès started producing accessories for the elegant equestrian in 1837, just a decade after Balzac's style manual dedicated to ties and a few years before Barbey d'Aurevilly's essay on dandyism. That same year the founder of one of today's biggest luxury conglomerates also arrived in Paris to train as an artisan and serve the elegant society: young Louis Vuitton entered his apprenticeship to become a trunk maker. The combinations of hat, gloves, and tie, but also of bag, trunk, or saddle that so perfectly captured the essence of the dandy—which formulated a sentence of fashion through accessories—is fundamentally no different to the careful association, by today's luxury consumer, of an Hermès scarf with a Vuitton bag. It reaffirms both the craftsman's authorship as a brand and the wearer's individuality—though this last point may sound as an oxymoron given the change in the scale of production of these items today. Nonetheless, and no matter how the trend for logo mania may diminish the subtle message of distinction that these accessories were first used for, the aura of the accessory remains one of the most powerful ones in fashion, able like no other artifact to establish this fascinating and intricate play between "self-branding" or self-fashioning.

Belaboring Dress
Literature of
Wear and Tear

196

Paula RABINOWITZ

Emerita Professor of English, University of Minnesota, USA

*For the philosopher, the most interesting thing about fashion
is its extraordinary anticipations…Whoever understands how to read
these semaphores would know in advance not only
about new currents in the arts but also about new legal codes, wars,
and revolutions.*

–Walter Benjamin (1999, 63)

*I said: "A line will take us hours maybe;
Yet if it does not seem a moment's thought,
Our stitching and unstitching has been naught…"
[…]
That beautiful mild woman…
Replied: "To be born woman is to know—
Although they do not talk of it at school—
That we must labour to be beautiful."*

*I said: "It's certain there is no fine thing
Since Adam's fall but needs much laboring…"*

–William Butler Yeats (1956)

97

Invisible Labor

As my two epigraphs—one published at the dawn of the 20th century by the Irish poet William Butler Yeats, the other penned as a musing by the German Jewish philosopher and critic in the middle of Europe's decimation by Fascism—suggest, fashion (or for Yeats, female beauty) makes meaning. And it does so in part through writing. Diana Vreeland summed up this 20th-century insight with her rhetorical question, while musing the gowns mentioned in *Anna Karinina*: "Where would fashion be without literature?" (Vreeland, 1984, 82) It is a semaphore to be deciphered, a line to be read, simultaneously hiding the effort required to produce it and revealing its possible effects. To read fashion, including the figure of the woman who wears it, who embodies it, is to see the past—inheriting in the materials and labor required to achieve its form—and forecast the future— glimpsed in the trends these objects (which include the fashioned body) portend. Yeats is of course using his female interlocutor and her pointedly feminist commentary to emphasize the invisible labor required to write a poem. This poem is an ars poetica. It insists on laying claim to the invisible yet material conditions— time spent musing, writing, and revising, in short labor, at once mental and manual—of crafting a poem as essential to its aesthetics. Moreover, when that beautiful mild woman chimes in with her own corpus poetica, you might call it, it is clear that her labor is also essentially an aesthetic practice, an unrecognized one because the eye sees its end product, not the stitching and unstitching necessary to the vision. It is this final form—let's call it fashion—that, by hiding how it happens, by refusing to bare its devices, anticipates, for Benjamin, the future becoming of social relations, including art but also the law, even revolution. It works as a constellation. So, to turn Vreeland's insight on its head, we might ask: Where would literature (or philosophy) be without fashion?

In each passage, something glimpsed, something as ephemeral as beauty or fashion, arrests the gaze and an abstraction is concretized. Paradoxically, this abstraction flows within the present because it has been already worked over to become a harbinger of that which has yet to occur. Both writers develop a theory of aesthetic labor that pushes against the present, encasing the past and foreseeing the future. Fashion, woman's beauty, a line of poetry, a social critique; to fully apprehend them is to see the threads left hanging, what should have been excised, or at least ignored, or covered over in its production. Like the "strapped pumps" that draw Roland Barthes's eyes to an otherwise mundane 1926 James Van Der Zee studio photograph of an African-American family in Sunday best posing for a portrait, the excess bares meaning. This "'detail,'" which Barthes highlights in quotation marks, is, he remarks, "a partial object." The strapped shoes "prick" him, calling forth his "sympathy": "Mary Janes— why does this dated fashion touch me?" he wonders. In revealing that this detail "arouses" more than the photograph's "studium," its subject matter, Barthes interleaves clothing, photography, and writing—connecting all of it to critique— because, as he concludes, "the punctum can be ill-bred" (Barthes, 1981, 43). It disturbs, it calls attention, it accessorizes. Moreover, it theorizes.

David Trotter calls attention to another item of women's footwear in his essay, "Lady Chatterley's Sneakers," and gives a full-throated exegesis on the matter of literary wear and tear. D. H. Lawrence presents Constance Chatterley as "a particular kind of modern woman," and we know this, in part, by what she puts on to meet her gameskeeper and lover in his wooded cabin. Trotter attends to the narrator's fleeting, off-hand mention that Connie had donned a pair of "rubber tennis-shoes" (as the second version has it), and carried "a bottle of perfume by Coty," for her illicit tryst with Oliver Mellors (Trotter, 2012). Trotter demonstrates the significance of this minor detail about an item of clothing and a small object in a novel with a "prose style…of molten lava," which after all is not about attire.

James Van Der Zee, "Family Portrait," 1926

Sneakers were brand new in the 1920s and Lawrence was, in Benjamin's sense, attuned to the revolutions (in footwear) to come. Teasing out many sides to these new-fangled footwear, part of the growing craze for sports among the middle class, Trotter unpacks the eroticism lodged in their plebian everydayness—and the versatility by which a modern woman could combine them with perfume— as they might enable the mistress of the house to sneak (as in sneakers) out unawares because the rubber soles muffle the sound of footsteps on the creaky floors of an English country house while her husband listens to the radio. These are "shoes that don't squeak," he declares.

But there is more to the story of Connie's sneakers. Their very existence as objects made of canvas and rubber point to the triumphant, if soon to be flagging, moment of British imperial power that captured the labor and resources of far-flung lands to provide the raw materials available through technologies of extraction— rubber and dyes—to the new industrial manufacturing processes treating them and transforming them into commodities for sale. Lawrence might have seen advertisements for sneakers in newspapers, magazines, or circulars, as in 1921, notes Trotter, the British Rubber Growers Association (RGA) had "established a publicity department to develop 'press propaganda advocating the use of rubber for all conceivable purposes.'" He must have seen an actual pair, described by the RGA as having crepe soles made without chemicals "to impair the natural live quality and nerve of the virgin product" (Trotter, 2012). In the United States, also, advertisements for the new sports shoes by Keds, were sponsored by the United States Rubber Company during the 1920s. These sneakers meant for the tennis courts also serve for dancing naked but perfumed in the woods; but they are

1
2

1. Advertisement for Keds, United States Rubber Company, 1919

2. Advertisement for Keds, The Boston Post (June 22, 1922). Source: The Shoeseum, Baltimore Maryland

actually the vital commercial residue of the forests of Malaya and Ceylon. Clearly, Lawrence knew enough about them to point our gaze to the (forest) floor. Thus Trotter alerts us to the changing visual, cultural, and economic landscape that would have been recognized—if in unspoken way—by Lawrence's contemporary readers. He shows how the economic exploitation of the invisible laborers working rubber plantations and chemical factories congeals within this lowly item of clothing made by still other workers. A more or less proletarian piece of her wardrobe, implicitly understood—or perhaps not, no matter—condenses into a rich theoretical node, and like fashion anticipates the future.

As does the "little bottle of Coty's Wood-violet perfume" Connie leaves behind in Mellors's cabin.[1] During the 1920s, this brand was widely understood as a new kind of populist luxury item. In Alexandra Kollontai's 1923 novella *Vasilisa Malygnia* about the struggle for women's sexual freedom immediately after the Russian Revolution (translated into English for a 1927 American edition as *Red Love* and published in Britain as *Free Love* in 1931), the heroine realizes that she must leave her comrade/lover Volodya despite both once being dedicated revolutionaries. She is pregnant with his child, but he is madly in love with another woman, his "monkey" Nina and she, in turn, is "insanely" in love with him. In her jealousy, Vasya reads a love letter from Nina to Volodya and comprehends that her no-nonsense communism is no match for tears, cosmetics, and capriciousness. What seals the deal for Vasya, who decides to give up Volodya and leave him and raise her child within a collective of other women, is the postscript to Nina's letter begging Volodya to run away with her. "Just think, I'm so happy, I found that powder I was looking for, L'Origan Coty!," she concludes (Kollontai, 1978, 156). Here, too, a new accessory for adorning a female body has signaled that this woman is an erotic object, a new kind of modern woman—open to her desire and openly displaying it.

Known as the "Napoleon of Perfume," François Coty was among the first perfumers to blend synthetic and natural scents into perfumes and an array of related products meant for a range of buyers—from high-end luxury purchases in bottles by Lalique (for L'Origan) and Baccarat to middle- and working-class women worldwide. He was the first to develop the "idea of a fragrance set, a gift box containing identically scented items, such as a perfume and matching powder, soap, cream, bath salts, lipstick, and cosmetics. With blending some of the perfumes in the process of the cosmetics [sic], Coty left the age of the craft to enter fully into the industrial age," sold at department store counters, according to the Coty website. "By 1925, 36 million women worldwide used Coty face powders."[2] Coty entered fully into the industrial age, which is modern times, by marrying natural scents—Connie's wood-violet perfume—to an array of humanmade chemicals and materials developed in the lab and introducing new products through slick advertisements and marketing them to department stores.[3] As Benjamin noted: "At the moment when the production process closes

1. In addition to her tennis shoes and Coty perfume, Trotter notes that Connie is also wearing "a lightweight mackintosh (first blue then in a later version violet)" (Trotter, 2012). In the second version, John Thomas and Lady Jane, she dons the mackintosh four times; in the first instance, it is "dark-blue" and "ugly," but later it becomes "old blue" and "warm." D. H. Lawrence, John Thomas, and Lady Jane (London: Heinemann, 1972), 46, 118. It, too, is a product of the marriage of organic and humanmade materials, and also has its origins beyond upper-class fashion, in this case the trenches of WWI. As Celia Marshik notes, its ubiquity in the modern British imaginary, and in others' imagination of Britain, makes the "Mac" almost as emblematic of national identity as the Union Jack—only more practical. It is exemplary of how an item of clothing can become a lifeform and instill itself in the identity of its wearer while simultaneously erasing the body underneath its rubberized exterior. As surface, it is deep. Its presence on the battlefield turned it into a marker of death; its mass appeal on the streets made it into a brand name. How does this two-fold process work? For an answer, see Celia Marshik, At the Mercy of their Clothes: Modernism, the Middlebrow, and British Garment Culture (New York: Columbia University Press, 2017), 66–101.

2. https://cotyperfumes.blogspot.com/p/history.html (Accessed January 3, 2019)

3. It is not by accident that Virginia Woolf ends her biography/novel (and her ars poetica) Orlando, with the poet, now a thoroughly modern woman, shopping in a department store, "Messrs. Marshall & Snelgrove," to be precise. Virginia Woolf, Orlando: A Biography [1928] (New York: Harvest Books, 1956), 300. Theodore Dreiser understood the department store, like the train that transports Carrie Meeber from Wisconsin to Chicago, as one of the signal technologies of modernity, allowing a young single woman access to the latest styles. "Carrie passed along the busy aisles much affected by the remarkable displays of trinkets, dress goods, stationery, and jewellery" to be found at "The Fair." Theodore Dreiser, Sister Carrie [1900] (Mineola, NY: Dover Publications, Inc., 2004), 15–16. See also Cristina Giorcelli, "Sheer Luxury: Kate Chopin's 'A Pair of Silk Stockings'" for another modernist tale of the department store's allure for young women. In Cristina Giorcelli and Paula Rabinowitz, eds. Habits of Being 2: Exchanging Clothes (Minneapolis: University of Minnesota Press, 2012), 78–96.

itself off to people, the stock in trade becomes accessible to them—in the form of the department store" (Benjamin, 1999, 367). Moreover, "The advertisement is the ruse by which the dream forces itself on industry," declares Benjamin (Benjamin, 1999, 171). Products, sales, advertisements—these were the key features of the new fashion industry aimed at the modern women who must labor to be beautiful.

LES PARFUMS

Les Parfums Coty, Advertisement, 1931
Source: https://cotyperfumes.blogspot.com/p/history.html

Kollontai, who was living in self-exile in Mexico when she wrote *Love of Worker Bees*, after stints in Scandinavia (as Soviet Ambassador to Norway), includes this detail—the brand name of the newly marketed commodity, face powder scented by Coty's fragrance—to indicate the powerful allure of heterosexual desire and passion. This commodified accessory for the female body surpassed revolutionary fervor. By the early 1920s, even among militants, the Bolshevik revolution was losing its radical appeal for this "sexually emancipated communist woman," as Kollontai called herself in her autobiography (Kollontai, 1971). The powder, or rather its brand name, worked as a charm, in Karl Marx's term, a fetish; powder as power. It signals to Vasya that she has lost her communist lover, already compromised as a bureaucrat in the New Economic Program, a NEP man, to a more feminine (and also pregnant) woman. In both these modernist novels framing the new woman's sexuality—and the labor she exerted on her body to be desirable—Coty works as a punctum, an ill-bred detail, in Barthes's words, signaling a dangerous sexuality that disrupts the heterosexual couple.

Trotter sees Connie's Coty perfume as another example of the "techno-primitivism," inhering in various garments—like rubber-soled tennis shoes, each of which relied on a melding of organic and inorganic materials. They are emblems of the modern woman. Trotter is certain that Lawrence had all this in mind when his heroine slipped her feet into her sneakers and dabbed her neck with scent. Lady Chatterley's Coty perfume and Nina's L'Origan Coty powder, each a detail that grazes the body and gives it olfactory form, theorize themselves and with them much about women's desires and class formation in modernity. They appear to answer affirmatively Naomi Schor's rhetorical question: "Is the detail feminine?" (Schor, 1987, 4) They (the items and the women wearing them), like Karl Marx's coat and the 10 (and then 20) yards of linen exchanged for it, are commodities, "something two-fold." In the two novels, they are at once insignificant accessories, yet objects of utility (to engage in earthy sex or seduce the man you love into leaving his pregnant common-law wife) and depositories of value (exemplary items for modern womanhood, herself become a possession both useful and valuable to her lover). Because it is value that "converts every product into a social hieroglyphic," according to Marx. "Later on, men try to decipher the hieroglyphic, to get behind the secret of their own social products; for the definition of the object of utility as value is just as much their social product as language" (Marx, 1967, 86). Thus, in language, to literature, we must seek the "secret" of this "social product," the form of labor concealed within the detail—meant to be overlooked, on the one hand, but the result of well-wrought effort of stitching and unstitching to catch the eye, on the other.

Fewer than 10 pages into *Capital*, Marx uses the coat as an exemplary object to make visible how use-value (to keep one warm) as well as exchange-value (to signal social status, depending upon material, craftsmanship, cut, style, and tailoring) intertwine and are reified under capitalism. But of course, the tailor's labor had been preceded by that of the weaver (of linen [his relative "equivalent" material] or wool) and before that of the farmer planting and harvesting flax or shepherd shearing sheep and then of the factory hands mass-producing clothing. "By making the coat the equivalent of the linen, we equalize the labor embodied in the former to that in the latter…their common character of human labor…abstract human labor" (Marx, 1967, 50). One might argue that the entire theory of abstract labor, which is the basis of the "Critical Analysis of Capitalist Production," i.e., volume 1 of *Capital*, depends upon these equivalences because "value can only manifest itself in the social relation of commodity to commodity"

(Marx, 1967, 47). Or, in Gertrude Stein's words: "A shawl is a hat and hurt and a red balloon and an under coat and a sizer a sizer of talks. A shawl is a wedding, a piece of wax a little build. A shawl…There is a hollow hollow belt, a belt is a shawl" (Stein, 1997). When everything is reduced to commodities, all transaction is exchange; and things (and the labor entailed in their production) appear interchangeable, but of course, they are not: Connie's and Nina's Coty assumes the guise of individuality because they are details, feminine details.

This is implicitly Peter Stallybrass's argument in his 1998 essay "Marx's Coat," perhaps the template for Trotter's inquiry into Connie's sneakers and perfume. Stallybrass shows how throughout the 1850s and 1860s, as Marx was undertaking the research and writing of *Capital* traveling to and from the British Museum, his overcoat determined his ability to leave his house and get to work. In a letter to Friedrich Engels, Marx wrote on February 27, 1852, ironically, "A week ago I reached the pleasant point that I was unable to go out for want of the coats I have in pawn" (Stallybrass, 1998).[4] Stallybrass declares, "What clothes Marx wore thus shaped what he wrote." They literalized "a vulgar material determination" that surrounded his opening move toward abstraction.[5] The threadbare coat in hock "counts therefore as embodied value, as a body that is value." Marx explains: "In the production of the coat, human labor-power, in the shape of tailoring, must have been actually expended. Human labor is therefore accumulated in it. In this aspect the coat is a depository of value, but though worn to a thread, it does not let this fact show through." (Marx 1967, 51) Later that year, Marx wrote again about his circulating coat: "Yesterday, I pawned a coat dating back to my Liverpool days in order to buy writing paper."[6] Stallybrass understands Marx's plight, like the commodity form itself, as two-fold: he is literally so poor that he cannot work because he lacks the materials necessary to perform as a researcher (at the British Museum, where he would be required to be more or less properly attired to enter); or as a journalist (for which he needs paper to write and newspapers to read in order to keep abreast of world events). That ragged overcoat enables him to gain the materials necessary for his work. Marx's coat morphs into Connie's and Nina's Coty: from material to abstraction.

Peter Stallybrass's dissects the first parts of *Capital* into the very tangible terms of the materials of bodily covering. He renders the history of pawnbrokers and their representations within European 19th-century literature as centrally about how working-class households made do, and did so usually on the backs of women who were the primary frequenters of the pawnshop. He elaborates the costs of dressing. Stallybrass insists we understand the affective and material

"Commodities." From Karl Marx 'Capital' in Lithographs by Hugo Gellert (New York: Ray Long and Richard R. Smith, 1934).

05 conditions endured during the writing of Capital through our attention to the quite pointed way in which the coat that figures as Ur-commodity, we might say as a *punctum*, in Marx's allegory also references the actual coats that trafficked back and forth from Marx's cramped quarters to the pawnshop. Allegorical and material, two-fold, a condensation that belabors the literary garment as an expressive form, an affective form; in this case worn by Karl, but borne by Jenny. In the exchanges of Marx's coat in and out of the pawnbroker's shop (labor, Stallybrass notes, performed by the women caring for Marx, wife Jenny and housekeeper Helene Demuth) (Stallybrass 1998, 191). Here, as well as the dynamic between Connie and her lover and Nina and hers, are dramatized the connections Yeats drew about invisible labor: "the goods," Jewish tailors' slang for fabric, are means to achieve ends.

Visible Labor

Tennis shoes, a pair of Mary Janes, Coty perfume, a ratty coat—these are the details accessorizing modern literature and philosophy. Like accessories, their very insignificance releases "anticipations," as Benjamin noted, about what lies beyond, behind, within the works. They point—as a punctum in Barthes's

---

4. Marx, 50; quoted in Stallybrass, 187
5. Quoted in Stallybrass, 188
6. Ibid.

sense—to openings for interpretation. But they are surely marginal to the texts themselves. The literary garment can also claim total attention; its characters actual participants in the wear and tear of fashioning and self-fashioning. Anzia Yezierska's 1923 novel, *Salome of the Tenements*, roughly based on the short-lived marriage of labor organizer Rose Pastor to philanthropist Graham Stokes (but also on Yezierska's complicated relationship to educational reformer John Dewey), unveils the behind-the-scenes labor of dressmaking—from tenement sweatshops to Fifth Avenue couture. Jewish immigrant Sonya Vrunsky, the titular Salome of the Lower East Side, meets American millionaire John Manning at a settlement house and decides to snare him into marriage, unleashing her "thrill of aesthetic delight" to cajole various Ghetto businessmen to aid her pursuit. Dressmaker Jacques Hollins (formerly Jaki Solomon) offers her a fine garment (along with undergarments) free of charge and she wheedles money from "Honest Abe," the pawnbroker, to decorate her apartment (Yezierska, 1995, 22). But shortly after her marriage, Sonya cannot abide Fifth Avenue and its snobbery; and the upper-crust WASP reverts to anti-Semitic type once her story of debt comes out. In the end, she joins Jacques/Jaki as a collaborator. However, instead of making finery for the wealthy women of Fifth Avenue, the two decide to design beautiful apparel for the working-class women of Grand Street.

Clothing motivates everything in this novel. At first, Sonya is drawn to Manning by "the cultured elegance of his attire. Not a detail of his well-dressed figure escaped her...A master tailor had cut his loose Scotch tweeds," she notices (Yezierska, 1995, 2). In her attention to refined male haberdashery, Sonya is akin to another restless daughter, Carrie Meeber, who escapes her drab Wisconsin town for Chicago. On the train, Sister Carrie meets "travelling canvasser" Charles Drouet and immediately takes in his suit "of a striped and crossed pattern of brown wool... The low crotch of vest revealed a stiff shirt bosom of white and pink stripes. From his coat sleeves protruded a pair of linen cuffs of the same pattern, fastened with large gold plate buttons, set with the common yellow agates known as 'cates-eyes.' His fingers bore several rings" (Dreiser, Sister Carrie, 3). Both young women see that clothes make the man—or think they do—and their vision sparks action. Manning's attire—carefully tailored yet casually worn—spurs Sonya to reject the "unspeakable cheapness of a dry goods shop...limp calico dresses of scarlet and purple, gaudy blanket of pink and green checks...banners of poverty" (Yezierska, 1995, 5). Once Sonya has tried on the dress of "nun-like grey with a touch of sheer batiste again the whiteness of [her] throat," she is transformed "like Fifth Avenue-born," as she declares to Jacques (Yezierska, 1995, 26). His generosity, markedly different from "the oppressive charity" from do-gooders she had received before as a child, alerts Sonya to a new kind of democracy. The art of dress becomes political: "All I want is to be able to wear silk stockings and Paris hats the same as Mrs. Astorbilt, and then it wouldn't bother me if we have Bolshevism or Capitalism, or if the democrats or the republicans win. Give me only the democracy of beauty" (Yezierska, 1995, 27). The democracy of beauty, as Hollins knows, traffics a two-way street: Fifth Avenue finery grabs the styles of Grand Street—he spends time wandering amid the cheap shops and department stores catering to waitresses—while Lower East Side knock-offs steal from fashion plates for these desiring working women.[7] It takes a dressmaker's eye to perceive the class connections clothing and accessories forge.

Lynn Nottage's brilliant play *Intimate Apparel* (2006) rips open the ways in which dressmaking, as a form of what Denise Cruz calls "exclusive labor," gestures at how clothing begets intimacy to form something two-fold—appearance and reality; the literal and the allegorical.[8] In this play about labor at the turn of the last century, a series of characters interact one-on-one across various discreet spaces cordoned off from each other by race, class, and ethnicity. These include a proper boarding house in Harlem for single African-American working women where Esther, who "sew[s] intimate apparel for ladies," lives (Nottage, 2006,

---

7. For an elaboration on the back-and-forth exchange of styles from rich to poor and vice versa at the turn of the twentieth century as a form of democraticization, see, Anna Scacchi, "Redefining American Womanhood: Shawls in Nineteenth-Century Literature," in *Habits of Being 3: Fashioning the Nineteenth Century.* Ed. Cristina Giorcelli and Paula Rabinowitz (Minneapolis: University of Minnesota Press, 2014), 181–209. For a discussion about the racialized sexuality of Salome of the Tenements as part of a longer history of urbanization, see Paula Rabinowitz, "Meeting on the Corner: Mediterranean Men and Urban American Women," in *America and the Mediterranean: Proceedings of the Sixteenth Biennial International Conference.* Ed. Massimo Bacigalupo and Pierangelo Castagneto (Torino: Otto Editore, 2003), 445–52.

8. Denise Cruz, conducting ethnographies of Filipino designers working in Dubai, also finds the affective links created by clothing to be both literal and allegorical connections forged between client and couturier. These intimate matters produce new theoretical models—in this case about global migration and labor. As Cruz puts it: "the visual dynamics that center on global Filipino laborer and veiled Muslim woman⋯this imagining of fashion elsewhere allowed one designer to achieve a form of queer intimacy" with his client. Cruz highlights the story of one designer, Gil, whose clientele consists of a single wealthy married woman for whom he might need to produce 10 gowns and 10 outfits a day as she sorted through samples for the ones she wanted. From this almost daily contact between wealthy client and her designer develops a subtle bond of intimacy that Cruz discovers opens to view "complications" of racial, religious, class, sexual, and gender orders. Gil's explanation of his relationship with his client who reveals secrets she keeps from her husband (her impending liposuction) and in her dresser drawer (loads of cash) details how "he was invited into private spaces, like the master's bedroom, just after her husband or she had just emerged in a towel. While their initial meetings began in the sitting room, they sometimes move to the kitchen, where he meets her and she asks him to slice or mix for her and then gives him food to take home." Cruz's tale of transgressive encounters between "a gay male designer from the Philippines and an elite Emirati woman" are made possible "because he offered a form of exclusive labor. He was expected to work for her late into the night, and in the end, he provided her not only with custom made clothing but another kind of care—a listening and empathetic ear, an opportunity for her to talk with him about her life, her insecurities." This intimacy born of "exclusive labor," however, is anything but reciprocal. Denise Cruz, "Filipino Couturiers: Manila, Dubai, Hollywood Collections," paper delivered at the American Studies Association Conference, Denver, November 2016. My thanks to Denise Cruz for permitting me to quote from her talk.

16); Panama, where George, a man from Barbados, works building the canal; a white woman's elegant Fifth Avenue boudoir inhabited by Mrs. Van Buren; a Lower East Side tenement where Orthodox Jew Mr. Marks (no accident this name) sells goods; and another boudoir behind a speakeasy where an African-American singer and prostitute Miss Mayme lives and works. These spaces contain characters primarily known through what they wear—or what they make or sell for others to wear. Esther keeps a picture of George, her pen pal, dressed in a "cambric walking suit...a heliotrope handkerchief stuffed in his pocket"; she knows him by this detail that entices and seduces her (Nottage, 2006, 23). Miss Mayme covets the risqué embroidered silk corsets Esther stitches from the remnants of Japanese silk Mr. Marks, who "always wear[s] black," has saved for Esther so she can make "a smoking jacket for [her] gentleman," along with the "cobalt hand-dyed silk" she fashions into a camisole for Mrs. Van Buren. Her employer has been assisting illiterate Esther's letter writing to George so her prose rises to the level of his descriptions of the Caribbean landscape (Nottage, 2006, 30; 18; 30). These two share the close encounter of underwear fittings (it is called intimate apparel for a reason) and letter writing: Esther asks, "Do you think we could describe this silk? Will you tell him what it feels like against your skin? How does it soften and supple to the touch?" (Nottage, 2006, 59)

Betrayals abound: Eventually George arrives to marry Esther, she in a handmade dress of fine silk given to her by Mr. Marks; he is not what he pretended—he too had someone else write his letters—and runs with Mayme, giving her the smoking jacket Esther made for him; Mrs. Van Buren does not pay for her garments but she bestows a kiss on Esther instead, claiming to demonstrate her love and friendship. In the end, Esther retrieves the smoking jacket, gives it to Mr. Marks and actually fits him in it, violating his admonishments against her touching him, then returns to the boarding house, pregnant and alone, but with her sewing machine with which she begins to piece together a quilt for her unborn child from all the remnants she has amassed.

Nottage's highly mannered drama trades on the series of exchanges of materials and the fine labor that transform cloth into clothing—intimate apparel—cultivating (false) intimacies. The playwright brilliantly manipulates the allegorical and material conditions of these fabricated relationships by naming each scene for the items of dress or fabric circulating among and between characters: "Wedding Corset: White Satin with Pink Roses"; "Gardenia Ball Corset: Pink Silk and Crêpe de Chine"; "Imperial Silk: Embroidered with Blue Thread"; etc. As with any fine garment or accessory, details are crucial, and, as Schor argues, clearly gendered feminine.

Intimate Apparel is set in various bedrooms of New York in 1905, the year Edith Wharton unleashed her skewering of New York society as she follows Lily Bart through another series of bedrooms and ballrooms, until she too lands alone in a sad rooming house for single working women. Wharton peers underneath the corsets containing Lily's aberrant upbringing to find the debased, if fine, handiwork by those whose bodies have been exhausted in the process of making Lily and her ilk beautiful. After all, Yeats's poem, "Adam's Curse," appeared in a 1904 volume, *In the Seven Woods*.

1

2

1. Advertisement for Hancock & James Court Milliners and Dressmakers. London, 1900

2. Millinery Workroom of T. Eaton Co. Toronto, Canada, 1904
   Source: Archives of Ontario. The Eaton Collection. Fond 229. 308-0-1819-2 AO 2329

When Lily Bart first appears to Lawrence Selden in Grand Central Station one hot summer day as a vision of serenity amid the bustle of commuters, Wharton's narrator observes that her beauty and flawless dress came at the expense of others far more drab and downtrodden—those whose efforts (as dressmakers, milliners, and as maids who dress and coif her) had made her into this desirable, delectable object. Wharton knows that poor women make the lives of the wealthy possible; on occasion even obtuse Lily senses this, sees herself as another kind of "slave" like her maid, dependent on the kindness and acquisitions of intimates' hand-me-downs. Ultimately, she joins the ranks of workers (which entails, she discovers, far more labor than "trimming hats"). By the novel's end, Wharton allows us to peek beyond the showroom into the millinery workroom in back—stifling and smelly with glue and geegaws, preserved birds, and flowers saturated with toxic chemicals.[9] This is where it all ends, fingers sluggishly moving ineffectually, until overcome with exhaustion. Lily's downward trajectory within society is mirrored in her move from front of the house (and customer) to workroom (and laborer) and finally to the cold flat where she dies. No longer consumer, she cannot make it as a laborer either. Millinery was seen as a "practical" skill, "with an aim to educate girls for everyday life, and, like needlework, and all subjects relative to it, it encourages habits of neatness, industry, and thrift," according to Amy Reeve, whose manual, *Practical Home Millinery* appeared in 1915.[10]

This spatialization, from front to back of the house, allegorizes the work that clothing and apparel perform in this work—and perhaps all—of literature; it produces volume. Dress as covering of body, as an object (and even a scent is an object) made for use, even at its most extravagant, signals that something of further value is underneath this surface. It constructs depth even as it insists on surface as the plane on which affect alights. The belaboring of the clothed body is an artifice requiring description, a literary process. Attention to the details of dress—not merely a corset but one of magenta silk; not merely a powdered cheek but one scented with Coty's L'Origan—is, within the world of the literary garment, the provenance of those who work with and care for these materials, even if they cannot possess them but can only dream of their beauty. As such, literary dress theorizes class differences through attention to the democracy of beauty as Sonya called it.

One hundred years after Wharton detailed Lily's slow demise, Spencer Reece's poem "The Clerk's Tale," presents a melancholy dissection of a young man working in an upscale men's haberdashery. Like Nottage's *Intimate Apparel* (first performed in 2004), it provides a template for understanding how the intimate service work of clothing (in this case, sales at a mid-level men's haberdashery rather than dressmaking) reconstitutes class, sexuality, and gender (and ultimately, age), even as it stabilizes them within proscribed hierarchies.[11] This exchange almost completes the literary labor of wear and tear. The salesman— interacting with customers, other clerks, and the luxurious materials displayed— produces subjectivities-in-relation (that is, class) by always being attentive to nuances of sexual, aesthetic, and social distinctions while he fits his customers and encourages them to make a purchase. Service work, mostly invisible in Wharton's novels (despite a keen awareness "that she [Lily Bart] must have cost a great deal to make, that a great many dull and ugly people must, in some mysterious way, have been sacrificed to produce her"), (Wharton, 1964, 7) achieves literary visibility here, as it does in *Intimate Apparel*. Nottage's play anatomizes the mysteries of beauty in the form of elegant silk undergarments through the sacrificed fingers that produce rich women's finery; Reece's clerk works in the largest indoor mall in the United States servicing white-collar men who work in downtown and suburban offices. He spends his day folding "pincord, houndstooth, nailhead, and sharkskin" behind the glass panes of the shop window in Minnesota's Mall of America, the largest indoor mall in the United States. Literary garments make legible precisely how discerning what to wear is something two-fold—always an exchange—a discourse and practice of class relations and more.

Dress (in its widest definition, including accessories), the stuff that adorns, even if with such a gossamer touch that it can only be sensed through smell, gives surface (and paradoxically heft [something two-fold]) to characters. The labor of dressing is materially manifold; from the farmers growing flax and cotton

---

9. As late as the 1970s, London milliners worked in "an unventilated basement into which twenty girls sat round tables with tiny workspaces for each. There was no protection from the gas rings and steamers for from the heady stench of glue. The pressure to work fast was relentless but so was demand for perfection and fingers became raw," recounts Wendy Edmonds. In Clair Hughes, *Hats* (London and New York: Bloomsbury, 2017), 27.

10. Amy J. Reeve, *Practical Home Millinery* (London and New York: Longmans, Green and Co., 1915), iii–iv. Before her death, Lily, who has not been known for her organizational skills (except when it comes to her personal attire and her social life), puts her house in order; she writes out a check for the amount of money she owes, which she has saved up by scrimping, and neatly arranges her clothing and papers, perhaps she did learn something from her otherwise unsuccessful efforts at millinery.

11. Spencer Reece, "The Clerk's Tale," appeared on the back page of the 2004 fiction issue of *The New Yorker*, https://www.poets.org/poetsorg/poem/clerks-tale

and tending sheep, through the millworkers' looms, and then seamstresses and sweatshop workers transforming raw materials into wearable goods, to the salespeople selling them, and on to the buyer who organizes her closet and tends to her clothing through its wear and tear—washing and mending—to the second-hand merchants and junk dealers and trash haulers carting the discards of yesterday's fashions into chic second-hand shops or landfill (but that's another story).[12] Dress is also an idea—a sensory idea animating literature's evocations of gender, race, class, and sexuality through descriptions of material: what it feels like; how it looks; even how it smells. To begin appraising dress in literature often means pulling at the threads not yet clipped from seams—belaboring details—theorizing the intimate work of fashioning. The literary garment, as Thomas Carlyle at once spoofs and conveys in *Sartor Resartus*, is "thought-woven or hand-woven," in either case, a manifestation of human labor—mental or manual, mental and manual: "Clothes, as despicable as we think of them, are so unspeakably significant," remarks Diogenes Teufelsdröckh.[13] They are avatars, as Walter Benjamin argued. "The eternal is far more the ruffle than some idea," says Benjamin, claiming fashion's details, its accessories, for philosophy (Benjamin 1999, 69). The very materiality of dress, its excess, the ephemeral rustle that yards of stiff fabric or dabs of complex earthy scents might excite, sends us to contemplate the hands that first rucked the cloth or mixed the chemicals into these stylized details and that wrote about their effects. Thus the literary garment works as Benjamin's semaphore or Barthes's *punctum* or Schor's detail or Marx's coat or Esther's camisole or Lily's hat or Connie's Coty; it crystallizes abstract labor, giving value to the wear and tear of clothes. Indeed, many more than two hands work material into allegory. Where would literature be without fashion?

---

12. For more on this story of cycling and recycling clothing, see Katalin Medvedev, "It Is a Garage Sale at Savers Every Day: An Ethnography of the Savers Thrift Department Store in Minneapolis," in *Habits of Being 2: Exchanging Clothes*. Ed. Giorcelli and Rabinowitz, 230–53.

13. Thomas Carlyle, *Sartor Resartus: The Life and Times of Herr Treufeldröckh* (1833–34). Ch. 9 "Prospective," Project Gutenberg. http://www.gutenberg.org/files/1051/1051-h/1051-h.htm#link2HCH0005 For an in-depth analysis of the philosophical power of Carlyle's work and its effect on Ralph Waldo Emerson's transcendentalism, see Giuseppe Nori, "Garment of the Unseen: The Philosophy of Clothes in Carlyle and Emerson," in *Habits of Being 3: Fashioning the Nineteenth Century*. Ed. Giorcelli and Rabinowitz, 52–81.

Acknowledgments

I first wrote about accessories when Cristina Giorcelli invited me to contribute to her on-going series, *Abito e Identitá* last century. That essay "Barbara Stanwyck's Anklet: The Other Shoe" (2001) led to my fascination with (and more essays about) various aspects of dress. I owe her for awakening this scholarly interest. Ultimately, she and I co-edited the four-volume series, *Habits of Being* (University of Minnesota Press): *Accessorizing the Body; Exchanging Clothes; Fashioning the Nineteenth Century; and Extravagances*. This engagement with the material, in all senses, refocused my teaching and research. I thank my students in the seminar "What to Wear: Clothing, Dress, and Fashion in Literature, Film, and Art" at the University of Minnesota for their attention to detail. I gratefully acknowledge the portions of this essay that began as a talk, entitled *What to Wear and (Why) Do We Care*, delivered at the 2017 Modern Language Association annual meeting in Philadelphia for the panel, "Fashioning Theory/ Theorizing Fashion" and were later developed into a review of "At the Mercy of their Clothes: Modernism, the Middlebrow, and British Garment Culture" by Celia Marshik, originally published in the *Journal of British Studies* (2017).

Reference

Barthes, R. 1981. *Camera Lucida: Reflections on Photography*. Translated by Richard Howard. New York: Hill and Wang.

Benjamin, W. 1999. "Baudelaire." In *The Arcades Project*, Translated by Howard Eiland and Kevin McLaughlin, 367. Cambridge MA and London: The Belknap Press of Harvard University Press.

Benjamin, W. 1999. "Exhibitions, Advertising, Grandville." In *The Arcades Project*, Translated by Howard Eiland and Kevin McLaughlin, 171. Cambridge, MA and London: The Belknap Press of Harvard University Press.

Benjamin, W. 1999. "Fashion."In *The Arcades Project*, Translated by Howard Eiland and Kevin McLaughlin, 63. Cambridge MA and London: The Belknap Press of Harvard University Press.

Kollontai, A. 1971. *The Autobiography of a Sexually Emancipated Communist Woman*. Translated by Salvator Attanasio. New York: Herder and Herder.

Kollontai, A., 1978. *Love of Worker Bees*. Translated by Cathy Porter. Chicago: Academy Chicago Publishers.

Marx, K. 1967. *Capital v. 1: A Critical Analysis of Capitalist Production*. Edited by Frederick Engels. New York: International Publishers.

Nottage, L. 2006. *Intimate Apparel/Fabulation*. New York: Theater Communication Group.

Schor, N. 1987. *Reading in Detail: Aesthetics and the Feminine*. London: Methuen.

Stallybrass, P. 1998. "Marx's Coat." In *Border Fetishisms: Material Objects in Unstable Spaces*, edited by Patricia Spyer, 183–207. London: Routledge.

Stein, G. 1997. "A Shawl." In *Tender Buttons*, 16. Mineola, NY: Dover Publications, Inc.

Trotter, D. 2012. "Lady Chatterley's Sneakers." In *London Review of Books* 3:7.

Vreeland, D. 1984. *D.V.* New York: Alfred Knopf.

Wharton, E. 1964. *The House of Mirth*. New York: Signet.

Yeats, W. B. 1956. "Adam's Curse." In *The Collected Poems of W.B. Yeats*, 78. New York: The Macmillan Company.

Yezierska, A. 1995. *Salome of the Tenements*. Urbana and Chicago: University of Illinois Press.

Accessories

Their Ontological Function as Superfluous/Essential Items of Clothing—
with Some Instances of Their Literary and Filmic Meanings

Cristina GIORCELLI

Professor Emerita of American Literature at the University of Rome Three, Italy

According to its first definition in the Oxford *English Dictionary*, an accessory is "a thing which can be added to something else in order to make it more useful, versatile, or attractive"; according to its second definition—more specifically attributed to apparel—an accessory is "a small article or item of clothing carried or worn to complement a garment or outfit." Consequently, an accessory is both an "addition," that is, an extra in respect to what is indispensable, and a "complement," that is, an item that contributes to something that is more important. Since the second definition highlights another of its characteristics—that of being "small"—an accessory should also be an item that is not of large dimensions. In other words, these formal definitions rule that an accessory does not occupy a central position, as it is an item on the periphery of what, on the contrary, is a prerequisite. In both definitions an accessory is thus identified as something that is non-basic, something that is secondary and rather trivial, even as far as size is concerned. At best, therefore, an accessory is an *ex-centricity*.

But, are these definitions still valid in this world of ours in which there are few boundaries, few limits, and few demarcations, and in which everything tends to be fluid and homogenized? In other words, do these definitions really sum up what an accessory is today? Especially since, for instance, shoes are still considered to be accessories.

In effect, like clothes, accessories can reveal individual traits, suggest intentions, manifest a propensity for play and irony, favor interpersonal encounters, hint at class and gender relations, and evidence various connections within what is pointedly called the social "fabric." In sum, exactly like—or even more so than—a dress, a coat, or a gown, the so-called accessory is an imperative element in the construction of a look. And this because, as Kaja Silverman observes, "clothing [including accessories] is a necessary condition of subjectivity...in articulating the body, it simultaneously articulates the psyche" (Silverman, 1986). Film scholar Sarah Berry maintains that accessories can even act as catalysts for new kinds of social behavior (Berry, 2000). As in Roland Barthes's opinion (Barthes, 1990) fashion items are also tools of social communication, accessories can disclose what the wearer—perhaps indirectly, perhaps only implicitly—intends to reveal about him/herself. Not by chance, I surmise, the word "accessory" etymologically derives from the medieval Latin word *accessorium*, taken from the verb accedere, which means "to approach," to come close to (a person/ality, for instance).

That accessories have become momentous items of clothing—especially at a time of economic crisis—is evident from the success that a chain of shops such as the British retail outlet "Accessorize"—that originally started its business as "Monsoon"—is enjoying around the world. Its generally inexpensive, frequently small, items entice consumers as "things" that may renew, or at least jazz up, an old dress (perhaps with a bright shawl), or a worn-out coat (perhaps with a silk flower or a costume brooch), or an out-of-date gown (perhaps with a necklace of costume pearls), or even render a dull face luminous (perhaps with costume diamond earrings).

Vis-a-vis the complexity that apparel represents, I really do not think that the aforementioned definitions describe the role and function of accessories today. I propose, instead, to call them details. That is, not just additions or, at best, complements—merely supplements—but items that are often the most telling parts of/in apparel. Details, in fact, have an interesting status and an intriguing ontological meaning.

Generally speaking, what we call details in garments are the many variations in which an item of clothing may be declined. In the case of collars, for instance, the details are the flounces, jabots, frills, and ruffles that can adorn a shirt. According to the *Oxford English Dictionary*, a detail is "a minor decorative feature." Not an "addition" to or a "complement" of something—not something that takes a secondary position in respect to something more important—but a "feature" that is self-standing and distinct, charged with specific characteristics. In other words, a detail is a "decoration" that may remarkably distinguish apparel. That it is designated as "minor"—similar to the "small" encountered for "accessory"—does not detract from the fact that the definition of "detail" does not single it out as flimsy, but as special (in the *Oxford English Dictionary* a feature is "A *distinctive attribute* or aspect of something" [italics mine]). Suffice to ponder that pearl of wisdom found in the famous proverb: "The devil is in the details"—the crux, that is, lurks in those apparently insignificant words and phrases that in a legal contract, for instance, may have devastating implications.

This change of name matters, as it does not simply entail the substitution of one word with another, but requires the substitution of one concept with another. In sum, these items of clothing—these accessories or, better, these details—need to be accorded their *real* prominence in our habits of being.

Indeed, in recent decades, through the prevailing technique of "mix and match," the parameters and hierarchies of fashion have shifted. In the mixtures and combinations of styles, colors, patterns, and materials, such details often capture—on first impact and in an exclusive way—the attention of the onlooker. He/she no longer observes the old dress, the worn-out coat, the out-of-date gown, or the dull face; that is, he/she is no longer taken by the context, but by such items as bright shawls, silk flowers, costume brooches, costume pearls, or costume diamonds, that "signify" more than the rest of the apparel or, even, more than their wearers (as, from different perspectives, both Sigmund Freud [2005] and Marshall MacLuhan [1951] have argued, and as Martin Margiela[1] has shown). Actually, these details stand out so prominently that the garment itself becomes a sort of backdrop for them. In fact, apparel turns into a sort of stage on which these items perform. In other words, they are crucial to the accumulative look. Indeed, they are what in rhetoric called metonymy: they stand as vital parts *of*—but *also for*—the whole.

If, regarding the ensemble of apparel, the onlooker loses a sense of entirety, of "harmony"—if we want to use such a pompous word and, as far as fashion goes, such an old concept—it is because these "small" items often end up acquiring a significance that transforms them into events. As the Italian semiologist Omar Calabrese explains, (Calabrese, 1992) details—a word that comes from the French "de-tailler," that means "to cut into pieces"—differ from fragments that are the result of random breaks. Details, on the contrary, presuppose the existence of both someone (in our case, the designer, the stylist) who cuts/draws them, who devises them in such a way as to make them individual or unique, and of onlookers who, gazing at them, visually/mentally distances them from their background (that thus loses much of its importance). As French art-historian Daniel Arasse declares, "A detail may bring an essential meaning to the whole image" (Arasse, 1992). Therefore, especially at times of economic crisis, and when a new aesthetics is called for to explain and justify the search for new types of beauty, these details, far from being banal, are of the utmost purport.

This is exactly what Jacques Derrida upholds in his essay on "parerga" (that is, on those decorations and embellishments that Immanuel Kant discussed in his *Critique of Judgment*): "the 'parergon'—Derrida writes—inscribes something

---

1. See Margiela's collections of the 1990s, for instance. See, Paola Colaiacomo, "Fashion's Model Bodies," *Habits of Being. Accessorizing the Body*, vol. I, ed. Cristina Giorcelli and Paula Rabinowitz (Minneapolis: University of Minnesota Press, 2011), 24–32.

which comes as an extra, exterior to the proper field...but whose transcendent exteriority comes to play, abut onto, brush against, rub, press against the limit itself and intervene in the inside only to the extent that it is lacking from itself" (Derrida, 1987). This is exactly what matters: the "parergon," the detail, is called upon when/because something is lacking. These items of clothing are therefore helpers that come to assist when/where there is a deficiency either in apparel or in the body or in both. Far from being superfluous, details thus become essential. Not only, but the tendency today to privilege details over the whole is what Calabrese defines as the new baroque (recasting the style and gusto that was prevailing in 17th-century European art). A tendency subsumes a way of living and of being, structurally and formally, characterized by instability, polydimensionality, and mutability. One has but to think of Rei Kawakubo's creations, for a case in point. Is this not, however, the very essence of fashion, that, over a century and a half ago, was declared by Charles Baudelaire to consist of an "ephemeral, fugitive, contingent" element (Baudelaire, 1995)? And, is this not what Walter Benjamin implied when he wrote that "the eternal... is far more a ruffle on a dress than some idea" (Benjamin, 1999)? In effect, in order to try and give garments a semblance of renewal, of novelty, these details may not only be changed endlessly, but, as they tend to become of increasing consequence, their ultimate goal is to be found in emphasis and excess. Today, in what Jean Baudrillard has defined as a civilization of images (Baudrillard, 1988), when in jewellery, for instance, precious metals and stones are no longer necessarily used—substituted by more inexpensive and readily accessible materials—the intended effect of details is to surprise, to be spectacular. In other words, these details take on the import of an emblem: the emblem of both the process of representation (for the designer and for the wearer) and the process of perception (for the onlooker).

This is the reason why they are so revelatory: regardless of their cost, they always have a prominent value as manifestations, as symbols of something else, that is, of what Martha Banta has called people's "inner impulses" (Banta, M., 2011).

Consider a few examples regarding authentic or costume jewellery both in art, in films, and in literature. In addition to beautifying, jewellery has traditionally stood for wealth and status. We have but to think of Bronzino's portrait of Eleanor of Toledo or, at the end of the 19th century, of the portraits of wealthy women by such painters as Giovanni Boldini and John Singer Sargent.

Billy Wilder's 1954 film *Sabrina*, with Audrey Hepburn in the title role, was a modern-day Cinderella tale. Sabrina herself, a driver's daughter, is presented as having come of age by living for two years in Paris, where she had gone to learn French cooking. When she leaves the City of Light and goes back home, the details in the apparel that he wears show how she has grown from an innocent girl into a fully fledged sophisticated woman: she dons a close-fitting cap over short curly hair—when she left she still wore a pony-tail—and gold hoop earrings. Earrings, being among the only kind of jewellery that—when not clasped or attached with a screw—necessitates the drawing of blood (Giorcelli, 2015), have a special significance, because they are inserted into, and thus become part of, the wearer's body. What is more, by being close to the face, they command special attention. In particular, because in past centuries a hoop earring was also worn by men (by sailors, but also by ancient Persians, and, during the Renaissance, by literary artists such as William Shakespeare and John Donne, as they appear in their portraits), this type of earrings is meant to suggest the wearer's strong personality. As far as women are concerned, hoop earrings have always been worn by Roma, and traditionally they have been associated with defiance and wanton sexuality. The latter is certainly not the case with Sabrina, because, apart from the delicacy with which her character is drawn, censorship in Hollywood movies was strict in 1950s United States. What these earrings (and oufit) lightly—but unequivocally—suggest, however, is that in Paris Sabrina has not only learned how to cook. As she herself says, there she also learned how to live—with all the possible connotations, including the sexual ones. And, in order to illustrate how sophisticated she has become, and—no longer shy and insecure about herself and her position—how she is determined to attract attention to herself by various means, she also parades a bejeweled French poodle around on a leash. That such an accoutrement was an indication of glamour and of maturity is shown by the fact that the most fashionable mannequin of the time, the Barbie doll, in 1959 was equipped with a bejeweled poodle or with a poodle on a bejeweled leash.

Animals, particularly bejeweled ones, are traditionally the pets of dangerous women (look no further than the panther motif in Cartier jewellery, where this rare feline became the symbol of luxury for strong and determined women, like Wallis Simpson, the controversial Duchess of Windsor). Poodles and terriers are certainly not ferocious dogs, but when, in F. S. Fitzgerald's *The Great Gatsby* (1925) Myrtle, the wife of poor George Wilson, asks her lover Tom Buchanan—who is married to Daisy—to buy her a terrier with a leash studded with costume diamonds, we know that problems are on the horizon. In fact, in her attempt to climb the social ladder, Myrtle wants to parade around New York with her bejeweled dog as if she were a member of a higher social class (as Sabrina will do). It is the expensive leash, however, that makes her husband, George, realize that his wife is unfaithful to him. Hence the catastrophe: Daisy kills Myrtle in a car accident, and George kills Jay Gatsby because, misdirected by Tom, he believes it was Gatsby who was Myrtle's lover and it was Gatsby who killed her.

Another recurrent type of jewellery, found both in literature and in film, is the pearl necklace: a symbol of love and marriage since Greek times. But the recourse to pearls is often full of dark omens, even if pearls are the epitome of luster, purity, perfect circularity, and, therefore, beauty: mythology has it that Venus herself was born from a shell. In the ancient world, pearls were believed to be the result of the marriage between heaven and earth: in the first century BCE, Pliny the Elder wrote in his *Natural History* that pearls are created when oysters come to the surface of the ocean before the light of day, open their shells and swallow the dew that comes from the sun, the moon, and the stars. In the Western world, it was the eighteenth-century Swedish naturalist Carl Linnaeus, who discovered that pearls, on the contrary, are the product of a disease, of an irritant to the oyster.

In that quintessential American literary work, Nathaniel Hawthorne's *The Scarlet Letter* (1850), it is not by chance that the daughter of Hester Prynne, born of an illicit relationship, is called Pearl. Henry James's protagonists Daisy Miller (1878), in the eponymous novella, and Milly Theale in *The Wings* of the Dove (1902)— both destined to die young—wear pearl necklaces. The same applies to Lily Bart, the tragic heroine of Edith Wharton's *House of Mirth* (1905), who, poor in a world of rich people, shows off a gold cigarette case attached to a long pearl chain in order to keep up appearances. She too will die young of poverty and neglect. Furthermore, going back to Fitzgerald's masterpiece, *The Great Gatsby*, Tom Buchanan presents his future bride with a string of pearls the day before their wedding: a necklace that Daisy throws into the waste paper basket that very evening when she receives a letter from Gatsby. While the pearls are precious, their marriage is not, as it is complicity—not love—that will keep this "careless" couple (as they are defined by the narrator, Nick Carraway) together. At the very end of the novel, when Nick sees Tom entering a jeweler's shop, he thinks that Tom might well have gone there to buy either a pair of cufflinks for himself or another pearl necklace for Daisy to definitively seal their criminal pact. Similarly, at the beginning of Fitzgerald's *Tender is the Night* (1934), Nicole Diver is introduced as "a young woman [who] lay under a roof of umbrellas...her bathing suit was pulled off her shoulders and her back, a ruddy, orange brown, set off by a string of creamy pearls, shone in the sun" (Fitzgerald, 1986, 14). Nicole is so closely identified with her pearls that, in the novel, she is more than once called "the woman of the pearls." Although she does not die young, she is damaged: she first was victim to her father's incestuous desires, and then her marriage to Dick Diver—a diver of pearls, one is tempted to surmise—will end in divorce.

In the 1920s Coco Chanel made it fashionable to casually wear multiple necklaces, made of such non-precious materials as Bakelite, fake stones, and wood, among others. In addition to attracting the onlooker's attention with their shapes, colors, and materials, these necklaces compensated for the flat (androgynous) chests that women of the time were proud to exhibit.

From the 1940s, also thanks to Franklin D. Roosevelt's so called "Good Neighbor" policy, a (Portuguese-born) Brazilian actress, singer, and dancer brought her abundance of necklaces made of cheap materials to Broadway and Hollywood, and then onto the international scene: Carmen Miranda. She candidly claimed that she owed half her success to her apparel: colorful turbans with exotic fruit or feathers stacked upon them, enormous rings and bracelets, platform shoes with fake gems and six-inch heels, and a great quantity of necklaces, called "balangandans." In her case, she was not so much inspired by Chanel, but by the costumes of women in Bahia—the Brazilian Northeastern state—who were strongly influenced by Africa as they were the descendants of slaves. "Balangandans" had originally been made of the most diverse materials—from Catholic metal crosses to animal teeth, to leather pockets containing lamb's blood, to tropical fruit and herbs—and were worn during syncretic religious celebrations. Miranda wore up to 20 strings of necklaces, made of beads of various forms and materials. Such necklaces became so famous, that a US Company, Leo Glass and Co., specialized in producing them. In the West, Miranda came to represent the stereotype of the Brazilian woman: impulsive, aggressive, irrational, and excessively adorned—in a word, exotic. While she lost her Brazilian public, who considered that she had sold out and had misrepresented them, her necklaces live on today, even if we do not always acknowledge our debt to her. Such details are, therefore, not only charged with meaning, but often convey a long, colorful, and still relevant history.

1

2

22

3

1. *Habits of Being.*
   Accessorizing the Body, vol. I (Minneapolis: University of
   Minnesota Press, 2011), (cover).

2. *Habits of Being.*
   Extravagances, vol. IV (Minneapolis: University of Minnesota
   Press, 2015), (cover).

3. Agnolo Bronzino, *Portrait of Eleanor of Toledo with her son*
   (Florence, Uffizi Gallery)

4. Antonio Boldini, *Portrait of Josefina Virginia de Alvear* (Buenos
   Aires, Museo Nacional de Arte Decorativo)

4

John Singer Sargent, Portrait of Isabella Stewart Gardner (Boston, Isabella Stewart Gardner Museum)

Reference

Arasse, D. 1992. "un détail peut être porteur d'une signification essentielle à l'ensemble de l'image." *Le Detail*, 23. Paris: Flammarion.

Banta, M. 2011. "Coco, Zelda, Sara, Daisy, and Nicole: Accessories for New Ways of Being a Woman." In *Accessorizing the Body: Habits of Being I*, edited by Cristina Giorcelli et al. Minneapolis: University of Minnesota Press, 82–107.

Barthes, R. 1990. *The Fashion System*, translated by Matthew Ward and Richard Howard. Berkeley: University of California Press.

Baudelaire, C. 1995. *The Painter of Modern Life and Other Essay*, translated by Jonathan Mayne, 30. London: Phaidon Press.

Baudrillard, J. 1988. *Simulacra and Simulation: Selected Writings*, translated by Mark Poster. Stanford, CA: Stanford University Press.

Benjamin, W. 1999. *The Arcades Project*, translated by Howard Eiland and Kevin McLaughlin. Cambridge, MA: Harvard University Press, 69

Berry, S. 2000. *Screen Style: Fashion and Femininity in 1930's Hollywood*. Minneapolis: University of Minnesota Press.

Calabrese, O. 1992. *Neo-Baroque: A Sign of the Times*, translated by Charles Lambert. Princeton: Princeton University Press.

Derrida, J. 1987. "Parergon." In *The Truth in Painting*, translated by Geoff Bennington and Ian McLeod. Chicago: University of Chicago Press, 55–56.

Fitzgerald, F. S. 1986. *Tender is the Night*, vol. II. London: Penguin.

Freud, S. 2005. *The Uncanny*, introduced by Hugh Haughton, translated by David McLintock. London: Penguin.

Giorcelli, C. 2015. "Earrings in American Literature." In *Habits of Being: Extravagances*, vol. IV, edited by Cristina Giorcelli and Paula Rabinowitz. Minneapolis: University of Minnesota Press, 56–77.

McLuhan, M. 1951. *The Mechanical Bride: Folklore of Industrial Man*. New York: Vanguard.

Silverman, K. 1986. "Fragments of a Fashionable Discourse." In *Studies in Entertainment: Critical Approaches to Mass Culture*, edited by Tania Modleski. Bloomington: Indiana University Press, 145.

The Body Common

Christine LÜDEKE
*Professor, Head of MA Design & Future Making, School of Design,
Pforzheim University, Germany*

The body. At once habitus and performative. Subject and object.

"It is the body which speaks" (Merleau-Ponty, 2002). The philosopher Merleau-Ponty refers to the body as a source of meaning through its characteristic of expressiveness and intentionality. "The body is our means to have a world at all, of relating to and shaping the world" (Merleau-Ponty, 2002). It transcends its own biological dimension, defining the world while concurrently being part of it. The immediacy of jewellery and clothing on our bodies amplifies our awareness of the relationship we have with our surroundings and others. It is directly related to our own sense of existence—a sense of body in context that we experience through physical and/or psychological communication. To dress, to adorn is to exist.

Laura Stachon, In Between, 2018
© Laura Stachon

Both dress in the global sense and jewellery create a frame in which the wearer projects who they are and perhaps more importantly, who they would like to be, both for themselves and others. Simultaneously our interaction with the world in general is shaped by a dependency on it and its integral limitations—real (such as attachment to matter) and virtual (confrontation of fantasy with reality)—which we experience through the body conduit.

As soon as we perceive and then shape something we give it meaning and significance. "Art does not reproduce the visible but makes visible."[1] Klee's insight is just as applicable to the general concept of making. This is a constant

1. Paul Klee, first published in Tribune der Kunst und Zeit, 1920.

endeavor that taps into the energies at the core of being, and whilst material and form help connect us to the physicality of perception, the crafted object transcends its own corporeal existence to communicate.

It is the material aspect of craft that often leads it to being misunderstood, the honing of skills directly related to forming material and materiality, the cultivation of tradition accompanied by a whiff of dreaded nostalgia. In itself not necessarily bad, but it tends to override the key essence of making—that it is a dialectic endeavor in which, to paraphrase Heidegger, the potential of both the understanding subject and the understood object is mutually developed and projected. Viewed in this context, it follows that meaning is the driving force of making, structured as it is by intention, all the while contributing to the understanding of something as something. The ensuing narrative transcends actuality, connecting the material with the immaterial, the collective cultural with the specifically contemporary, the physicality of the object with that of the body.

Signifying meaning in context of the body, gesture as well makes the invisible visible. Gesture begins in the mind, is directed to the body, and then is amplified or transferred into an artificial signifier. Knowledge, formed by experience and emotion, informs decisions regarding adornment through both real and perceived material and form. The ensuing interaction in turn forms and informs the body. As manifested in posture and movement, for example, this interaction can in itself then be coded like a gesture. Fashion and jewellery's gesture is their primarily non-verbal rhetoric and communication, always functioning with or in reference to the body. Codes related to the body also take place indirectly. An intriguing example of this is Cornelia Parker's "Wedding Ring Drawing" (Circumference of a Living Room). The materiality of gold allows her to draw two wedding rings into a wire that equates the circumference of a living room. The body, divorced from it's wearable object, is implied through the context of sanctuary associated with the described living room or is perceived as being confined through the transference of meaning to the golden wire. Reflected within the prism of the initial wedding rings, both interpretations function as different perspectives on the social construct of marriage.

Coding that simultaneously takes place on and abstracted from the body, contextually amplifies. The work of Helen Chadwick embodies this concept. She physically holds traces of her body, captured at specific intervals of her life and recorded on abstracted objects that were significant at those moments.

Her work is visceral in its exploration of the past, memory, space, and the now. These metaphorical dimensions give body, shape, and contour to meaning and reciprocally participate in the invention of that meaning.

One of the key essences of jewellery, in all its definitions, is its constant juxtaposition to the body—the physical as well as the implied presence. It is through this relationship that the body imbues meaning into the object. The act of being worn is the moment when the wearer intersects with both the maker and the viewer, each thereby manifesting their individual projections. It goes without saying that fashion is also worn directly on the body, but by their very nature clothes are able to fuse with the body, making it difficult to distinguish between the "body" of flesh and blood and the "fashion body" of fabric or other materials. Fashion condenses and projects the historically changing (self-) understanding of a culture, and is thus an important cultural medium in defining and positioning the body and its relationship to one's surroundings and world.

Interestingly, while both jewellery and fashion share similarities in their individual intersubjective relationships to the body, object, and viewer, the relationship between them is often defined in terms of superior and subordinate. In the workshop Jewellery Virus Fashion Infiltration, students from Pforzheim University, Central St. Martins, and Politecnico Milano were interested in rethinking jewellery's status and flipping the dynamic. They asked questions through design such as "Can jewellery redefine the relationship between body and fashion?" or "Can jewellery reciprocally influence fashion?" As a consequence of this line of design enquiry, new relationships on the body were proposed and developed that made the body complicit, and new perspectives were discovered not just on jewellery and fashion's mutual roles but also how we perceive each one.

Etymology provides us with another approach to understanding the body within the concept of making. Specifically, directly derived from another meaning of fashion, ie., the verb "to fashion," it means to create something with the hand; to create something, using the hands or the imagination.[2] This definition describes the ability to change perspectives—literally and metaphorically. The sense of body in relation to craft becomes even more interesting when regarded both in terms of craft as vessel (as in the nautical sense—the bearer as well as the

---

2. Cambridge Dictionary, https://dictionary.cambridge.org/de/, acessed 9/12/2018

1

2

1. *Cornelia Parker, "Wedding Ring Drawing" (Circumference of a Living Room), 1996*

2. *Helen Chadwick, Ego Geometria Sum, The Labors IX, 1983-86*
   © Mark Pilkington

3

4

3. *Silvia Schröck, Infiltration,
   2014 © Jan Keller*

4. *Moritz Rasch, C6H11NO,
   2014 © Petra Jaschke*

5. *Puyuan Carrie Yuang,
   2014 © Petra Jaschke*

5

projector of fashion and jewellery communication) and as verb, creating the objects that define us and by which we simultaneously define ourselves.

The haptic quality of the object matters to the wearer because it literally touches us in our subjectivity. The wearer, in a direct way—and the body in an extended, abstract sense—defines the object as much as the maker. The body is affected by fashion/jewellery and vice versa. There is a holistic, symbiotic relationship in defining the object and the craft that lies between the outcome and the subjectivity of the processes that determine its existence. This extends to the making in itself and the active role the body plays in the development of craft. This intelligence of the body, it's capacity to innovate and retain new meaning, is constantly being altered. Repetition—refinement—honing. Habit is actually a competence that can be mobilized under different conditions to achieve different effects. According to Merleau-Ponty "it is knowledge in the hands, which is forthcoming only when bodily effort is made, and cannot be formulated in detachment from that effort" (Merleau-Ponty, 2002). This mirrors the essence of handcraft in it's historical meaning: learning through hands, developing mastery through repeated, sensitive, and empirical working with—and thereby gaining knowledge of—materials and processes.

Craft is intrinsic to what it is that makes us human. The word used in Greek antiquity to describe the skill of the practitioner, tekhnethe, comes from tasha, taksan [Sanskrit for axe, carpenter] and taksati, shaper or maker [Sanskrit for the one who fashions]. Texere [Latin verb for "to weave"] comes from precisely the same root (Tim, 2010). The unique characteristics of crafts originate from the emotion passed to the crafted object by its creator through its production, and by the owner through the possession and usage of it. Skill in making, which lies at the heart of all craft practice, is attained through the integration of embodied knowledge with technical understanding, injected with imagination. The balance of conscious and rational technical knowledge while intuitively working the inherent characteristics of the material informed through touch, can be interpreted within context of Christopher Bollas's concept of "the intuition of the unthought known" (Philpott, 2012). Body memory, developed through experiences without the construct of spoken language, is expressed through behavior that contributes to how we craft and interpret the object world.

Exploitation of the profound haptic knowledge of materiality, gained unconsciously yet consciously developed throughout our lives leading to mastery, can significantly impact the process of making. Tactility is a key associate of craft and a confirmation of humanity, functioning both on a conscious and subconscious level. The haptic experience is grounded in the physical sensation of touch, which can be ambiguous, subjective, and open to varying interpretation. It forms a direct connection to the physicality of ourselves and our surroundings, functioning on a subliminal level as a confirmation of "I exist." Craft(ed) objects are things that embody agency derived intentionally through the direct exchange of tacit and explicit forms of substance and process, knowledge between humans and non-humans, tools and touch.

"The desire of the craftsperson to see what a metal can do, rather than the desire of the scientist to know what a metal is, enables the former to discern a life in metal and thus, eventually, to collaborate more productively with it" (Bamford, 2016). This becomes—in addition to the underlying concept—a defining factor in the character of the pieces. "It is not only craft as 'handcraft' that defines contemporary craftsmanship: it is craft as knowledge that empowers a maker to take charge of technology" (Dormer, 2015). Knowledge comes not just in the learning and planning, but in the doing. Materials present a particular set of criteria, the craftsman responds, back and forth, repeat. The resulting synergy of functionality and expression of human values transcends the boundaries of space, time, and social mores and meaning manifests itself as sensory-embodying.

Frieda Dörfer, Terror Vacui, 2013.
© Petra Jaschke

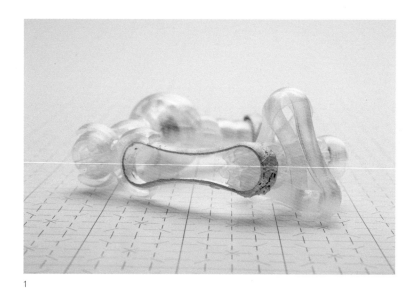

1

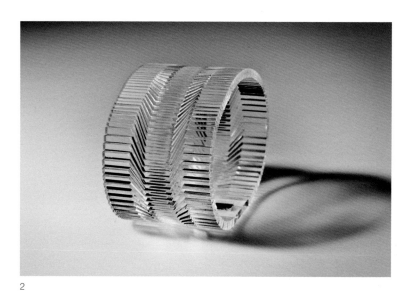

2

1. *Marc Limper, Chronüp, 2016*
   © Isolde Golderer

2. *Janika Slowik, 21 grams, 2017*
   © Petra Jaschke

Phenomena such as brain activity, micro-organisms, or other invisible forms of energy become "real" because they have been "translated" by technologies into perceivable experiences. Such "realities" could not otherwise be perceived by humans, or even interpreted by them. Thus, "thinking that flows into things and manifests itself in a objectified and materialized form is clearly ahead of abstract thinking that defines itself solely through the act of thinking" (Burckhardt, 1997). This recognition, coupled with the democratization of technology and the advent of maker labs, has contributed to a new understanding of what a final, crafted material can and can't be, as well as placing digital technologies squarely into the handcraft purview.

One aspect that accompanies the current revival and contextual evolution of crafts is the internet. It enables a concurrent development of skills via exchange through strangers, as opposed to the traditional more linear and side-by-side evolution. Through the imperceptible play between reality and the perception of various possible realities, new truths are discovered that in turn facilitate new interpretations and uses of technological applications. At best, the disembodied dissemination of information leads precisely through its nature to inventively new body-specific understanding and development. The blurred boundaries between amateurism and unencumbered new insights, while requiring a new attentiveness, accelerate exchange and thus their evolution.

Unsurprisingly, as all tools and technology have a distinct character, these leave impressions—be it the anonymity of perfection or the possibility of new formal languages or materials, hitherto not possible. Thus, as we collectively become more sophisticated in dealing with new technologies, we begin to augment them beyond being a direct tool substitute, discovering and adding new functions and abilities inherent in the new technology's DNA. Digital object space moves with us, the opposite of physical space, which exists in contrast to us. Digital technology also holds a capacity to interchange huge amounts of information via communication channels linking different fields of action. The use of interoceptive senses in direct relation to the body (pressure, temperature, tension, position in space, sense of pain, etc.) by artists that combine, mix, intensify, and diminish them over time, generates unknown and uncertain transmutations, densities, colors, rhythms, and intensities. This goes far beyond the dualistic correspondence between vision and audio, vision and touch, smell and taste. And yet, as the integration process of new technologies is not a consecutively linear but rather an overlapping concurrent phenomenon, we as a

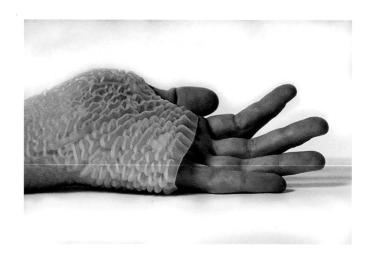

Neri Oxman and Media Lab, MIT, Carpal Skin
© *MIT Media Lab*

society are currently redefining technologies, while at the same time augmenting them. While this entails the expected pendulum swing to a more discriminating analysis of the digital and it's effect on our lives, it also embraces a creative understanding and exploration of what this technology can do, inherent to its own capabilities, and not just as an extension or the development of existing technologies. Digital fundamentally means creating bridges of understanding and communication between the unseeable and the tangible, decoding abstract behavior; as does jewellery.

As we learn what the new technologies can do and understand their potential beyond technical efficiencies and respect to the reciprocal nature between body and object, we begin to modify not only how we use them but also the the contexts within which we interpret and position our understanding of craft and, by extension, design. For example, 3D printing has superseded it's role as an efficient intermediate step to being the goal of manufacturing, and as a result introduces new materialities and body-object interactions. Developments in bio-based materials go hand in hand with the advancement of digital possibilities, resulting in new potential in the body-jewellery-fashion paradigm. The attentive and empathic cultivation of craft principles in evolving concepts of materiality and technology augment our understanding of ourselves.

Regardless of process or variance in tools, craft is defined by intention and attention, caring about the outcome and in relation, caring about the body.

This is why craft matters, why the notion of digital craft has emerged. It is the potential for humanism to reassert itself at the far reaches of mass culture. It allows craft and the perception thereof to move beyond solely nostalgic associations, clarifying its fundamental role in the collective creation process.

Through amplification—enlarging, repeating, extending, abstracting, and materializing the invisible—we posit our relationship to each other and to our surroundings and thus to ourselves. The making and wearing of jewellery and fashion are amplifications of one's own body, of one's self—physical and immaterial projections illuminating the facets of being human. The more abstract the more specific, the larger the closer, the more focused the more amplified the statement.

The body provides the context, the body is the context.

The body common.

Reference

Bamford, R. 2016. "Accident, Determinism and Hermeneutics: Relationships between Analogue and Digital Fabrication." *Making Futures*, 4(1): 1–6.

Burckhardt, M. 1997. *Metamorphosen von Raum und Zeit. Eine Geschichte der Wahrnehmung (Metamorphosis of Space and Time: A History of Perception)*. Frankfurt am Main: Campus Verlag.

Dormer, P. 2015. *The Culture of Craft: Status and Future*. Manchester: Manchester University Press.

Loschek, I. 2008. "Von der Geste zum Ritual in der Mode (From Gesture to Ritual in Fashion)." In *Eine Frage (nach) der Geste*, edited by Alba D'urbano and Tina Bara. Salzburg: Fotohof Edition.

Merleau-Ponty, M. 2002, *The Phenomenology of Perception*, translated by Colin Smith. New York: Routledge.

Philpott, R. 2012. "Crafting Innovation: The Intersection of Craft and Technology in the Production of Contemporary Textiles." In *Craft Research*, 3(1): 53–74.

Tim, I. 2010. "The Textility of Making." In *Cambridge Journal of Economics*, 1: 91–102.

CHAPTER

3

BELONGING & INTERDISCIPLINARY
Sustainability and
New Technology

Introduction

Jie SUN

National Distinguished Expert, Professor at Tongji University, Shanghai, China

The revolution of science and technology has a profound influence on design and fashion. Technology has liberated the means of express fashion design and enriched its quality, communication speed, and dimension. Sustainability is one of the focuses of contemporary design and fashion discussion. As one of the theories of design, sustainable design includes thinking about design and practice from four aspects: environment, economy, society, and culture, and attempts to minimize the negative impact of human activities on the environment through smart and sensitive design and methods. Sustainable fashion and design are often supported by the development of science and technology. The process of design itself is a creative process, and its diverse contents also provide many methods and definitions for it. It also serves as a method of interpreting and studying society and people, beyond the form of aesthetics and representation. As an early stage of design, modern design has already proved itself as an important means of social development, and to some extent it is also a kind of value judgment standard for the endorsement of future. Therefore, it is important how to create a design object ingeniously. It can be simply a necessity, such as the need for self-expression, or the need for life function, or the need for sustainable development, but the design method created by each need is different, whether it is the need for class, society, or economy. Of course, there is still a need that designers and artists are often more sensitive and intense than sociologists. They use design to provide feedback on the development of society, whether it is the need for self-expression, the need for life function, or the need for sustainable development. Stella McCartney, a British fashion designer, emphasized in her forum with me in Tongji Design

Week in 2019 (see figure in page 233) that she particularly emphasized sustainable fashion as the core and thinking of her design from the beginning of the brand. Whether it is from materials or technological processes, sustainable fashion is not only a concept and theme, but also a systematic thinking and lifestyle. Since 2016, Kering Group has started to develop the app of "Innovative Luxury Lab," (see figure in page 234) in which "Environmental Profit and Loss Statement" (EP&L) can provide a visual model for designers and even the entire fashion industry to understand the impact of products on the environment from raw material production to sales. On the one hand, it also provides a brand-new perspective for the creation of design and R&D teams, to truly integrate sustainable development into the whole design process. On the other hand, it also provides Kering with an accurate environmental assessment on a global scale, from procurement, raw material processing to sales in stores, helping the group to formulate better business strategies and boost disruptive innovation and research and development.

Conversation on Fashion Sustainability Prof. Sun and Stella McCartney

The four articles in this chapter have different perspectives on the relationship between science and technology, sustainability, and design. Dr. Elizabeth Shaw thinks that sustainable design has different meanings in different contexts. She points out two completely different general views on technology. One is that the rise and adoption of technology is an inevitable result of social progress, and the other is that technological progress has completely changed history, which is "inevitable and not subject to human control." From the perspective of balance and empowerment, technology is the ability to change the world around us and create value. It reflects the existence of social value with deep social structure and cultural connotation and affects the way we communicate with the world around us and our views between each other. From environmental and cultural perspectives, she discusses sustainability around the impact of new technologies and their applications. Katharina Sand's research mainly focuses on the speculative design thinking of fashion technology and the real-world apparel tactile experience, and analyzes the technological

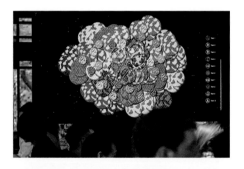

Innovative Luxury Lab Workshop in Shanghai 2017

innovations in production, retail distribution, fashion communication, and human clothing interaction. She tries to explore how to apply the latest scientific and technological innovations such as augmented reality and radio frequency identification technology systems to the industries of fashion and jewellery related products, so as to create a more sustainable future.

Dr. Maarten Floris Versteeg focuses on the application of technology in the jewellery field, according to his own design practice, especially the relationship between wearable jewellery design and fashion. Similarly, Dr. Chiara Scarpitti analyzes a series of cases of contemporary jewellery cases as her research object, and there are some examples from fields other than the jewellery industry (such as medicine and engineering), or the horizontal application design of digital products with jewellery as the medium, emphasizing the intersection and interaction among contemporary art, design, and media. Finally, she also gives a philosophical perspective of the value of the intersection of science and technology and disciplines.

Lessons We Should Learn

Elizabeth SHAW

PhD, Senior Lecturer, Queensland College of Art, Griffith University, Australia

Sustainability has different meanings in different contexts. I am conscious that my own understanding has evolved over time and still is. In this paper I am considering sustainability from an environmental and cultural perspective in relation to new technology and the impact of its adoption. I will draw on a historical introduction of new technology, the Industrial Revolution, that continues to have a lasting impact on societies internationally.

Objects and jewellery play an important role in the human world, they enrich our lives. As an academic involved in teaching and research in the field of jewellery and small objects, I focus my research on jewellery that is worn on the body and objects that are carried or kept near the body, these are things that are inherently part of human society. Archaeologists refer to jewellery and objects as "portable art" and I like that nomenclature. They study ancient jewellery and personal objects to uncover information about individuals and societies and I find it extraordinary what they recognize an object can convey and what it can mean.

Hands © Sabine van Erp from Pixabay

People imbue the jewellery they wear with emotions and stories. In turn, we view the jewellery people wear and the objects they surround themselves with as part of them, part of their story. A ring or a cup from a departed loved one can act as a poignant connection to the human we associate it with. This is regardless of whether the ring or cup was made by hand or machine. This observation sits in an awkward relationship to the ideas I held when I completed my first university study in silversmithing. At that time the ideas of William Morris and the arts and crafts movement resonated. In essence I graduated with a belief that the handmade was superior in its capacity to represent the individual and that the mass-produced product was inevitably impersonal and anonymous. A lot has changed in my thinking since then. The texts and ideas covered in my early study were heavily influenced by a response to the Industrial Revolution in Britain several centuries earlier.

The Rise of Industrialization

The 18th-century rise of industrialization in the United Kingdom was the start of what would become known as the Industrial Revolution. What was then "new technology" revolutionized how things were made and the quantities of things that were made. The impact of this reverberated around the world. It led to massive changes to international trade, the world economy, as well as changes to the cultural traditions of communities both in the UK and in many countries across the globe. I won't pretend that the points I will mention are comprehensive, rather they are ones that have informed my thinking.

Over time the new technology meant production capacities were greatly increased and the costs of production dropped, so goods became more affordable. This did not happen instantly, and the benefit was not spread equally at a local level or internationally. The increased production also enabled the owners of manufacturing businesses to expand their markets and in turn increase their profits. While freeing workers from "menial" tasks, industrial tools removed the manufacturing of goods from common sight and understanding. In effect, most makers of the goods became anonymous.

The introduction of the new technology was not embraced by everyone in the UK. From 1811 to 1812, a group of workers known as the Luddites "sent threatening letters to employers and broke into factories to destroy the new machines." They wanted "to get rid of the new machinery that was causing unemployment among workers." This included "Hand weavers" who "did not want the introduction of power looms." Their protests were "against changes they thought would make their lives much worse."[1] I note that losing jobs was not confined to workers in the UK; some weavers in India also lost their jobs to industrial looms in Britain. So, India, which had once been a major world exporter of textiles, became an importer of British textiles.[2]

A less aggressive form of resistance to industrialization in the UK was the arts and crafts movement in which designer William Morris was a key 19th-century figure. Morris championed the qualities of the handmade object as having values that were a result of the skilled human maker, qualities that the machine-made object was inevitably devoid of. This didn't correlate with the industrial "progress" focus of the era in which Morris was living.[3]

Lewis Mumford, a noted American historian, sociologist, and philosopher of technology, initially criticized "the effects on society of mechanization and industrial capitalism" (Green, 1995), but in the 1930s he offered an alternative to the popular perception in America at the time that high technology and mechanized industry were the enemy of "organic human culture." He wrote:

Our capacity to go beyond the machine rests upon our power to assimilate the machine. Until we have absorbed the lessons of objectivity, impersonality, neutrality, the lessons of the mechanical realm, we cannot go further in our development toward the more richly organic, the more profoundly human (Mumford, 1934, 363).

As mentioned previously, the ideas of Morris and the arts and crafts movement featured heavily in my early training as a silversmith. This focussed my attention on the value and importance of the handmade, but in my lifetime the dominance and the prevalence of the mass-produced, machine-made products has always been clear.

Fashion Revolution

In 2013 the collapse of the Rana Plaza factory in Bangladesh made international news headlines. The images of the collapsed factory, the wounded, and the dead confronted people around the world. What was a terrible event in another country could not be dismissed as disconnected to other places. The victims were workers in a clothing factory, which made clothes for foreign companies. An extraordinary revelation after the event was that many of the clothes were being made for international brands, and some claimed that they had no idea that Rana Plaza was the location of their production. The subsequent media scrutiny exposed that fashion supply chains were complex and confusing tangled webs and greater transparency was called for.

The innovations of technology enabling mass production introduced during the Industrial Revolution had sped up production and had also helped remove

---

1. Who were the Luddites and what did they want? http://www.nationalarchives.gov.uk/education/politics/g3/

2. Kevin Murray. Social sutra: A platform for ethical textiles in partnerships between Australia and India. http://www.academia.edu/8119128/Social_sutra_A_platform_for_ethical_textiles_in_partnerships_between_Australia_and_India

3. https://www.vam.ac.uk/articles/introducing-william-morris

manufacturing from common sight and understanding. The makers of the majority of the world's goods had become anonymous and the Rana Plaza disaster drew international attention to the ugly side of what this anonymity and invisibility of the making process had enabled. The global Fashion Revolution movement formed in response.

The first Fashion Revolution week was held in 2014 and has since been held annually in April to mark the anniversary of the Rana Plaza collapse. "We use this week to encourage millions of people to ask brands 'Who made my clothes' and demand greater transparency in the fashion supply chain."[4] Through harnessing the popularity of social media the impact of the campaign continues to grow annually, regular updates, clearly compiled reports, files for educators, and opportunities to become involved are just some of the ways the Fashion Revolution is growing its audience.

The Fashion Revolution 2018 Consumer Survey Report is positive but sobering as it shows just how much more there is to do in terms of raising awareness. Orsola de Castro, co-founder of Fashion Revolution said in an interview in 2013, "the shift is toward change, and changing takes time and is challenging. It won't happen overnight, and we are still dealing with resistance, skepticism, and miss-information along the way."[5]

For the *Fashion Revolution 2018 Consumer Survey Report*, five thousand people between the ages of 16 and 75 from the five biggest European fashion markets—Germany, the United Kingdom, France, Italy, and Spain—were surveyed.

The survey questions were designed to correlate with the following United Nation's Sustainable Development Goals:

- *1 – End poverty in all its forms, everywhere.*
- *5 – Achieve gender equality and empower all women and girls.*
- *8 – Promote sustained, inclusive and sustainable economic growth, full and productive employment and decent work for all.*
- *12 – Ensure sustainable production and consumption patterns.*
- *13 – Take urgent action to combat climate change and its impacts.* [6]

"The majority of people" surveyed "think it is important for fashion brands to reduce their long-term impacts on the world by addressing global poverty (84%), climate change (85%), environmental protection (88%), and gender inequality (77%)."[7]

1

2

1. *Fashion Revolution Week, 2019 Save the Date. Source: www.fashionrevolution.org*

2. *Fashion Revolution Consumer Report. Source: www. fashionrevolution.org*

4. Fashion Revolution, Get Involved, Brands, Wholesalers, Retailers, and Distributors (Fashion Revolution information booklet, 2017).

5. Bruno Pieters. Interview with Orsola de Castro, co-founder of Fashion Revolution Day. https://www.fashionrevolution.org/uk-blog/interview-with-orsola-de-castro-co-founder-of-fashion-revolution-day/

6. See Fashion Revolution. *Consumer Report, Results Only* (Fashion Revolution booklet, 2018), 2.

7. See Fashion Revolution. *Consumer Report, Results Only* (Fashion Revolution booklet, 2018), 3.

The Fashion Revolution collects and shares information and stories that inspire and encourage initiatives internationally. For the last three years my students have organised Fashion Revolution-inspired events, hosting an annual "I Made Your Jewellery" event where they discuss with the public their choices of techniques, processes, and materials—including the origins of materials and why this is important to know and their approach to having minimal to no waste. As jewellers they are following the example of the Fashion Revolution and applying the need for transparency to their own practices. Their "I Made Your Jewellery" event is as much about educating themselves about the hidden impact of their chosen materials and processes as it is about educating the buying public.

Ethical Metalsmiths

The ethics of the supply chain and sustainability is also a focus of Ethical Metalsmiths. Formed in 2004 it "is a community of caring buyers, jewellers, designers, and suppliers. (Who are) Committed to responsible, environmentally sound practices for all facets of the Jewellery Industry." The organization works to "connect and educate people globally from mine to market."[8] I am a member of and am on the advisory council of Ethical Metalsmiths.

An educational program that Ethical Metalsmiths runs is the "Radical Jewellery Makeover," which draws attention to the resources that are hidden in households and the potential for their reuse. It "is an international community jewellery mining and recycling project. It brings together jewellers, working together to examine mining issues while making innovative jewellery from recycled sources."[9] It also serves an educational role for the university students and jeweller participants and the public. In the lead up to an RJM a call is put out to the wider community to "mine their drawers." What this means is members of the public are asked to sort through their things and find jewellery they no longer wear or want and that they are willing to donate. They are warned that what they donate may be deconstructed, melted, cut, and altered beyond recognition, their donations will become materials for new works to be made from. The donated materials will be treated with respect and the jewellers in the RJM will be challenged to make new pieces. The works created are launched in an exhibition. The donors receive a credit for their donations and can use that to purchase works that have been created during the RJM. It is quite extraordinary what people donate, I have been involved with delivering two RJMs in Australia

Do you wonder what resources it takes to make a single piece of jewelry?

www.EthicalMetalsmiths.org

Ethical Metalsmiths. Source: www.ethicalmetalsmiths.org

and one in New Mexico, USA and at each version the donations provided an insight into the objects that people hold close. "Donated jewellery is rich with sentiment, and lends itself to conversation about source, future thinking design, and collaborative problem solving."[10]

The circumstances that led to the idea for the Radical Jewellery Makeover can be traced back to issues that have emerged in the world altered by the Industrial Revolution. Mass production has led to a surplus of objects. I want to be clear it was not the technology that led to these issues, but how the technology was used to build consumerism.

What Can We Learn?

In her 2015 book *Digital Handmade*, author and cultural commentator Lucy Johnston stated that the "first industrial revolution revealed a new order, refining, accelerating and regulating the process of manufacturing objects for wider appreciation and consumption" (Johnston, 2015, 7). She attributes this

8. Ethical Metalsmiths, *About Us*, https://www.ethicalmetalsmiths.com/about-us/
9. Ethical Metalsmiths, *Radical Jewellery Makeover*, https://www.radicaljewellerymakeover.org/
10. Ethical Metalsmiths, *Radical Jewellery Makeover* RJM https://www.ethicalmetalsmiths.com/about-us/

with the diminished role of the craftsman, while researcher Glenn Adamson has identified the industrial revolution as the origin of modern craft, arguing that "craft was invented as industry's other" (Adamson, 2013). Johnston identifies that the new industrial revolution focussed on digital technologies is reenabling the "skill and vision" of the craftsman through technologies enabling on-demand manufacture.

A significant difference between the first Industrial Revolution and the New Technology Revolution is that the first was focussed on enabling efficient mass production, and the power to do so was in the hands of a relative few who profited handsomely, whereas the new revolution includes technology that is relatively low cost and flexible and can be used by individuals for individualized outcomes. Professor Jen Loy has noted that "in some ways, this technology has crept up on us." She says, "because we've been using 3D printing as a prototyping technology for so long. It is only recently that developments in technology and materials have allowed us to create end use products through direct manufacturing...if we look at 3D printing in the context of the digital revolution—the internet, data generation, and manipulation and many more digital developments, there has been a whole shift in business practice thinking made possible by the technology." [11]

In 1987 the United Nations published a Report of the World Commission on Environment and Development, which defined sustainable development to be "development that meets the needs of the present without compromising the ability of future generations to meet their own needs." [12] History has shown that we are not necessarily capable of knowing what impacts our current activities will have on future generations. Indeed, researchers Sarah M. Grimes and Andrew Feenberg noted in their *Critical Theory of Technology* (2015) that "Most technology was shaped for success on markets where many externalities could be ignored for generations" (Grimes and Feenberg, 2015, 9).

In 2002 chemist Michael Braungart and architect William McDonough released the book *Cradle to Cradle* with the subtitle of *Remaking the Way We Make Things*. Braungart and McDonough identify that the popular mantras of reduce, reuse, recycle, and upcycling are about minimizing damage. They refer to the still dominant manufacturing model that dates back to the Industrial Revolution, a model that creates huge amounts of waste and in turn pollution, a model they call Cradle to Grave. This is where the waste and pollution generated through production, and the product at the end of its life is destined for landfill. Built in

Garbage © Adege from Pixabay

obsolescence and fashion-led obsolescence have heightened the speed with which products reach their end of life. Cradle to Cradle looks at a product's whole life cycle, from extraction to production, to distribution, to use and ultimately its return to raw material. The idea being that nothing is wasted, nothing is thrown "away."

The number of articles, programs, and podcasts focussing on "decluttering" are evidence of just how much manufactured product there is in the world. In 2016 Steve Howard, Head of Sustainability at "the world's biggest furniture retailer," Ikea, said, "If we look on global basis, in the west we have probably hit peak stuff" while others such as Chris Goodall, a British environment writer, have suggested we reached it far earlier than 2016.[13]

Think back about Grimes and Feenberg's 2015 statement that "most technology was shaped for success on markets where many externalities could be ignored for generations." The indications are that it is increasingly becoming apparent

11. Jen Loy, "Embrace the future of 3d Printing," https://app.griffith.edu.au/sciencesimpact/embrace-the-future-of-3d-printing/

12. United Nations, Report of the World Commission on Environment and Development, http://www.un.org/documents/ga/res/42/ares42-187

13. Usborne, Simon, 2017. "Just do it: the experience economy and how we turned our backs on 'stuff.'" In *The Guardian*, UK, Saturday, 13 May. https://www.theguardian.com/business/2017/may/13/just-do-it-the-experience-economy-and-how-we-turned-our-backs-on-stuff?CMP=share_btn_link.

that many of the externalities that have been ignored through industrial development and mass production, such as the cost to the environment, can no longer be ignored.

A World Economic Forum discussion paper authored by Thomas Philbeck, Nicholas Davis, and Anne Marie Engtoft Larsen, identified "two most widely held views of technologies." The first is the rise and adoption of technologies as inevitable progress for society, and the second is that history has been defined by technological advancement and this advancement is "inevitable and out of human control." Philbeck, Davis & Larsen argue that:

A more balanced and empowering perspective recognizes technologies as capabilities that interpret, transform and make meaning in the world around us. Rather than being simple objects or processes that are distinct from human beings, they are deeply socially constructed, culturally situated and reflective of societal values. They are how we engage with the world around us. They affect how people order their lives, interact with one another and see themselves. Far from an academic observation, this more nuanced view has practical importance for strategic needs as well as implications for successful governance of technologies.[14]

25

There are inspiring examples of how digital technologies are enabling extraordinary life-changing improvements. An Australian example is the work of Mat Bowtell, an engineer who "was retrenched from his car manufacturing job" and used his severance pay to buy himself 3D printers. He has been designing and making 3D-printed, purpose-built prosthetics free of charge for those who need them, regardless of where they are. "His designs carry a creative commons licence that allows people to download, but not sell or profit from them."[15] A prosthetic, due to its need to fit and work for an individual is not suited to mass production. Bowtell's engineering and design skills combined with the efficiency of design adaption and production has meant that his pro-bono initiative can and has benefited people far beyond his immediate territory.

While global movements continue to raise awareness of ethical and environmental issues, our activities will increasingly be judged against the

14. Thomas Philbeck, Nicholas Davis, Anne Marie Engtoft Larsen. Rethinking Technological Development in the Fourth Industrial Revolution (discussion paper, World Economic Forum, August 1, 2018).
15. Lazzaro, Kellie, 2018. "I don't even charge postage": Phillip Island engineer uses 3D printers to make free prosthetic limbs. https://www.abc.net.au/news/2018-10-23/retrenched-engineer-makes-3d-prosthetic-limbs-for-free/10418050.
16. United Nations, Report of the World Commission on Environment and Development, http://www.un.org/documents/ga/res/42/ares42-187.

measures that are being applied to assess all other industries, and so they should be. We are in the position to draw on the lessons from history to ensure the environmental and cultural impacts of the new technology we use and the items we produce are considered. It is undeniable that there is surplus of product in the world and designers need to be intelligent about how they deliver new things in this environment, to consider the material and production impact, the lifecycle and the need.

Digital technologies are enabling alternative ways of approaching production, such as producing personalized, bespoke products through variations to a design. Bowtell's prosthetics are a good example of this. There are examples of the "cradle to cradle" theory being applied to the development of printer filament in part driven by the DIY maker movement, hacker spaces, and makers labs that are investigating new technologies and alternative materials. Fortunately, the digital revolution is occurring at a time that digital media means we can be involved with the innovations wherever we are. So far my assessment is that the digital revolution is benefitting more people and a wider cross section of society more immediately than the industrial revolution did, and hopefully this one will be "without compromising the ability of future generations to meet their own needs."[16] I am conscious that we need to be proactive in asking the questions, sharing the information, discussing the ideas, and striving for best practices from an environmental, cultural, and community perspective, and along the way be willing to shift our thinking and practices to embrace new ideas.

Reference

Adamson, G. 2013. *The Invention of Craft*. London: Bloomsbury.

Green, H. 1995. "The Promise and Peril of High Technology." In *Craft in the Machine Age*, edited by Janet Kardon. New York: Harry N Abrams, 36–45.

Grimes, S., and Andrew Feenberg. 2015. *Critical Theory of Technology*. London: SAGE.

Johnston, L. 2015. *Digital Handmade*. London: Thames and Hudson.

Mumford, L.1934. *Technics and Civilization*. New York: Harcourt Brace.

Could Innovations Such as Augmented Reality, the Internet of Things, and Artificial Intelligence Render the Fashion Industry More Sustainable?

Katharina SAND

Lecturer at the Geneva School of Art and Design (HEAD) Switzerland and Parsons Paris (the New School), France

Fashion allows us to reinvent ourselves. It is all about experimentation, about constantly moving forward. Fashion is about change—at a pace that keeps accelerating. Garments have become disposable more quickly than they are being produced. According to a McKinsey report, nearly three-fifths of all clothing ends up in incinerators or landfills within a year of being produced.[1] As a result, the area where change in the fashion industry is the most necessary is sustainability, especially in regard to pollution, waste, and labor issues.

In the same vein, technology also constantly creates obsolescence. Smartphones have an average lifecycle of two years. A United Nations report estimated electronic waste at 44.7 million metric tons in 2016.[2] Technological innovation in production and distribution is what makes fashion faster. But could we repurpose those innovations to empower creativity and increase sustainability?

There are definitely challenges. For any fashion innovation technology to work, it first has to be worn. Google Glass and Google Jacquard didn't really catch on. Nor did the Tommy Hilfiger Xplore collection, which launched in 2018. The Guardian simply called it "creepy."[3] You can find the video of how it was hacked by Leanne Luce on fashionrobot.com. So you might ask why are companies like Google and Tommy Hilfiger not succeeding in producing fashionable innovation that people want to keep? The answer is: they put technology first.

Many of the questions around fashion innovation and sustainability currently focus on fabrication. There have been incredible improvements in production methods and astounding innovation in textile engineering, new biotech fabrication methods, and even biodegradable fabrics, as in the case of Swiss company Freitag. *Yet key to sustainability is why and how we consume fashion. What makes a fashion item wearable and valuable—and what makes us throw it away?*

My fashion practice as a fashion journalist and fashion entrepreneur has allowed me to observe how we interact with clothes and accessories and what

---

1. Remy, N., et al. 2016. Style that's sustainable: A new fast-fashion formula. Sustainability & Resource Productivity : McKinsey & Company. Retrieved from http://www.mckinsey.com/business-functions/sustainability-and-resource-productivity/our-insights/style-thats-sustainable-a-new-fast-fashion-formula

2. Baldé, C. P., Forti, V., Gray, V., Kuehr, R., Stegmann, P. 2017. The Global E-Waste Monitor 2017, United Nations University : "The Global E-waste Monitor, developed by the International Telecommunication Union, United Nations University and International Solid Waste Association has highlighted the increasing generation of e-waste; in 2016 some 44.7 million metric tonnes of e-waste were generated globally."

3. Wolfson, Sam. 2018. Track-suits: Tommy Hilfiger's creepy new clothes know how much you wear them. *The Guardian*. July 26.

Robbie Barrat. Medium: Neural Network Generation. 2018

makes them meaningful to people for more than 20 years. This involves not just reviewing thousands of fashion shows, but also watching a lot of people getting dressed. It means asking a lot of questions and not just listening but deep listening. It entails observing how people inhabit and interpret clothing both online and offline and how these relations change over time. It is a research practice that allows for an understanding of how fantasy and wearability merge in real life and how they impact long term use in a way most engineers and fashion designers never see.

Analyzing data instead of people to answer these questions can lead you to a lot of wrong conclusions. For example, numbers tell us that customers are massively returning online orders claiming "it didn't fit." As a result, innumerable fashion technology startups are focusing on custom sizing and fit. An infamous recent example is the Zozo suit, launched (and now discontinued) by Japanese entrepreneur Yusaku Maezawa. The—data-based—assumption being that a personalised fit would reduce returns and encourage customers to keep these garments. But people do not buy and wear and keep something just because it fits. Nobody buys a 50,000-dollar watch—or keeps it—because it fits. A lot of women buy shoes and clothes that don't fit at all. It is a plus if it fits. First, it has to mean something, to be of value to the wearer.

In architecture, Steven Holl refers to the "psychological space" of spatial experience (Holl, 1991, 11). The sociologist Appadurai refers to our "social imaginary." Joanna Entwistle addresses the fashion imaginary "to understand fashion is analysis of the symbolic production of meanings and values within fashion" (Entwistle, 2016). In other words: it is about how you think you look. Those clothes and those earrings you are wearing all exist not just in physical space but in imaginary space.

Augmented Fashion Reality

Therefore, it makes perfect sense that we are increasingly wearing garments and accessories in digital space, like Instagram or Weibo. Even more interesting is that we can now overlay digital fashion on top of the real world.

One of the most talked-about fashion collections during the last New York fashion week was A.Human. Rather than a traditional fashion show, it was an immersive fashion experience, which was really about selfies. People were willing to pay 28 dollars for tickets to try on unusual accessories and tae selfies with them. It allowed for being extravagant, for simply playing with fashion. It allowed for fashion experiments that were as impermanent as they were immediate. It is a very interesting business model that compares to pay-per-view for fashion.

Those of you who have teenage daughters will probably have tried snapchat filters. You might also know that "virtual makeup" is a thing. Imagine the augmented reality IKEA catalog, except that you "furnish" your face. It seems to be paving the way for consumers to ease into virtual wearables. During fall 2018 Paris fashion week the designer Virgil Abloh, also known as Kanye West's best friend, the designer of the off-white clothing collection and currently the designer of Louis Vuitton's menswear, proposed the possibility of "wearing" his sunglasses by using an Instagram filter. Though it doesn't look like a real pair of glasses yet, those start ups who have researched optimal fit could use their skills for creating Augmented Reality Fashion that fits virtually perfectly.

If fashion is, as José Teunissen explains, "performing identity in space (Teunissen, 2013) it makes perfect sense that many shoppers would only buy clothing for the sake of Instagram posts and them return them. [4]

The advantage of AR fashion is that it is the fastest fashion possible—it is

---

4. Kozlowska, H. 2018. Shoppers are buying clothes just for the Instagram pic, and then returning them. Quartz. Aug 13.

immediate. It is also very sustainable. You can wear the most extravagant and surprising things, share these fashion experiments with other people, and all this fashion never needs to be washed, produces no waste, requires low production costs, and has a very low environmental impact. It can let us make as many fashion mistakes as we want, completely guilt-free. It could help us rethink the whole system.

Amber Jae Slooten only designs for virtual space—to avoid pollution. The designer has been using artificial intelligence algorithms and 3D-modelling technology to develop collections that only exist in digital space.[5] Virtual fashion coud be not only the missing link for fashion sustainability. Young independent designers who cannot afford expensive prototypes and production costs—and are conscious of the environment—could make their designs available worldwide just like Zara. It could be the most lowcost, environmentally friendly, and most far-reaching way to produce avant-garde fashion, allowing radically innovative fashion to be worn virtually and shared anywhere and everywhere at the price of an app.

For large luxury groups it could reduce counterfeiting—allowing them to provide everybody with luxury design at a cheaper price than a copy. Groups like LVMH who have been losing the middle-class market and are increasingly dependent on the more affordable "masstige" beauty products for revenue could make their virtual luxury products affordable for a large market, dramatically reducing logistics, costs, and labor issues. Meanwhile, actual physical production could remain reserved for the happy few with immaculate craftsmanship, returning to what true luxury used to be.

IOT (Internet of Things), RFIDs, and the Sharing Economy

Most of us are already interacting with fashion technology every day: the RFIDs (radio-frequency identification tags), which many retailers and manufacturers use to track their products. They do a lot more than just beep if you leave the store without paying. RFID tags read and emit data, transmitting information to a radio-frequency reader about the identity, or location, of a given product without needing a battery. It is one of the innovations that has allowed companies like Zara, Uniqlo, and Mango to manage their production and distribution logistics with the utmost precision, tracking garments and accessories from production right to the movements on the store floor.

Beyond supply chain logistics, it has for example allowed for analysis of wearability. If a pink dress gets taken into the changing room hundreds of times yet never gets taken to the check-out counter, then in-store tracking would indicate that it is appealing on the hanger, but there is a problem with the fit. The retailer can then deduce that either the pattern-making needs to be adjusted or that it needs to go on sale. These RFIDs could also be used to transmit the meaning and cultural significance of materials, origins, and production practices They could be used to transmit—and increase—value to consumers, as well as creating consumer networks.

Companies such as Alibaba are investing in RFID tags to fuse offline and online shopping. Avery Dennison, which creates barcodes and clothing labels for brands such as Nike and Hugo Boss, announced a partnership with the technology company Everything in 2018 to embed unique "digital identities" into 10 billion garments and accessories over the next three years. Many items of the world's biggest fashion brands will be able to connect to smartphones to trigger services. In France, the company Primo1d has developed an "e-thread" that allows for seamless RFID integration into clothing without tags.[6] In fact, the World Economic Forum forecasts that 10 percent of the population will be wearing internet-connected clothing by 2022. Though privacy will be a concern, all this is establishing a trackable knowledge base of wearable clothes worldwide.

As people on average wear only about 20 percent of their wardrobe[7] this huge knowledge base could also be used for a shared economy of clothing. We are experiencing a shift in concepts of ownership: car companies like Ford are reinventing themselves to become mobility providers—their new goal is not just to sell more cars but to minimize the time cars are not being used. Just as a private car is parked 95 percent of the time,[8] 80 percent of our closet is idle. Shared ownership, exchange, and rental could both allow the repurposing of clothes and be a solution for the constant desire for renewal without requiring new production. Besides reducing waste and carbon footprint, it could also foster human exchange.

5. https://www.amberjaeslooten.com

6. Swedberg, C. 2017. Company Boosts Sensitivity and Shortens Length of Its RFID Yarn. RFID Journal, May 9: "The E-Thread is an RFID yarn for which the antenna is built into the yarn strand itself (see E-Thread Provides Discrete Anti-Counterfeiting or Tracking Solutions). The company uses standard RFID chips which typically measure 445 micrometers (0.018 inch) by 490 micrometers (0.019 inch) or smaller."

7. Smith, R. A. 2013. *The Wall Street Journal*. A Closet Filled With Regrets. The Clothes Seemed Great in the Store; Why People Regularly Wear Just 20% of Their Wardrobe. April 17.

8. Morris, D. Z. 2016. Today's Cars Are Parked 95% of the Time. *Fortune*. March 13.

One hundred billion items of clothing are being produced annually. Fifty percent of fast-fashion pieces are disposed of within a year. According to a 2016 report from state news agency, Xinhua,[9] China alone throws away 26 million tonnes of textile waste each year, of which less than 1 percent is reused. At the same time, short-term rental of clothing is becoming a reality in China, for example through a clothing rental app called Yi23. One way the clothing and accessory industry could use the desire for novelty would be to repurpose RFID codes to allow renting and sharing. RFIDs could make constant change sustainable.

How can AI make fashion more innovative and sustainable?

It is impossible to speak of innovation these days without addressing artificial intelligence as well. According to the MIT Tech review, Amazon started using AI last year to design clothes (Knight, 2017). My main concern with AI-designed mass production by global companies is that we will end up with fashion that is based on repetition of best-selling items, a selection of the worldwide common denominator of the banal. It could dramatically reduce the amount of playful experimentation that is possible through clothing.

In fact, it is precisely for that experimentation process that AI is also being activated. Thanks to computer vision, algorithms (and some human input), Amazon offers Echo Look style assistants, Stitchfix offers predictive outfit suggestions, and Yoox is offering AI generated styling advice. Earlier in 2018, Alibaba launched a Fashion AI platform that provides fashion styling and product recommendations for consumers based on over 500,000 sources of data collected from stylists on Taobao and Tmall shops.

I am pretty sure none of the above would recommend some of the fashion mistakes I have committed. But after years of working in the fashion industry, I also realize people—myself included—do keep some of their most adventurous choices. Sometimes a strange geometric kaftan can give you a new perspective of your whole wardrobe. Sometimes it can refresh your outlook on life. Some clothes can inspire reflection on traditions, cultural heritage, and values. Others are valuable because they are memories of experiments. We enjoy and hold onto such items not because they make getting dressed easier but for their imaginary potential.

9. http://www.xinhuanet.com/politics/2016-03-28/c_128838861.htm

The moment garments and accessories are discarded is when they do not correspond to who we imagine we are anymore and how we want to represent ourselves to the world. But one of the most fascinating aspects of fashion is how we all compose and recompose old and new items and identities together, and how through these recompositions we constantly give things new meaning. So perhaps instead of using AI recommendations for new items, algorithms could be used to repurpose the billions of existing fashion garments and accessories. With a little help from RFIDs and AI, we could be accessing the whole world's closets. The creative compositions could be endless.

The virtual clothing created by Amber Jae Slooten was created with artificial intelligence and GAN (Generative Adverserial Networks) and 3D-modelling technology. She fed it images from previous Paris Fashion weeks and the algorithms created virtual entirely new pieces of clothing. A 19-year-old developer, Robbie Barat, also created a fashion show video with algorithms, feeding the GANs only Balenciaga catwalk images. Both have worked with items that were created before to recompose something virtually new. The beauty of Barrat's work is actually that both him and the AI are still learning—the results are memorable and striking because there are so many weird glitches. It is a little creepier, but also a reminder that the process of designing an outfit with technology as a tool can be playful.

One of the biggest challenges for sustainability is to make people enjoy it. Perhaps rather than just accelerating efficiency and production, machine intelligence could be used to encourage avant garde experiments and to make us play with clothes that already exist. Rather than play for us it could play with us, encouraging exchange and experimentation.

Reference

Appadurai, A. ed. 1998. *The Social Life of Things: Commodities in Cultural Perspective*. Cambridge: Cambridge University Press.

Entwistle, J. 2016. "The Fashioned Body 15 Years On." In *Fashion Practice* 8(1): 19.

Holl, S. 1991. *Pamphlet Architecture 13: Edge of a City*. New York: Princeton Architectural Press.

Knight, W. 2017. "Amazon Has Developed an AI Fashion Designer." In *MIT Technology Review*, August 24.

Teunissen, J. 2013. "Fashion: More than Cloth and Form." In *The Handbook of Fashion Studies*, edited by Sandy Black et al. London: Bloomsbury, 198.

Where Fashion, Jewellery, and Technology Meet

Maarten VERSTEEG, Elise van den HOVEN,
Caroline HUMMELS

At the end of the 19th century, French electrical engineer M. Gustave Trouvé designed and realized his *bijoux électriques lumineux* (see below), in order to enchant ballet performances and soirees. Unfortunately, most of his pieces did not survive [1].

Fig. 108. — La Signora Zanfreta, première danseuse du théâtre du Châtelet, à Paris, parée, dans la « Poule aux œufs d'or », des bijoux électriques lumineux de M. Gustave Trouvé.

Miss Zanfreta, first dancer at the Chatelet Theater in Paris, in "Hen with Golden Eggs," trimmed in electrically illuminated jewels by M. Gustave Trouvé (Barral, 1891)

This early example nicely illustrates some of the topics, which we will address in this article. It is interesting that these pieces are designed by an engineer. Of course, the application of electronics on the body involves many technical challenges in terms of the size of the components, the lifetime of the power-source, and the durability of the circuit during use, to mention a few. The figure "Miss Zanfreta," which features byoux électriqs lumineux being worn, also shows the relation to the dressed human body and the expressive potential of electronic jewellery.

We believe that, in order to exploit the full potential of electronics on the human body, a thorough understanding is needed of the fields of fashion, jewellery, and wearable technology, their similarities and differences, and their intersections. In this article we sketch a dynamic and multidisciplinary perspective on this topic, by regarding fashion, jewellery and wearable electronics as three partly overlapping fields (See next page).

1. The only still existing piece that we know of, is a pin with an electro-mechanically animated skull, kept in the Victoria and Albert Museum in London.

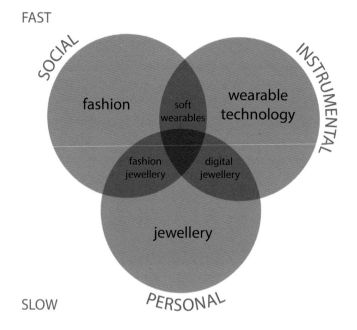

FAST

SOCIAL

INSTRUMENTAL

fashion
soft wearables
wearable technology

fashion jewellery
digital jewellery

jewellery

SLOW
PERSONAL

Overview of the fields of fashion, jewellery, and wearable technology.
The vertical axis shows the pace of the product lifecycle.
The newly identified design space is found in the middle of the figure

Different Paces

The fields of fashion and wearable technology have a much higher pace than the field of jewellery. Fashion is characterised by a constant need for change. Flügel (1930/2016) explains this need using the balance between *decoration* and *modesty*: on the one hand humans feel the innate urge to decorate their body, on the other hand social conventions require us to restrain from attracting attention. As the conventions change over time and differ from place to place, fashion keeps changing. Next to that humans imitate the social class they (aspire to) belong to, striving for upward social mobility. At the same time, social classes tend to differentiate themselves from lower classes: as soon as a lower class starts to imitate a certain fashion, a new fashion is adopted (Simmel, 1957). This process is called "the trickle-down effect" (see right, above). [2] For a long time,

2. With the emancipation of diverse minorities and the rise of sub- and youth-cultures throughout the second half of the 20th century, fashion is no longer one-directional, but spreads itself also across (trickle-across) social classes and in upward direction (trickle-up) (Field, 1970).

fashion marketing has supported this mechanism by offering an increasing number of fashion-collections and accompanying accessories per year. In recent years the awareness starts to dawn that this pace is not sustainable in the long term.

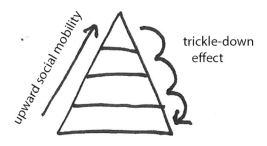

Visualisation of social ladder and trickle-down effect
inspired by Simmel (1957) and Field (1970)

The fast pace in the field of wearable technology originates in the on-going quest for smaller and more powerful electronics. Since Trouvé's Bijoux Electriques Lumineux, electronics have miniaturized, microchips have been introduced with increasing storing capacity and a growing number of functions. Moreover, devices are no longer stand-alone, but are connected to the cloud.

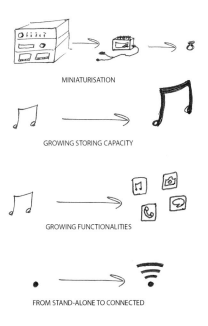

MINIATURISATION

GROWING STORING CAPACITY

GROWING FUNCTIONALITIES

FROM STAND-ALONE TO CONNECTED

Overview of developments
in wearable technology
(© visual by authors)

Compared to the other fields, jewellery tends to be of a more timeless nature. This slower pace can partly be explained by the enduring value of the used materials—like precious metals and gemstones—and partly by the fact that jewellery tends to hold a strong personal and emotional value. In the next paragraph we will take a closer look at the different emphasises within the fields of fashion, jewellery, and wearable technology.

Different Emphasises

When compared to each other, each of the three fields has a dominant emphasis. As we already described in the previous paragraph, the *social* context is relatively important in fashion.

The motives to wear jewellery are of a more *personal nature* (Unger and Leeuwen, 2017, 139):

- *Adornment: to adorn our body in order to feel more beautiful and accentuate certain body parts*
- *Prosperity: to easily take financial resources with us and show our financial wealth*
- *Protection: to protect ourselves against evil forces*
- *Identity: to reinforce our identity to ourselves and show our social position to others*
- *Desire: to express our desires (for example a longing for past times, pure nature, or a certain place)*
- *Memento: to be reminded of our personal history, roots, and relations*

(Unger-de Boer, 2010; Unger and Leeuwen, 2017)

The figure below illustrates the most personal motives with a concrete example.

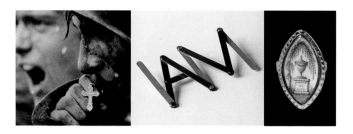

Motives to wear jewellery, left to right: Psychological Protection (Russian soldier, 1943), Confirming Identity (Chp63, I'm by Dinie Besems), Memento (Hairwork mourning ring © Victoria & Albert Museum)

Wearable Technology is of a more *instrumental* nature. The Beecham Research Group (2014) divided the field of wearable technology in the following sectors:

- *Glamour: expressive designs often with dynamic patterns or lights;*
- *Communication: extensions of one's cell phone. Incoming calls, messages, and notifications are filtered according to rules set by the user;*
- *Lifestyle computing: combines functions of the previous and following sector with lifestyle advice like meditation exercises;*
- *Sport/fitness, wellness, and medical: three sectors that track activity and/ or collect physiological data, respectively aiming at physical training, improved vitality, and health monitoring;*
- *Security/safety: basically, wearable alarm-buttons that can be used to alert relatives, other users nearby, or emergency services;*
- *Business operations: wearables used to interact with the internet of things through gesture control or used as a wireless identifier.*

(Wearable technology: enabling the connected lifestyle—outline, 2014)

The diverse emphasises of the fields become very clear when we compare them (see below). For example, there is a clear relation between "adornment" (jewellery field), "glamour" (wearable technology field), and "decoration" (fashion field, see previous paragraph). Yet, the field of fashion makes the connection to modesty and social conventions. In the field of jewellery, the relation with the human body and the personal perception of beauty is accentuated. And within the field of wearable technology the focus is more on the dynamic and expressive quality of the piece as an *instrument* to achieve a certain effect.

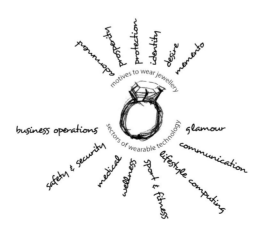

Overview of the motives to wear jewellery (Unger-de Boer, 2010;
Unger and Leeuwen, 2017) and sectors of wearable technology (Beecham Research Group, 2014)

Intersections

Where the fields overlap, we find four subfields: fashion jewellery, soft wearables, digital jewellery, and, in the middle, a fourth yet unnamed field.

Fashion or costume jewellery is decorative jewellery made from ordinary and semi-precious materials. The first industrial revolution created the circumstances for fashion jewellery to emerge: a higher social class of people with plenty of free time and money to spend in the newly invented department stores and innovative materials like Bakelite. The relatively cheap materials and ephemeral character of fashion jewellery allows for expressive and voluminous designs (Cera, 1997, 10). Key figures in the popularization of fashion jewellery in the 1920s are French couturiers Gabrielle (Coco) Chanel and Elsa Schiaparelli, who convinced the upperclass to leave their "real jewellery" in the safe and replace it by or mix it with fashion jewellery. It is interesting to realize that many of the accessories that we nowadays refer to as jewellery actually fall into the field of fashion jewellery. Next to that it is fascinating to see how fashion jewellery initiated the democratization of jewellery, which contributed to the emergence of contemporary art jewellery in the second half of the 20th century.

On the intersection of fashion and wearable technology we see the emergence of *soft wearables*: the integration of wearable electronics within textile wearables. Within soft wearables we find fashionable examples (see right, above) and functional ones (see right, middle). Soft wearables is an interesting and quickly developing field, with very specific challenges in terms of fitting, integration, sustainability and washability (see for example Seymour [2008] on this).

On the intersection of jewellery and wearable technology the subfield of *digital jewellery* emerges: design concepts that try to balance the instrumental opportunities of wearable technology and the personal meaning of jewellery. Wearable technologies have been criticized for lacking an understanding of the implications of the proximity to the human body in terms of aesthetics and personal significance (Wallace and Dearden, 2005). During the last decade the integration of jewellery and wearable technology has been addressed in the academic world by scholars with a background in technology, interaction design, and/or craft, mainly through design explorations (Ashbrook, Baudisch, and White, 2011; Miner, Chan, and Campbell, 2001; Perrault, Lecolinet, Eagan,

1. *Ilja Assimila SS16, Ilja Visser and Marina Toeters*
2. *Closed loop smart athleisure fashion, by-wire.*
   net and Holst Centre
3. *Memento, left: recording sound, right: playback*

1

2

3

and Guiard, 2013; Silina and Haddadi, 2015; Versteeg, van den Hoven, and Hummels, 2016; Wallace, 2007; Werner, Wettach, and Hornecker, 2008; White and Steel, n.d.). Other scholars sketched the field and advocated a specific approach (Kettley, 2005; Koulidou, 2018; Wallace and Dearden, 2005; Wallace and Press, 2004). As an example of digital jewellery—Memento (see p. 269) is a soundlocket developed by Karin Niemantsverdriet in cooperation with the first author. Memento can be opened on two sides. By opening the one lid it starts recording. When the other lid is opened playback starts. The volume is such that the locket needs to be held close to the ear during playback. In order to navigate through the samples one pulls the chain. The more often a fragment is listened to, the easier it can be found. Samples that are hardly listened to, will diminish and ultimately disappear from the locket's memory.

Lastly, by creating the figure in page 264, we identified a so far unnamed intersection in the middle, where the three fields overlap. To our knowledge this field is not yet explored by academics. It promises to be an interesting design space though, as it perfectly balances the three fields. The exploration of this field requires a separate study, which goes beyond the scope of this article.

A Dynamical Approach

So far we have sketched an overview of the different fields, their relations and characteristics. Such a scheme helps us gain insight but can also easily be interpreted as static and over-simplification. Therefore, we would like to stress that it should be approached dynamically, meaning that we have to switch between different levels of detail. The figure in page 271 shows several levels of abstraction. On the left side, we see the three fields from such a distance, that the innerlines start to fade. It creates awareness that fashion, jewellery, and wearable technology—despite differences in pace and emphasis—in the end share the proximity to the human body. Moreover it shows a partly blank canvas on which related and probably inspiring fields like accessories and wearable aids could be positioned (Tamminen and Holmgren, 2016). When we zoom in, the subfields as described in the previous paragraph, emerge (see right, middle part). Further zooming-in shows that the oldest and more mature fields are heterogeneous in themselves (see right, right part). Within the field of fashion we for example find the unique handmade haute couture pieces, ready-to-wear collections that are made in small series, and mass-produced clothing. Comparable segmentations can be found within the fields of jewellery and fashion jewellery. Zooming in even further will reveal the gray dots to be brands and eventually individual designers and makers. On this level we will find the tacit merits of true craftsmanship: unique sensitivity for material qualities, sublime handling of tools, age-old skills that have been past from generation to generation and subtle understanding of the characteristics of the human body.[3]

In order to successfully further develop the (sub)fields, we need the holistic overview shown on the left, as much as we need the refined craftsmanship hidden on the right.

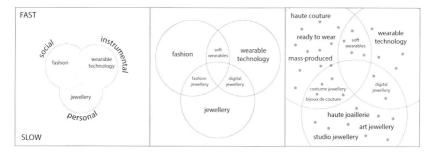

Overview of the three fields on different levels of abstraction

Some Concluding Thoughts

There lay more than a hundred years between *les bijoux électriques lumineux* by M. Gustave Trouvé and today. What seemed promising back then is within reach now. Electronics have become wearable and are entering the intimate proximity to the human body. For ages this space was reserved for clothing and jewellery, rooted in the human urge to adorn, express, and identify. What is new is exciting, but the unknown can also be uncertain and scary. In order to deal

---

3. For further reading about the merits of craftsmanship we refer to Sennett (2008).

with that, mutual understing is needed. Therefore, we sketched an overview of the fields of fashion, jewellery, and wearable technology and their intersections, and we identified an unexplored design space where the three fields overlap. Yet, an overview is inherently a simplification of reality. Therefore, we advocate a dynamical approach, switching between the holistic overview and the richness of the details. We believe the field is in need of such a dynamic and multidisciplinary approach, cherishing and challenging both similarities and differences, in order to explore the full potential of fashion, jewellery, wearable technology, and all possible intersections.

Reference

Ashbrook, D., P. Baudisch, and S. White. 2011. Nenya. *Proceedings of the 2011 Annual Conference on Human Factors in Computing Systems - CHI '11*, The 2011 Annual Conference, 113. http://doi.org/10.1145/1978942.1979238

Barral, G. 1891. *Histoire d'un inventeur*. Retrieved from https://github.com/uvicmakerlab/trouve d.d. 15-1-2019.

Farnetti Cera, D. 1997. *Costume Jewellery*. London: ACC Art Books.

Field, G. A. 1970. "The Status Float Phenomenon: Upward Diffusion of Innovation." In *Business Horizons* 13(4): 45–52.

Flügel, J. C. 2016. "The Fundamental Motives." In *The Fashion Reader*, edited by L. Welters and A. Lillethun, 2nd edition. London: Bloomsbury, 169–73 (original work published in 1930).

Kettley, S. 2005. "Framing the Ambiguous Wearable." In *Convivio Web-Zine* 2: 1–15.

Koulidou, N. 2018. "Why Should Jewellers Care About the Digital?" In *Journal of Jewellery Research* 01(February): 17–33. Retrieved from http://www.journalofjewelleryresearch.org/wp-content/uploads/2018/04/JOJR-vol-1-Koulidou.pdf.

Miner, C. S., D. M. Chan, and C. Campbell. 2001. "Digital Jewellery: Wearable Technology for Everyday Life." In *CHI EA '01: CHI '01 Extended Abstracts on Human Factors in Computing Systems*, 45–46. http://doi.org/10.1145/634067.634098.

Perrault, S. T., Eagan J. Lecolinet, and Y. Guiard. 2013. "Watchit: Simple Gestures and Eyes-free Interaction for Wristwatches and Bracelets." In *Proceedings of CHI 2013*, 1451–60. http://doi.org/10.1145/2470654.2466192.

Sennett, R. 2008. *The Craftsman*. London: Penguin Books.

Silina, Y., and H. Haddadi. 2015. *The Distant Heart: Mediating Long-Distance Relationships through Connected Computational Jewellery*. eprint arXiv:1505.00489. Retrieved from http://arxiv.org/abs/1505.00489.

Simmel, G. 1957. "Fashion." *American Journal of Sociology*, 62(6): 541–58.

Tamminen, S., and E. Holmgren. 2016. "The Anthropology of Wearables: The Self, the Social, and the Autobiographical." In *2016 Ethnographic Praxis in Industry Conference*. 154–74.

Unger, M., and S. van Leeuwen. 2017. Jewellery Matters. Rotterdam: nai010 publishers.

Unger-de Boer, M. 2010. *Sieraad in context: Een multidisciplinair kader voor de beschouwing van het sieraad [Jewellery in context: a mulitidisciplinary framework to study jewellery]*.

Versteeg, M., E. van den Hoven, and C. Hummels. 2016. "Interactive Jewellery: A Design Exploration."In *Proceedings of the TEI '16: Tenth International Conference on Tangible, Embedded, and Embodied Interaction*, 44–52. http://doi.org/10.1145/2839462.2839504.

Wallace, J. 2007. "Emotionally Charged: A Practice-centred Enquiry of Digital Jewellery and Personal Emotional Significance." In *Development*, (July), 1–228. http://doi.org/10.1258/jrsm.100.8.368.

Wallace, J., and A. Dearden. 2005. "Digital Jewellery as Experience." In *Future Interaction Design*, edited by Antti Pirhonen, 193–216. Cham: Springer.

Wallace, J., and M. Press. 2004. "All This Useless Beauty: The Case for Craft Practice in Design for a Digital Age." In *The Design Journal*, 7(2): 42–53. http://doi.org/10.2752/146069204789354417.

Wearable technology: enabling the connected lifestyle—outline. 2014. Retrieved from http://www.beechamresearch.com/files/BRL Wearable Tech Report Outline.pdf.

Werner, J., R. Wettach, and E. Hornecker. 2008. "United-pulse: Feeling Your Partner's Pulse. ""*Proceedings of the 10th International Conference on Human Computer Interaction with Mobile Devices and Services*, 535–38. http://doi.org/10.1145/1409240.1409338.

White, H., and E. Steel. 2007. "Agents of Change: From Collection to Connection." In *The Design Journal* 10(2): 22–34. Retrieved from http://www.tandfonline.com.dianus.libr.tue.nl/doi/pdf/10.2752/146069207789272703.

Post Digital Jewellery

The Future Scenarios of Contemporary Jewellery Design

Chiara SCARPITTI

PhD, Lecturer in Design and Innovation. University of Campania "Luigi Vanvitelli," Italy

Far from a short-term inspiration, the contemporary designer is nourished by a cultured design study through an analysis of shapes, materials, the idea he/she wants to communicate, and his/her vision of the world. It is not just a question of embellishing the person through an operation of decoration, but of embedding within the product an immaterial value. It concerns the creation of thought able to stimulate the mind and produce knowledge. In this perspective, the design of a jewel is aimed also at an intellectual consumption.

In light of this, the international debate on jewellery-making production requires new perspectives, focused at deepening the design role in the digital age. Industry 4.0 is widespread and affordable while contemporary project culture interfaces with digitalization in an increasingly integrated and inclusive way.

It is quite clear that the transition from digital to post digital is underway and the theories of Mel Alexenberg bear witness to this: "Postdigital pertains to art forms that address the humanization of digital technologies through interplay between digital, biological, cultural, and spiritual systems, between cyberspace and real space, between embodied media and mixed reality in social and physical communication, between high tech and high touch experiences, between visual, haptic, auditory, and kinesthetic media experiences, between virtual and augmented reality, between roots and globalization" (Alexenberg, 2011, 11).

The paper analyzes a series of case studies of contemporary jewellery that highlight a renewed relationship between design and technology, as for example, the construction of bio-inspired ornaments. However, several examples arise also from the transversal use of processes and post digital productions related to sectors other than the world of jewellery, such as medicine or engineering. This typology of disruptive design often investigates a wider spectrum of themes, including material experimentation or the political, sustainable, and ethical issues that affect today's society.

Contemporary Jewellery toward the Post Digital

The international debate on digital production requires a greater awareness of the role of design within the future scenarios of jewellery. The 4.0 industry is now widespread, but the places of production, if they really want to innovate, have to be sensitive cultural systems, within which stratified know-how must be constantly renewed.

Already in 1998, Negroponte affirmed, "The Digital Revolution is over...Like air and drinking water, being digital will be noticed only by its absence, not its presence. The decades ahead will be a period of comprehending biotech, mastering nature, and realizing extraterrestrial travel, with DNA computers, microrobots, and nanotechnologies the main characters on the technological stage. Computers will be a sweeping yet invisible part of our everyday lives: We'll live in them, wear them, even eat them" (Negroponte, 1998).

In the outlined scenario, it is clear that the relationship between human and digital is becoming increasingly complex, since technology—which has always been an expression of civilization—now assumes a crucial aspect. The speed with which computer systems are progressing[1] together with the arrival of the I.o.T. (internet of things)—which is now evolving towards the I.o.E. (internet of everything)—places the world in a global network that connects people, things, and living beings.

In the I.o.E. the human world, the natural world, and the world of the web coexist in a unique experience of life. "The Internet of Everything (I.o.E.) brings together people, process, data, and things to make networked connections more relevant and valuable than ever before—turning information into actions that create new capabilities, richer experiences, and unprecedented economic opportunity for businesses, individuals, and countries."[2] Surrounded by such an articulated relational dimension, design, in its role as a transformative tool of reality, now completes a new path of research, mixing atoms and bits, physical reality, and cyberspace.

As Mel Alexenberg states in his writings on post-digital, with the elimination of barriers between materials and virtual, design uses new working methods, hybrid tools, and matters. The digital component has become an essential element in a contemporary project that looks to the future, even more so if these technologies were to be integrated with science and nature toward an inclusive and hybridizing productive horizon.

Innovative software, 3D scanners, manipulation of new materials, and contamination between skills shape new product scenarios and completely subvert the old way of designing. This is the landscape in which a series of pilot experiments highlight a renewed relationship between design, jewellery, and technology.

Devices have taken over our lives. The omnipresent screen culture is responsible for a social transformation. The chat app is what the cigarette was in the last century: a symbolic consumption good that makes a significant contribution to the running of the economy. In the case of the cigarette, lungs are slowly destroyed. But what is the hidden cost of becoming device people? And how can a piece of jewellery respond to this transformation? [3]

These are the questions through which Gijs Bakker invites to imagine new jewels for the exhibition Device People, presented at the Milan Design Week 2018 at the Alcova space. Among the displayed works, the EXT. project by Bart Hess is built with very thin copper wires taken from cables through which electricity and the network data pass. The necklace looks like an extra-body organ, meticulously composed just like an organic element and woven through the use of primary materials for the physical transmission of bits.

With *Black Transparency, the duo Conversation Piece*, composed by Beatrice Brovia and Nicolas Cheng, proposes a brooch with a shape similar to the screen of the first iPhone 2G ever produced. The reflective surface of these objects seems to be composed of gold chips and crystals that reflect the human image of the viewer, allowing a contemplative reflection on sustainability issues.

In the book *Postdigital Artisans*, Jonathan Openshaw analyzes a series of brands and creative studios that work with the digital merging of different media and transdisciplinary approaches, including architecture, fashion, art, and jewellery. The book traces a futuristic post-digital scenario that divides the creative act into several categories of action: forces, bodies, surfaces, particles, structures, and matter. "A JPEG of a sculpture and the physical sculpture are not the same thing, but they are related. They are able to live separate but entangled lives, and so the overall object that they constitute is neither physical nor digital, but an amalgamation of both" (Openshaw, 2015, 7).

1. Moore's Law. By Dominic Basulto April 14, 2015. Website: https://www.washingtonpost.com/news/innovations/wp/2015/04/14/10-images-that-explain-the-incredible-power-of-moores-law/?utm_term=.92253fe901d8

2. Cisco. 2013. Internet of Everything. Website: http://share.cisco.com/IoESocialWhitepaper/#/

3. Device People is a project curated by CHP···? Website: http://www.chpjewellery.com/device-people/

Toward a new kind of meanings and values, a design of a digital jewel can also represent the most negative moods. In this interstitial space Dorry Hsu conducts her research. With *Aesthetic of Fears*[4] the Korean designer tries to materialize phobia for insects through the creation of a limited series of pins, masks, and rings, combining a robotic modeling through a haptic arm and colored resins. The final result responds to the initial concept by the creation of jewels that are repulsive and at the same time fascinating, occupying a borderline between the unconscious emotions and matter.

1

2

1. Conversation Piece, Black Transparency, 2018
2. Dorry Hsu, Aesthetic of Fears, 2014

4. Hsu, D. 2014. Aesthetic of Fears. Website: http://cargocollective.com/Dorry_hsu/Aesthetic-of-Fears

The Physical Body: An Exploratory Map for the Digital Project

From atoms to bits to return to atoms—or rather to physical matter and the importance of our corporeity—one of the future scenarios of jewellery design consists in a total customization that takes the individual as the starting point and arrival of the project. In the post-digital era, the design production no longer means repetition identical to itself, but it is a process of singularization of an object that, combined with a person, reveals its most intangible component. "The body is our first technique, but it is also our first material. It is the medium with which we construct and modify the world. To call the body into question, building up our own subject, means to be rooted in the sensitive being that we are, and in perception and action" (Fiorani, 2010, 51).

The tangibility of our existence passes through a revisitation of the body, understood as a field for a project exploration of both analogical nature, through the adoption of traditional goldsmith techniques and artisan production, and digital, through the use of new technologies and computerized tools.

Among the most recent researches, the generative biometric design can generate a diversified multiplicity of objects adopting as formal parameters the measurements of the body. Through 3D scans and virtual mapping of a single part—such as the neck or the wrists—it is possible to build, with the help of algorithms, unique jewels that perfectly fit the human anatomy. Experiments of this kind are already widespread in the biomedical field, for the generation of prostheses and custom-made limbs. But in fashion and design, these can give rise to a new wearability for the jewel, in close relation with the aesthetic and functional needs of each person.

Among the most innovative examples in this sense, we find the work of Rein Vollenga, who creates biomorphic sculptures through a mix of techniques such as lacquering and resins, or the research of Ana Rajcevic, who, with her wearable sculptures, moulds objects that cannot be categorized in any type of product. In the text presenting the project "Animal: The Other Side of Evolution," Rajcevic states: "The project is grounded in a unique visual interpretation of animal anatomy, building upon existing skeleton structures to create a series of sculptural pieces that appear as natural properties of the human body, suggesting strength, power, and sensuality. Concepts of mutation and evolution are explored in order to develop a contemporary cross-image of human and animal, an atemporal, supreme creature, beyond past and future."[5]

In relation to the human-animal theme and its hybridization, the transdisciplinary research of Jorge Alaya Atelier is oriented toward a post-human scenario through the modeling of new living species. "Post-digital Curiosities" is a synoptic installation that recalls the periodic table of chemical elements by Mendeleev. The project exhibits a series of parametrically generated biomorphic artifacts, which are subsequently reworked using a skillful mix of particular pigments, chemical agents, and drying times. Far from the traditional computerized aesthetics, Alaya stages a reshaping of digital objects as animated and imperfect beings, each representing a possible evolutionary universe.

In this perspective, the designer appears as an alchemist who investigates the logic of nature from the inside, reconstructing its dynamics, processes, and differences. However, his reflections do not always positively reconnect humans with the natural environment, but rather lead to a destabilization of the dichotomies of human–nature, human–human, and human–technology. It is the beginning of a phase of the project that places humans at the center of technology, not only as the final recipient, but as an actor in the "construction" of their own process and of a reciprocal relationship.

28

As Alexenberg says, differently from digital, the post-digital horizon feeds on material and physical reality, in an increasingly inseparable reciprocity. The most experimental approaches are using sensitive information from the network, bio-hacking practices, and the entire human body as bio-digital inputs to be inserted into new production systems.

Jewels connected to the external or internal anatomy of the body, because they are linked to organs and clinical parameters, return outputs that can be transformed into shapes, colors, and emotions—all singular and unrepeatable. The morphology of the iris, the heartbeat, the neuronal frequencies, or the breath, a strand of hair, a fingerprint: each element of the body can condense into a precious object.

5. Rajcevic, A. 2012. Animal: The Other Side of Evolution by Ana Rajcevic. Website: http://www.anarajcevic. com/work/animal

1

2

1. *Ana Rajcevic, Animal.*
   The Other Side of Evolution, 2012
2. *Rein Vollenga, Essences, 2011*

On the borderline between biological and digital, several designers and artists are investigating the intersection between practices related to microbiology. From a production point of view, the gradual shift we are witnessing is from a homologated manufacture of equal multiples—clearly exemplified by a previous industrial paradigm—to a manufacture of unique multiples, toward a renewed 1:1 ratio between human and product.

In 2006, as part of a transdisciplinary research project called Bio Jewellery, a group of designers from the Royal College of Art in London, together with researchers from King's College, investigated and created a series of bone tissue rings for couples. "In the course of the project we drew upon the skills and experience of many different disciplines and professions: materials engineering, cell biology, oral surgery, media imaging, computer-aided jewellery design, graphic design, interaction design, product design, fine art, media relations, journalism, science communication, sociology and ethics" (Thompson, Stott, and Kerridge, 2006, 35).

Through the use of these laboratory processes, body and nature are investigated in a way that is no longer mimetic, but from within their real scientific dynamics. The tissues were taken directly from the couples who, after written consent, underwent a small surgical operation that would allow the extraction of the sample. It's obvious that the idea of a wearable object containing parts of the beloved is a very ancient and powerful image. And in this direction, the technologies of the future, taking inspiration from the past, can reinforce those anthropological values, placing the jewel in another sphere of perception and thought.

Technologies as Envisioning Tool

In light of these experiments, technology can be one of the most evocative frontiers of a contemporary jewellery project because of its ability to open horizons and explore new material possibilities. But despite this, it is also essential to support it by a vision that binds itself to the anthropological dimension of humans, for a deep awareness of human beings. Whenever the design of a jewel takes on a new technological challenge, its presence offers the viewer a reflection on what and how it is possible to exist.

It is a question of reflecting on the relationship between the metaphorical capacity that the object has to evoke other than its properly technical connotation. In this sense, moving away from the rational domain, technology goes beyond the acquired knowledges and suggests new research paths through which the most humanistic and sensitive component of the project finds space.

We should not forget that a jewel is a device with a strong symbolic power that binds the wearer to an emotional and perceptive sphere and amplifies it. Jewel, subject, and thought are connected when there is an exchange of energy and mutual influence. According to this research perspective—theoretical and practical—technology is not only used for an aesthetic or functional optimization, but it becomes a tool for envisioning and the establishment of a new relationship—corporeal and intellectual—with the human being.

83

Reference

Alexenberg, M. 2011. *The Future of Art in a Postdigital Age*. Bristol: Intellect Ltd.

Fiorani, E. 2010. *Leggere i materiali*. Milano: Lupetti.

Negroponte, N. 1998. "Beyond Digital." In *WIRED Magazine*, 12(6).

Openshaw, J. 2015. *Postdigital Artisans: Craftsmanship with a New Aesthetic in Fashion, Art, Design and Architecture*. London: FRAME.

Thompson, I., N. Stott, and T. Kerridge. 2006. *Biojewellery: Designing Rings with Bioengineered Bone Tissue*. London: Oral & Maxillofacial Surgery, King's College London.

CHAPTER

4

DIALOGUE &
COMMUNICATION
Curation

Introduction

Jie SUN
National Distinguished Expert, Professor at Tongji University, Shanghai, China

In the book *Thinking through Exhibition* published more than 20 years ago, the following conclusion was sugguested: "Exhibitions are the primary site of exchange in the political economy of art, where signification is constructed, maintained and occasionally deconstructed...exhibitions—especially exhibitions of contemporary art—establish and administer the cultural meanings of art" (Greenberg, 1996,2). Today, with the acceleration of globalization and the emergence of new network technologies, as well as the increase of cross-border exchanges among people, art, capital, culture, and the "experience economy" in different cultural contexts, the exhibition does not only serve as a display of collections and research results, but also builds its more important cultural and research practice value. The exhibition itself constructs multi-dimensional and multi-level cultural and social exchanges, and the production and process of curations are used as research methods. In addition to the relationship between its content and the current life, the open and diversified forms of contemporary fashion and design exhibitions are more and more interested by art galleries and museums and welcomed by the public. Contemporary curation, as a creative form of practical research, has produced many achievements, including the exhibition itself, digital archives, and related publications, etc. However, how do we understand the value of contemporary curation, how to position the role of the curator, and what is curation as a research method? In the article of this chapter, I took the TRIPLE PARADE Biennale for Contemporary Jewellery as a case to analyze and discuss these issues.

Broadly speaking, curation is an important part of the fashion industry. Whether it is a dynamic fashion press conference or a static exhibition of cultural institutions, curation can effectively spread fashion themes and product-related content to the public and the media. On the other hand, even though the combination of fashion and museum has a history of nearly 100 years, how to treat contemporary fashion in museum exhibitions still raises new arguments. In this regard, associate professor Hector Navarro launched his discussion. He believes that from the establishment of fashion-themed museums in the early 19th century to fashion exhibitions in art museums held by well-known fashion curators such as Diana Vreeland, Harold Koda, Richard Martin, Valerie Steele, etc, that there are more and more fashion-themed exhibitions and curatorial activities, which have become a new trend of art museums. This trend also influenced Spain, which led to the establishment of permanent museums such as Museo del Traje and Museo Balenciaga. In addition, some museums combine art with fashion. For example, in the exhibition "Sorolla and fashion," the paintings of the artist Joaquin Sorolla are displayed together with fashion, and fashion is also regarded as another way of presenting paintings. Taking this as a starting point, he put forward his views on the importance of curation and management.

Introduction

Reference

Greenberg, R. 1996. *Thinking through Exhibition*. London and New York: Routledge.

Research Methods and Strategies of Contemporary Design Curation

Take the TRIPLE PARADE Biennale for Contemporary Jewellery as an Example

28

Jie SUN
National Distinguished Expert, Professor, College of Design and Innovation, Tongji University, Shanghai, China

In the traditional mode, there are great differences in curatorial methods and management, exhibition methods, and attitudes of museums of contemporary art (art galleries/design museums/art centers) and museums of history and culture. The latter shows the display of objects based on historical chronological context, while the former not only shows the relationship between people and objects and the development of human society, but also a field is built to try to ask questions and map problems on this basis (Martinon, 2013; Ferguson, 1996). Therefore, although they are all culture and art institutions and exhibitions, they present a completely different curatorial framework (Barker, 1999). In museums of history and culture, most of them are "permanent" exhibitions based on collections. However, in the field of contemporary art and design, the "short-term" exhibitions have formed an important "breathing" function to maintain the vitality and influence of the institutions. It can usually be an exhibition or an event with a specific theme, rather than having a direct relationship with the collection (Heinich, 1996). Especially at present, with the strong development of art galleries and museums and the growing culture of international biennales, coupled with the increasing demand for "cross-border cooperation" from high-end brands and some commercial activities, more and more exhibition contents and forms appear. Visiting the exhibitions in contemporary art museums (museums/art, museums/galleries) has also become a new mode of popular lifestyle and social mode (Marstine, 2006). Therefore, the quality of "short-term" exhibitions in the context of contemporary art has become an important bargaining chip for the development of institutions.

It is obvious that people are paying more and more attention to various contemporary exhibitions, because with the acceleration of globalization, new network information and science and technology, as well as the increase of the exchanges between public and lifestyle, art and capital, culture and communication, as well as "experience economy," and cross-border culture. In order to gain the interest of the public and professionals (Kirshenblatt-Gimblett, 1998; Marincola, 2002), the diverse roles and cultural values of exhibitions are being promoted and expanded, and different curators are required to provide diversified exhibitions and to constantly strive to find new exhibition forms, new curatorial means, theme researches and activities, and promote the knowledge exchange and participation of audiences/visitors. The relationship between contemporary cultural institutions and the public or specific groups is constantly changing (Bauer, 1992; Obrist, 2016). This change reflects that, in the contemporary context, the exhibition has begun to change from paying attention to the display of collections and their historical stories to paying attention to how to interact with viewers/participants and rethink the role of the audience. This shift of focus requires art galleries and museums to better consider the research of visitors, cross-border cooperation models (Billing, 2007), digital interaction, and new communication models (Cook, 2002). On a more important level, due to the increased external demand for knowledge and content of exhibition output and academic researcher in art galleries, the staff of art galleries have become an indispensable part in the implementation of exhibition curatorial practice, which has changed the role and status of exhibitions in cultural institutions to a certain extent (Hooper-Greenhill, 2014). In the past, they only displayed the completed research results, and they have become an important platform for integrating resources and a place for knowledge creation and production (Gardner and Green, 2016).

The practice and research of contemporary art curation has become a relatively independent ideology and form of expression, and the exhibition is no longer confined to collections and single historical research. The brand-new curatorial motive makes the exhibition become a new research language or art practice; a field where the curator (author, director), exhibits (practical works of artists' thoughts), and the audience interact, think, and explore, providing a multitude of freedoms and possibilities for contemporary curators, but also presents great challenges. This new form exposes that the traditional curatorial methods and systems can no longer adapt to the new vision and discipline development of current society, which also implies that the traditional curatorial methods and art museum studies are facing a challenge, because the traditional curators probably lack the knowledge and judgment of the real context as well as the means and ability to deal with complex tasks and objects. As the art historian Terry Smith (Smith, 2012) asserted in his monograph *Thinking Contemporary Curating*, in this new era, in addition to the changes in the relationship and role between art museums and exhibitions, curators need to be prepared for transformation (MacLeod, Hanks, and Hale, 2012).

However, contemporary exhibitions are more than just meeting the needs of attracting audiences and maintaining the growth of cultural institutions in the experience economy (Pine and Gilmore, 1999). As Caroline Thea said, "Contemporary art exhibition or biennale: a laboratory for experiment, exploration, and free aesthetics; a place to test the curator's ability and knowledge; a venue to integrate knowledge and knowledge production. When they negotiate for artistic expression, knowledge criticism and humanistic care in their own society and others, they are challenged by the certainty and uncertainty of the evolving future." It is undeniable that contemporary exhibitions are also places for research and knowledge output, and the process of contemporary curation can also become a means of academic research (Drabble, 2008).

There are two ideas and models about curatorial research: one is based on literature and specific works or people as research objects, with curatorial research as methods and means to verify knowledge. In addition to papers, exhibitions can also be used as a part of knowledge output, which is not difficult to understand. Most of the scientific research of explicit knowledge is in this mode. The other is based on the design exhibition curation practice, the main form of which is the exhibition itself, which is not only regarded as a verification form of research (Thomas, 2002), but also as a place to conduct research and a place to conduct existing research (Herle, 2013; Bjerregaard, 2019). The research is not only carried out before the exhibition is realized, but also during the whole realization process of the exhibition. It is also considered as a scientific means to transfer knowledge, such as the method of selecting works, the structure of curatorial management and organization, the interpretation of the concept of scenography aesthetics, the structure of space design, the architectural models and documentary records displayed in exhibitions, or subjective and perceptual experiments, etc. These are all components of a curation model with academic research attributes, and a means of its content output. Of course, the former is curation and research, and the latter is curatorial research, which can also be understood as exhibition practice-based research and exhibition practice-led research. The relationship between these two is not difficult to understand, nor is it new. Although the two kinds of research are intrinsically related, there is also a split role in methods. This kind of "split role" is basically two modes of knowledge output: academic research in the scientific sense and practical research in the professional sense of the discipline. In fact, these two modes are always transformed between conflict and complementarity, rather than being opposed or irrelevant. On the one hand, curation is recognized as a scientific form of academic research, and at the same time, the behavior of curation is regarded as a research practice in exhibition forms of galleries, museums, biennales, and other cultural institutions. As far as curatorial research is concerned, what is the specific research object, what constitutes the research problem, and what mode and method to carry out research have become the means to distinguish the two research models of knowledge output.

Critical contemporary curatorial research (Bjerregaard, 2019) is an emerging

ARTISTS DESIGNERS ART WORKS

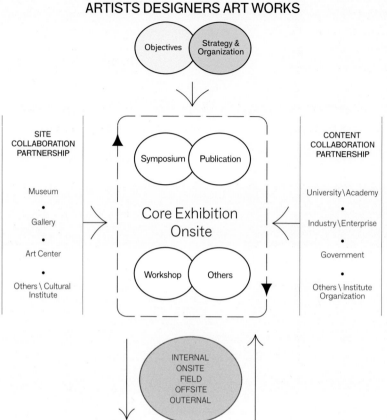

Based on "3D Mode" Five Levels of Communication

The stages and process of contemporary curation

international research direction that belongs to a wide field of museology and art research (Thomas, 2010). Professional independent art curators appeared in 1960s, and until 1980s colleges and universities trained curators based on different disciplines, professional fields, and professional needs: such as design curation (graphic and product) architectural curation, photography curation, and fashion curation (clothing), with contemporary curation with the theme of fashion and jewellery developing only over the last 20 years (Obrist, 2008). Contemporary curatorial research is mostly based on the methodology of art museology and anthropology, which mainly explores the research value of the exhibition itself as an "expression form of artistic practice." While the producer of the exhibition is the author, it is often overlooked that a contemporary exhibition is curated by planning using multiple-level knowledge for six months to two years (or even longer), and there are three stages (levels) (see left). The first stage is based on the exhibition before it takes place. This stage is like the "foundation," which contains a lot of planning and organization work, including determining the purpose of the exhibition, carrying out strategic research, feasibility study, theme and content, artists and works, the possibility of budget, and communication levels. The second stage is during the exhibition, which is usually the completion stage of the exhibition planning and the beginning of the exhibition. At this level seminars based on exhibitions and themes are held, publications released, workshops organized with a series of lectures. At this stage the curator communicates with the visitors, audience/peer scholars, and the public from various angles through the planned exhibitions, seminars, workshops/lectures and publications, so as to achieve the verification and dissemination of knowledge. The third stage is the end of the exhibition. The curator summarizes the positioning of the exhibition and sorts out the report. The three stages have realized a logical relationship of contemporary curation. From a perspective of research, these three stages have also constructed three discourses, which progress step by step. Besides discussing the different dimensions of the research content and theme, five different levels of communication have taken place (see left)—internal communication, on-site communication, professional and disciplinary communication, off-site communication, and external communication—all of which is used to verify and disseminate the research.

The appearance of contemporary curators has always been in a relatively abstract existence: selecting artists and works, and planning and organizing with clear themes, concepts, or narratives (Ventzislavov, 2014). What is the model and method of curatorial research on contemporary fashion and jewellery? How is

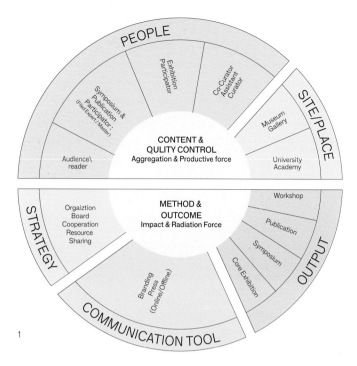

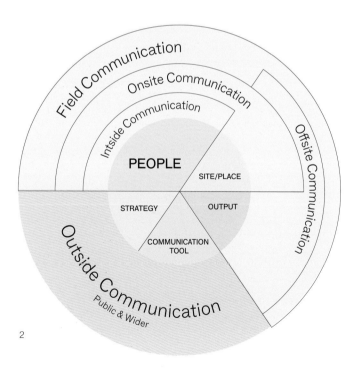

2

1. The content and structure of contemporary curation

2. Five levels of communication

curatorial research used as a mode to produce new knowledge? Based on the case of the TRIPLE PARADE Biennale for Contemporary Jewellery, [1]this paper addresses two dimensions of curation, the first being the curator as the author. Through the strategies and methods of my curation practice, contemporary curation is analyzed not only to reflect and disseminate the existing knowledge, but also to serve as the production method and research means of new knowledge. The second dimension is the curator as a producer. Guided by the system of contemporary art curation the curator must combine the particularities of the fashion and jewellery field to discuss the curatorial management model and practical framework through a systematic strategy and framework.

This study explores the framework of curator's role and the methods of curatorial research. Contemporary curators not only play the role of curators and managers of exhibition as producers, but also play the role of contemporary curators as authors, which complement each other and jointly build the value of curators' roles and the quality of their output. From the perspective of knowledge production, the planning of an exhibition is actually guided by the curator and consists of the joint activities of participants: artists (authors of works), institutions, and the public. Based on the case study of TRIPLE PARADE Biennale for Contemporary Jewellery, this paper investigates how the exhibition can be understood as a place and a production platform for knowledge collection and provides methods and means for the curation and research of contemporary fashion and jewellery design.

The Role of Contemporary Curators

"Cross-shaped" mode: the curator is a collection of two roles and functions as the author and the producer of the exhibition (Hiller and Martin, 2002; MJ Manifesta, 2010).

In the past 10 years, the role of curators has been one of the most discussed topics in visual arts, because the role of curator and curatorial practice has become an independent field of expertise, theory, and methods. From a research

1. http://tripleparade.org

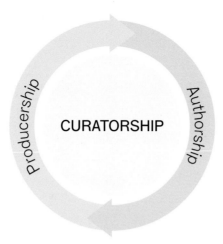

The role of curator

perspective, it also involves a wide range of interdisciplinary knowledge such as sociology, anthropology, management, and art. It has been discussed a lot that curators are researchers and authors in the curatorial process. However, through the research of the theme and the production of the exhibition, the curatorial behavior, as a way of artistic practice, also plays a very important role. Although sociology tends to regard the identity of the curator as a producer (Benjamin, 1970) through the application of implicit or concrete knowledge, the knowledge and plans of the curator may be affected by the contextual behavior in the process of exhibition production.

In contrast, in traditional museums, the curator's role tends to refer to the person doing research in the collection, showing a more isolated and single position. However, as theorists and practitioners begin to treat exhibition as the research object and as a means of research practice, exhibition and curation also present a new outline and extension of concepts in the contemporary context, and there is curatorial professional segmentation and method exploration based on different industries: such as fashion curation (Vänskä and Clark, 2017), architecture curation, design curation, and so on. Not only do contemporary curators need to constantly reflect on the status and relationship between exhibitions and culture, but also must improve their own professional transformation and research and critical awareness. For example, one of the more representative conferences is the academic symposium entitled "The Critical Edge of Curating" held at the Solomon R. Guggenheim Museum in 2011. In addition to hoping for a better theoretical analysis and practical analysis of

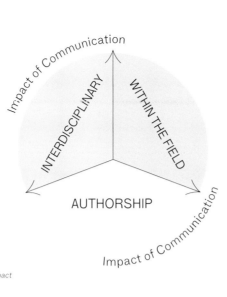

Dimensions of exhibition impact

curatorial studies based on art galleries and museums, another key topic of the conference was "curatorial agency in an expanded field of production," in which the author relationship, curatorial methods, ideology, and other issues based on contemporary context are put in a prominent position. Although this seminar took place 10 years ago, it has led to the multi-dimensional exploration of curatorial theories and practical methods in contemporary times. This exploration also illustrates a trend and tendency that the exhibition itself is a special place to generate knowledge and present the ideas and creativity of curators, rather than just a place to verify and disseminate research results (Thea, 2010). Obviously, when curation is a practice, it means that contemporary curators not only have one and only one role, but also have roles and functions of other dimensions and levels.

From the practical level, in order to facilitate analysis and understanding, I position the core role of curator as "author of the exhibition" and "producer of the exhibition." Throughout the whole curatorial process—early stage, middle stage, and completion—stage, these two roles need to face and deal with different contents and methods. With the advancement of curation, they complement each other and supplement each other, presenting a cross-shaped crossover, and the contemporary curator is a collection of two roles and functions of the author and the producer of the exhibition. In the cross-shaped model, the vertical is the curator's professional knowledge ability in the discipline field of curatorial science or exhibition content, which includes the depth of professional research capabilities, including the setting of the core theme of the exhibition, the cutting-edge issues of discipline and professional development, the choice of artists and the interpretation of art or design works, the design and scenography of the exhibition, the screening of forum experts, and the formulation of themes. The horizontal cross section is the curator's management and planning ability in addition to professional research capability, including the promotion of exhibition projects, strategy formulation, budget control, team management, exhibition and museum policies, publicity and interaction, media and activities, and so on.

What is important is that the curation of contemporary art design and fashion contributes another layer of meaning or explanation to the outside world through the in-depth analysis of the artist's original intentions and creative methods, and then conveys it to the outside world through the exhibition practice (Davallon, 1999). Many artistic creations of practical artists and designers are an experimental and inspiring emergent properties process, including the creator's own intentional cognition and artistic expression of real objects and spaces (Elkins, 1999). Sociology tends to classify the curatorial practice as based on theory and guidelines rather than subjective emotional knowledge and the production process; I will now analyze my curatorial practice to see if this is the case.

Strategies for the Cross-shaped Mode of Curatorial Research

The analysis of curator's role by the concept of the cross-shaped mode reveals how tacit knowledge, aesthetic criteria, and meaningful methods are generated and communicated in the process of curatorial interaction and actions. It can also provide a better understanding of the dynamic process of the curation. Such qualitative research is of value to the study on culture and sociology and art theory based on practical behavior.

Discourse Building 1: Theme, Raising and Defining Questions, Frame of Research

In traditional curation in art museums, most of the works and contents of the exhibition are based on the strategic planning by the museum and its collections and how to communicate and display the output to the public/audience/peers.

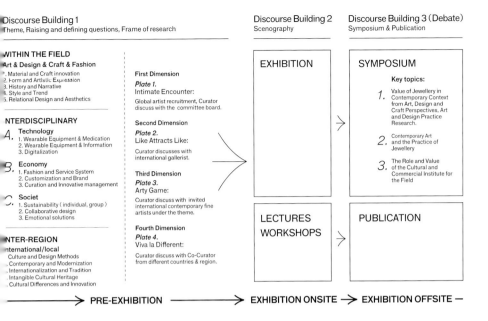

Discourse Building 1
Theme, Raising and defining questions, Frame of research

Discourse Building 2
Scenography

Discourse Building 3 (Debate)
Symposium & Publication

WITHIN THE FIELD
Art & Design & Craft & Fashion
1. Material and Craft innovation
2. Form and Artistic Expression
3. History and Narrative
4. Style and Trend
5. Relational Design and Aesthetics

INTERDISCIPLINARY
A. Technology
 1. Wearable Equipment & Medication
 2. Wearable Equipment & Information
 3. Digitalization
B. Economy
 1. Fashion and Service System
 2. Customization and Brand
 3. Curation and Innovative management
C. Societ
 1. Sustainability (individual, group)
 2. Collaborative design
 3. Emotional solutions

INTER-REGION
International/local
 Culture and Design Methods
 Contemporary and Modernization
 Internationalization and Tradition
 Intangible Cultural Heritage
 Cultural Differences and Innovation

First Dimension
Plate 1.
Intimate Encounter:
Global artist recruitment, Curator discuss with the committee board.

Second Dimension
Plate 2.
Like Attracts Like:
Curator discusses with international gallerist.

Third Dimension
Plate 3.
Arty Game:
Curator discuss with invited international contemporary fine artists under the theme.

Fourth Dimension
Plate 4.
Viva la Different:
Curator discuss with Co-Curator from different countries & region.

EXHIBITION

SYMPOSIUM
Key topics:
1. Value of Jewellery in Contemporary Context from Art, Design and Craft Perspectives, Art and Design Practice Research.
2. Contemporary Art and the Practice of Jewellery
3. The Role and Value of the Cultural and Commercial Institute for the Field

LECTURES WORKSHOPS

PUBLICATION

PRE-EXHIBITION ⟶ EXHIBITION ONSITE → EXHIBITION OFFSITE —

99

Strategy map for curatorial research

However, in contemporary curation, as I mentioned in the previous part of the article, due to the changes in the role of curators and curatorial research in the contemporary context, the curator has evolved from an author who simply goes through and studies the content into a screenwriter, director, and producer. The planning of the first stage is the core of the success of the entire exhibition, and it is the foundation of an exhibition.

The 4th TRIPLE PARADE Biennale for Contemporary Jewellery, hosted by the College of Design and Innovation, Tongji University in Shanghai on October 19, 2018, opened at the Shanghai How Art Museum, including core exhibitions, symposiums, and a series of lectures and workshops. The theme of the Biennale was "Dialogue Between the Past, the Present, and the Future." In time, it explains the past—tradition and singleness—the present—the existence of multiple values and multiple dimensions—and the future: reality does not exist and everything is possible. It connects Shanghai, an emergent global city, China—a rising nation—and the changing world. The dialogue here emphasizes the core content of time and space beyond the formal representation—the understanding of "contemporary value." Jewellery has with many diverse elements in its thousands of years of historical development, and has evolved into a special symbol, which is enough to reflect society and culture's perception of "value" in time and space. The existence and development of jewellery is not only a form, but also a content, exploring the relationship between people and objects, people and people, people and society, and people and the world. The development of jewellery reflects the social trends and cultural changes, especially in the field of jewellery specialty, because the traditional concept has always restricted the material value, historical value, and craft value of its materials used in the development of jewellery design and creation. In regard to the value of design and artistic creation, emotional value, and humanistic value of jewellery design, especially with the current rapid development of science and technology and information technology, the intersection and interaction of disciplines has become extremely important. The exploration of professional theories and methods is imminent, and the discussion of value is an attempt to answer this question. The existence of each value promotes the core of the development of this profession and industry. Contemporary jewellery itself should not have specific rules and boundaries.

Through its thousands of years of historical development, jewellery has evolved in diversified content; each leap starting with revolutionary design talents, the development of exquisite craftsmanship and technology, the change of materials, or the presentation of certain ideas and ideologies. No one can deny that it is not difficult to understand the theme of jewellery from a contemporary perspective. But what is the value of jewellery design in our time? How do we understand and recognize the existence of a work of art that can be independent and related to the body? How does one interpret and express the research on new materials, craftsmanship, culture, or forms, concepts, and new aesthetics from a three-dimensional perspective? How do different jewellery creation methods perform based on the cultural, social, commercial, and political contexts of different countries and regions? Based on these four research questions, the structure of the exhibition is composed of four sections: "Intimate Encounter," "Like Attracts Like," "Arty Game," and "Viva La Different." The selection and delivery of the works in these four sections discussed the theme from four angles in terms of content and research in order to gain greater influence from the communication and exchange dimension of the exhibition from a perspective of curation.

In the first dimension, the Biennale set up an academic committee. As the director of the academic committee and the joint art director I have reviewed works from 100 outstanding artists and designers from all over the world from a one-and-a-half-year global public solicitation and selection of works. They have all made outstanding contributions or innovations in the content, form, method, theory, and practice of jewellery to varying degrees (Section 1. Intimate Encounter). In the second dimension, I invited three international jewellery art galleries with important professional and industry influences in different regions. They are the 42-year-old Gallery RA in Amsterdam, the Netherlands, and the world's first truly contemporary jewellery art gallery, acting as the agency of the world's most important jewellery masters and pioneer artists; HANNAH Gallery in Barcelona, Spain (formerly known as Klimt02 Art Gallery), which manages the most important online platform in the field of international professional exchange (Klimt02.net International Contemporary Jewellery); and FROOTS Gallery, the only mainland Chinese art gallery invited, with two galleries located in Beijing and Shanghai, representing more than 40 international jewellery artists. The galleries needed to select and send ten artists as exhibitors according to the theme, setting, and research questions raised in my curation (Section 2. Like Attracts Like). In the third dimension, the intersection and interaction between disciplines and majors is also an important part of "contemporariness." Sixteen active contemporary visual artists were specially invited to create cross-border jewellery, including the famous oil painter Hong Yu, sculptor Wang Zhan, the installation artist Jian'an Wu. They provide a new perspective for contemporary jewellery creation from an interdisciplinary perspective (Plate 3. Arty game). The fourth deimension "Viva La Different" takes countries and regions as a unit, and invites curators from five continents and 10 countries and regions (China, Taiwan, the Netherlands, Italy, Finland, South Korea, the United States, Canada, the United Kingdom, and Australia) as co-curators of the Biennale, including Xiao Liu, Heng Li, Morgane De Klerk, Eija Tannien-Komulainen, Maria Rosa Franzin, Rebecca Skeels, Elizabeth Shaw, Ezra Satok-Wolmam, and Yong-il Jeon. Each selected 10 outstanding artists from their respective regions that concentrated on the impact and thinking of cultural and regional differences of contemporary jewellery creation. Based on the research questions raised by my curatorial framework from different levels, these four dimensions were researched, discussed, and combed for the first time. The final aspect of the exhibit was the display of 500 excellent works by 300 artists and designers from 34 countries and regions. Almost all artists and designers college/university educated and have their own careers.

American artist Lauren Kalman has a strong concept of contemporary art in her works, and her conceptual drive is to look at feminism from the perspective of jewellery. Some artists' work methods can also be considered creative explorations of relationships, such as personal emotions and emotional communication between themselves and others. In Chinese artist Xiao Liu's works, he recorded and described many small changes in his personal behavior, emotions, understanding, and self-awareness, and then created these recorded spiritual changes— the jewellery he creates is a result of this self-reflection. In the same way, the German artist Jivan Astfalck was in attendance—now living in Britian. The creations of Chinese jewellery artist Xiaochuan Zhang and Danish artist Annette Dam also address relationships, but their original intention is to explain the relationship between the change of nature and the existence of the individual, so as to think about the change and invariance, showing a strong Chinese style and complex. The other two Chinese artists Yi Zhao and Dongdong Zhuang are exploring the relationship between objects, seeking inspiration from some traditional Chinese cultures, and grafting new and old beauty and value of China with contemporary art design methods by reconstructing content or conceptual material forms. Similar ideas are also found in the works of Chinese artist Zheng Fang. Indeed, as one of the contemporary visual arts, contemporary jewellery not only possesses a practical use (wearability), but also has the characteristics of narration, ideas, concepts, and sculptural characteristics. For example, Turkish artist Aisegul Telli and Chinese artist Kai Ren's works are more based on exquisite craftsmanship. The research and exploration of material beauty is also a major theme in contemporary art and design, and it is no exception here. For example, Chinese artist Zhao Shijian, Danish artist Marie-Louise Kristensen, Turkish artist Snem Yildirim, French artist Sébastien Carré, Israeli artist Nirit Dekel, South African artist Gussie van der Merwe, and Swedish artist Karin Roy Anderson all take materials as objects. Of course, there are also Chinese artists like Xin'an Yu in the exhibition, trying to explore the possibility of design methods among technology, materials and concepts. British artist Lin Cheung skillfully masters conceptual design in the realization of jewellery language in the control of materials, reflecting her distinctive personal characteristics. Chinese design brand Dong Chang (artist Shuo Zhang & Xiaowen Chen), and designer Pinyu Deng have more direct cooperation with fashion design, trying to create limited editions of works, while Danyi Zhu is more clearly positioned as entry lux. This is the most benign and diverse artistic ecology. No matter what formal language or working methods these artists use, from the exploration of spirit to material, or from focusing on themselves and others, and then to cross-disciplinary cooperation, they always explore contemporary attributes in the world of jewellery and their values shine.

Therefore, the selection of works has become particularly important. Their works carry a lot of tacit knowledge and uncertainties that they themselves cannot recognize, including the creators' design methods, ideas, concepts, cultural concepts, thoughts, feelings, experiences, information, research, materials, craftsmanship, and attitude. Curators need to judge based on their understanding of artists and their works and extensive literature research. How to show the public the knowledge of contemporary works of art is usually considered an important part of their knowledge of art (Tobelem, 2005), whether this work can be put into the content framework of the exhibition, or can be included in the framework, and in what form can it appear in the exhibition. In addition, curators need to digest and reorganize this information through their own professional knowledge and necessary case studies, and transform a large amount of tacit knowledge in jewellery works into contextual words and new creations, which are re-presented to the audience in a curatorial way, including thinking about the design and scenography of the exhibition, setting the theme of the symposium, guiding the media and comments, and describing the relationship between the works and the exhibition.

03

Discourse Building 2: Scenography

The advancement of curatorial progress leads to the second level of research and discussion, which takes place during the scenography design and production of the exhibition (Scorzin, 2011). Exhibits are one of the contents that make up the whole exhibition. The way the curator sets the display to the public requires that they think about the creation of the scenography, which depends, to a great extent, on the exhibits. This stage involves many discussions and tests. First of all, some contemporary art exhibitions exhibit brand-new commissioned works, which means that the invited artists are commissioned to create their interpretation of the theme by the curator. The curator and the artist will have a long and detailed discussion on the medium and methods of the works, and this process is highly variable. On a more practical level, the curator may adjust or change the curator's ideas and reorganize the presentation mode of the exhibition because of the unpredictable artistic works in reality (DeNora, 2000). Second, most of the time, before the curator receives the work, he/she usually knows the work by looking at the image files, directories, folders, or websites, and then makes a statement on how to present the work. In most cases, this may be completely different from the cognition of the work in person. For example, it is related to the scale of exhibits, their true colors, or the lack of ideological logic of their display. This may also be due to subtle features of the artwork that are imperceptible in low-quality images, such as reflective surfaces, textures, small details, or the true scene of the artworks that is not shown in the images. Thirdly, although professional curators have a good understanding of the exhibition space and can also draw scenography display images of the exhibition, exhibits may still need to be adjusted according to actual space constraints, lighting systems, and display capabilities (Yaneva, 2003). Of course, the discussion on the construction in the process of exhibition scenography is not only limited to these three points, but it is enough to prove that this stage is a process of reaction and adjusment between these three: exhibits, the curator's thoughts, and research and space.

The exhibitionary complex was...a response to the problem of order, but one which worked...in seeking to transform that problem into one of culture, ...its constituent institutions reversed the orientations of the disciplinary apparatuses in seeking to render the forces and principles of order visible to the populace—transformed, here, into a people, a citizenry—rather than vice versa Bennett, 1996.

Sociology theorist Tony Bennett appropriately named the relationship between knowledge and exhibition production an "exhibitionary complex"—it describes the process of curation as a collection of integrating architecture, scenography, display, works, and ideas that represent the characteristics of creation, planning, production, management, and other fields.

In the second TRIPLE PARADE Exhibition for Contemporary Jewellery, the theme of that year was "Dialogue on International Contemporary Jewellery across Three Countries: Finland, Belgium, China," which discussed the exploration and differences of creative design methods between designers and artists based on local culture and craftsmanship. The exhibition is set up in the TAFA Art Museum of Tianjin Academy of Fine Arts. The square exhibition hall of 500 square meters has no partition, but 56 pieces of jewellery works need to be displayed. Meanwhile, the relationship and the interaction between the audience and the works and the audience and the design of the exhibition need be considered. Therefore, the application of scenography becomes indispensable, which is also one of the core differences between exhibitions and display quality. As an exhibition with clear contents, the differences and integration of national and regional cultures, the scenography design scheme is based on the concept of "icebergs" scattered in pieces. An iceberg is a wonder in the ocean. It drifts on the sea surface and can be in contact with the seabed or another iceberg, and each iceberg has its most unique shape. This also implies the multi-level expression of "differences & similarities" and "dialogues." The "Iceberg Block" will be located in the open museum space, and the audience had to walk through and float freely between the icebergs to see the works, which enriched the immersive interactive exhibition viewing experience from another level, and at the same time it brings the audience into the exhibition as a part of it.

The visual appeal of the exhibition is amazing. Experimental and contemporary jewellery is displayed in various iceberg scenes of different sizes, reflecting the interpretation of future jewellery development and creators' creativity. Obviously, the intention of the scenography design is to create a unique sensory experience based on the art museum as a cultural and artistic institution, which is a jewellery display mode that is not commonly available in any other jewellery stores, museums, exhibitions, and other spaces. The display of each work has been included and carefully designed in the experience of viewing the exhibition. The works of artists from different countries are not separated, but are narrated by nine themes in contemporary design, such as sustainability, digitalization, crafts and forms, craft and materials, social concept, fashion and beauty, and gender identity. In addition to on-site exhibition scenography, the application of digital media and new media in exhibitions has also been tried a lot by contemporary curators in recent years. For example, in the first TRIPLE PARADE Exhibition for Contemporary Jewellery in 2014, the exhibition offered an online virtual tour.

The entire experience and specific atmosphere are also created by selecting lighting and mapping. The dark art gallery room is dramatically illuminated, and the projector rotates from one display object to another. The route of the exhibition is guided by lights, and the audience's interest and the perception of jewellery works are continuously enhanced by the illumination of lights in different ways and the visual stimulation presented by the works under the influence of light and shadows. The richness of vision and the sense of experience are very important parts of scenography design as curation. This also fundamentally changed the traditional curator's simple display of exhibits, instead incorporating the exhibitions into artistic practice, research theories and thought as a way of knowledge exploration, so as to create an interactive experience of conveying meaning, content, and emotions, and maximally convey the way of knowing jewellery works that are static in nature and works of art that cannot communicate with the audience in essence. At the same time, before entering, every audience will get a brochure about the exhibition, which

1

2

3

1. Scenography of TRIPLE PARADE Biennale Exhibition 2015,
   TAFA Art Museum.
2/3. Online Virtual Tour of TRIPLE PARADE Exhibition 2014,
   Shenzhen OCT Museum.

introduces the theme of each exhibition with words and pictures. This text explains the historical background, vision, and analysis of designers and artists' creations, which also transforms the simple viewing experience of exhibition into a process of knowledge interaction and communication. Even if the audience does not have any basic knowledge of art, philosophy, and cultural history, they can get the information from the curator during the exhibition.

In recent years, the concept of scenography has been derived from the professional fields of theatrical context and stage art, and its influence has been continuously expanded in contemporary art and fashion exhibitions. How do we understand modern scenography then? As the name implies, it comes from the same root as "scenario" in English which comes from the Greek word "scenegrapho" (Small, 2013), which consists of *scene* and *grapho*. Scene refers to space, the stage and booth. Grapho refers to creation, recording, and description. The literal meaning is similar to that of Chinese word for scenography, which means building the scene, but it is very important that scenography, as an expression method of stage and drama, traditionally implies the identity of the author in the process of space creation and design, just as the scenography designer Frank (Oudsten, 2011) "interpreted as 'hut'...and...'to write'...Altogether, scenario suggests the meaning of authorship in a space." In other words, scenography is not equal to the setting or display design. On the contrary, it includes the overall design and creation of research, exhibits, booths, stages, lights, props, colors, audio, and video (Howard, 2002). Scenography has become a force to transform the single mode of traditional exhibitions. When curators apply scenography to their planning and the expression of themes, they have created an unprecedented meeting point. This meeting point (exhibition) has become the communication way among curator, artist/work, and audience. Although the application of scenography in the production of contemporary visual art exhibitions is not new, what value can it bring to the curatorial practice and discipline development of contemporary fashion and jewellery design in the context of art galleries? How can curators communicate and exchange their curatorial thoughts and research topics through public cultural platforms such as art galleries? These problems seem to be related to the development of contemporary museology. As economists B. J. Pine II and J. H. Gilmore mentioned in their books, driven by global knowledge and experience economy, contemporary art galleries are no longer just warehouses of pure historical collections. They need to strengthen the dissemination of new knowledge and public education, and at the same time, driven by knowledge economy, it is also necessary to enhance the audience experience (Basu, 2007), with a special focus on attracting young audiences to experience cultural institutions. Especially with the current emergence of a large number of private art galleries and museums and the huge consumption of infrastructure, cultural institutions have to rethink the diversity of their roles to face the contradiction among the survival, competition, and the development of art galleries. Scenography has a wide range of values and functions to meet cultural needs, and museums and exhibitions are regarded as a very important part in the curatorial process.

In recent years fashion and jewellery exhibitions have appeared within the scope of contemporary art galleries. Whether it is a professional research exhibition, an interpretation of famous designers, or a brand-specific exhibition of, on the one hand it shows that fashion and jewellery have great potential in the exhibition field (Valerie, 2015), while on the other hand it also presents the diversity of contemporary art curation. TRIPLE PARADE to me, as a curator, has discussed the professional research and development of jewellery in exhibitions and curation, creating a wonderful knowledge journey and experience for lovers of art, fashion, and jewellery, as well as exploring the diversified development of contemporary art galleries and contents. It successfully presents fashion and jewellery, both of which used to be considered themes of popular culture, as a more elitist form of contemporary art, which provides effective methods and theoretical support for the practice of contemporary fashion and jewellery curation. Fashion and jewellery exhibitions can be interpreted as new models in galleries and art museums (Andersson, 2000). This model understands fashion and jewellery as a phenomenon similar to the expression of contemporary art and the development of multiculturalism. Under this cognition, fashion and jewellery are liberated from the "commercial temperament" of "material and kitsch."

Discourse Building 3: Symposium & Publication

Undoubtedly, in addition to the curatorial practice process itself, symposiums and publications, as well as workshops and lectures are all very important forms of knowledge output and verification in the traditional research process. From the second TRIPLE PARADE Exhibition for Contemporary Jewellery in 2015 to the fourth Biennale in 2018, regardless of the scale of the exhibition, the symposiums and publications of contemporary jewellery design held during

1

2

1/2. Photography of the selected works on TRIPLE PARADE Biennale. Photographer Kuai CHE.

1

2

3

4

1. Symposium of TRIPLE PARADE Biennale 2018,
Shanghai HOW Art Museum.

2/3/. Symposium of TRIPLE PARADE Biennale
2016 in Tianjin.

4. Workshop of TRIPLE PARADE Biennale
2018 in Shanghai.

the exhibition have always become another climax after the opening of the exhibition. The symposium was held not only open to the jewellery field, but also to a wider range of art and fashion design fields, industries, the public, and students interested in this topic. The research results are exchanged, which also becomes the third discourse construction and discussion in the curatorial process. As an effective network and platform for knowledge discussion and sharing, the symposium itself brings together important world experts and scholars or industry elites related to the theme so as to achieve the most effective intercommunication in the academic field.

In 2015, the theme of TRIPLE PARADE International Jewellery Forum was "Jewellery as the Language—Boundary of Culture and Design." Twelve leading scholars from the Netherlands, Belgium, Finland, and China were invited, including design critics, famous collectors, college professors, art historians, famous gallery founders, designers, artists, and art museum curators. In 2016 we returned to explore the professional content of jewellery with the theme of "Dialogue Between You and Me to Them: Creator, Wearer, Viewer." In addition to academic symposiums, the editing and distribution of publications were also based on the theme of dialogue. Fourteen international scholars were specially invited to be interviewed into literature documents, which extended the thinking on the theme of research from the perspectives of design and creation, higher education, art museum curation, association management, collection and wearing, and art gallery management. The 4th Biennale Symposium in 2018 discussed the "Contemporary Value of Jewellery Design and Creation" from four aspects: "Cognition of the contemporarity and value of jewellery from the perspective of art, design, and craftsmanship," "Jewellery creation and research methods," "Cross-border practice of contemporary visual art and jewellery," and "Thoughts on the value and role of cultural and art institutions in the development of regional and jewellery industry." Special guest speakers and industry leaders from more than a dozen countries, including the United Kingdom, the United States, the Netherlands, Italy, China, Finland, Denmark, Canada, and Australia discussed these issues in depth.

Conclusion

The critical research is carried out under the context that the curator, the role of the curator, and the method of the curator are getting more and more attention.

Critical curatorial research is an emerging international research focus, which belongs to a wider field of museum and design research. Taking curatorial practice as a research method is also a means of exploring the development of disciplines for majors in colleges and universities. For an international jewellery biennale that has been successfully held four times, there are too many materials and documents worth discussing, including my own curatorial practice and research. It's hard for me to throw it out in one article. This article is a preliminary review of the curation as the research method and framework from the perspective of contemporary curators. Contemporary curation still has many challenges, especially curation of fashion and jewellery, because it should not only display and show works, but it should explore the complex nature of fashion and jewellery itself in the development process of the field, involving more interdisciplinary, social relations, and anthropological thinking.

Reference

Andersson, F. 2000. "Museums as Fashion Media." In *Fashion Cultures: Theories, Explorations and Analysis*, edited by Stella Bruzzi and Pamela Church Gibson. London: Routledge.

Basu, P., and S. Macdonald. 2007. "Introduction: Experiments in Exhibition, Ethnography, Art and Science." In *Exhibitions Experiments*, edited by Sharon Macdonald and Paul Basu. Malden, MA: Blackwell.

Bjerregaard, P. 2019. "Exhibitions as Research: An Introduction." In *Exhibitions as Research: Experimental Methods in Museums*, edited by Peter Bjerregaard. London and New York: Routledge.

Bennett, T. 1996. "The Exhibitionary Complex." In *Thinking about Exhibitions*, edited by Bruce W. Ferguson, Reesa Greenberg, and Sandy Nairne. London: Routledge.

Barker, E. ed. 1999. *Contemporary Cultures* of Display. London: Yale University Press.

Billing, J., M. Lind, and L. Nilsson. 2007. *Taking the Matter into Common Hands—On Contemporary Art and Collaborative Practices*. London: Black Dog Publishing.

Benjamin, W. 1970. "The Author as Producer." In *New Left Review* 1/62, July-August.

Becker, H. S. 1982. *Art Worlds*. Berkeley: University of California Press.

Bauer, U. M. 1992. *Meta 2 A New Spirit in Curating?* Stuttgart, Künstlerhaus Stuttgart.

Cook, S., and B. Graham. 2002. *Curating New Media*. Newcastle Upon Tyne, Baltic & University of Newcastle.

Drabble, B., and D. Richter. 2008. *Curating Critique*. Frankfurt, Revolver Verlag.

Davallon, J. 1999. *L'exposition à l'oeuvre: Strategies de communication et médiation symbolique*. Paris: L'Harmattan.

DeNora, T. 2000. *Music in Everyday Life*. Cambridge: Cambridge University Press.

Elkins, J. 1999. *What Painting Is*. New York: Routledge.

Ferguson, B., R. Greenberg, and S. Nairne. 1996. *Thinking about Exhibitions*. London, Routledge.

Gardner, A., and C. Green. 2016. *Biennials, Triennials, and Documenta: The Exhibitions that Created Contemporary Art*. New York: Wiley-Blackwell.

Guggenheim. 2011. "The Critical Edge of Curating', Guggenheim." <http://www.guggenheim.org/new-york/calendar-and-events/2011/11/04/the-critical-edge-of-curating/989> [accessed 12/08/13.

Heinich, N., and M. Pollak. 1996. "From Museum Curator to Exhibition Auteur: Inventing a Singular Position." In *Thinking about Exhibitions*, edited by Bruce W. Ferguson, Reesa Greenberg, and Sandy Nairne. London: Routledge.

Hooper-Greenhill, E. 2004. "Changing Values in the Art Museum: Rethinking Communication and Learning." In *Museum Studies*. edited by Bettina Messias Carbonell. Oxford: Blackwell Publishing Ltd.

Hiller, S., and S. Martin. 2002. *The Producers: Contemporary Curators in Conversation*, Vol. 4. Baltic.

Howard, P. 2002. *What is Scenography*. London: Routledge.

HOW's review on the symposium | THREE TIMES—Dialogue on World Contemporary Jewellery (Part I) (HOW 论坛回顾 | 三世之界: 全球当代首饰对话(上)). HOW Art Museum Shanghai (上海昊美术馆). (2018) < https://mp.weixin.qq.com/s/D791mu0td5XjRc2hk3zowg >.

HOW's review on the symposium | THREE TIMES—Dialogue on World Contemporary Jewellery (Part II) (HOW论坛回顾 | 三世之界: 全球当代首饰对话(下)). HOW Art Museum Shanghai (上海昊美术馆). (2018) < https://mp.weixin.qq.com/s/c4NW0QvoZreYYJcNji4GpA >.

Herle, A. 2013. "Exhibitions as Research: Displaying the Techniques That Make Bodies Visible." In *Museum Worlds*. Volume 1(1).

Marincola, P. 2002. *Curating Now: Imaginative Practice/Public Responsibility*. Philadelphia: Philadelphia Exhibitions Initiative.

Martinon, J. P. 2013. *The Curatorial: A Philosophy of Curating*. London: Bloomsbury.

MacLeod, S., L. H. Hanks, and J. A. Hale. 2012. *Museum Making: Narratives, Architectures, Exhibitions*. London: Routledge.

Marstine, J. 2006. *New Museum Theory and Practice*. Oxford: Blackwell Publishing.

MJ Manifesta Journal: v. 10 (January 1, 2010). *The Curator as Producer* (Paperback).

Obrist, H. U. 2016. *Ways of Curating*. New York: Farrar, Straus and Giroux.

Obrist, H. U. 2008. *Curating: A Brief History*. Zurich: JRP, Ringier.

Oudsten, F.D. 2011. *Space. Time. Narrative: The Exhibition as Post-Spectacular Stage*. London: Routledge.

Pine II, B. J., and J. H. Gilmore. 1999. *The Experience Economy: Work is Theatre and Every Business a Stage*. Boston: Harvard Business Press.

Smith, T. 2012. "Thinking Contemporary Curating." In *Independent Curators Inc.*

Scorzin, P. C. 2011. "Metascenography: On the Metareferential Turn in Scenography." In *The Matereferential Turn in Contemporary Arts and Media: Forms, Functions, Attempts at Explanation*, edited by Werner Wolf. Amsterdam: Rodopi.

Small, J. P. 2013. "Skenographia in Brief." In *Performance in Greek and Roman Theatre*, edited by George W. M. Harris and Vayos Liapis. Boston: Brill.

Steele, V. 2019. *Paris, Capital of Fashion*. New York: Bloomsbury Visual Arts.

Thea, C. 2010. *On Curating: Interviews with Ten International Curators*. New York: Distributed Art Publishers.

Thomas, N. 2010. "The Museum as Method." In *Museum Anthropology* 33(1): 6–10.

Thomas, C. 2002. *The Edge of Everything: Reflections on Curatorial Practice*. Banff: The Banff Centre Press.

Kirshenblatt-Gimblett, B. 1998. *Destination Culture: Tourism, Museums, and Heritage*. London: University of California Press.

Ventzislavov, R. 2014. "Idle Arts: Reconsidering the Curator." In *Journal of Aesthetics and Art Criticism* 72(1).

Vänskä, A., and H. Clark. 2017. *Fashion Curating: Critical Practice in the Museum and Beyond*. New York: Bloomsbury Academic.

Yaneva, A. 2003. "Chalk Steps on the Museum Floor: The 'Pulses' of Objects in an Art Installation." In *Journal of Material Culture* 8(2): 169–88.

Tobelem, J.M. 2005. *Le nouvel âge des musées: Les institutions culturelles au défi de la gestion*. Paris: Armand Colin.

Valerie, S. 2015. "Museum Quality: The Rise of the Fashion Exhibition." In *Fashion Theory* 12(1): 7–30.

Fashion and Museography
The Space as an Ally

Héctor NAVARRO

Professor, International Vice-Dean of CSDMM-UPM, Universidad Politécnica de Madrid, Spain

Curation in its widest meaning could be understood as a key part within the fashion process to communicate all the relevant contents of the final product to the general public. Communication through the physical space between the creator and the fashion product includes many questions to be considered. It is essential to show the produced pieces attending to the context and the fashion world must contemplate the many ways costume can be shown. In this sense, this article aims to share some professional works of museography made by Manuel Blanco and myself and other practical experiences made by the students from Centro Superior de Diseño (Universidad Politécnica de Madrid) designing window displays.

When an exhibition is designed, this work can be attempted from multiple points of view. The different strategies to be considered must relate the content to be shown and the space. The exhibition must contemplate the difficulty of two spheres: the curatorial and the design part. Both combined must produce a proposal capable of linking the visitors and the pieces to be shown. This content could be focused on architecture, painting, art, photography, and fashion. In any case, curator and designer, or both represented by one figure, have to analyze this material in order to create an appealing result that will facilitate the transfer of knowledge from the content to the user.

This article will start analyzing different exhibitions created by Manuel Blanco and myself in which every single commission is seeking different objectives, and all of them are giving the role play to the pieces to be shown. The whole strategy is giving form to an experience that pretends to transcend the object. And for that purpose, a spatial solution must be designed creating a complex proposal that provides different kinds of experiences. In other words, some users will just walk around the space and others will prefer to go deeper and get the most out of the pieces.

Santiago DC
Location: Santiago de Compostela, Spain. 2007

1

2

3

1. *Spain [f], we the cities*
   Location: Venice, Italy. 2006

2. *Childhood. Photographies by Isabel Muñoz*
   Location: Guggenheim Museum Bilbao, Spain. 2011

3. *Campo Baeza, the creation tree MAXXI Museum,*
   Rome. 2012

"Santiago DC" is one of the exhibitions selected to exemplify this idea, a work commissioned by the council of Santiago de Compostela, a northern Spanish city. One of the contents to be shown was a collection of old photographs of the city. Instead of hanging them on the wall, an interior landscape was created. For this purpose, a floor with the map of the old city occupied the space, a city that also presents a changing topography. This flooring had to include a careful graphic design work serving as the base to place all the pictures, printed in backlighted pieces of glass. The difference of heights was also representing the referred changing topography. So the proposal aimed to create an experience, where pictures were placed attending to a topographic reality. Even in the walls of the perimeter, users could see views from the old city toward the new urban plannings. The solution encouraged visitors to recognize old spots, compare them to the present city and, therefore, the exhibition turned into an experience that transcended the objects, elevating their value.

"Spain [f], we the cities" designed back in 2006 was the Spanish pavilion for the Venice Biennale. In this case, the referred experience was created based, not just on the objets, but also on oral contents. The different showcases included screens with women giving their vision of the city, from famous architects to teenagers or older citizens. They were filmed in a way that visitors could interact with these women in a scale of 1:1. Every user had a headphone, so the intention was to create a conversation, a dialogue between these women and the users attending the exhibition. Drawings, photographs, models, and other relevant materials were also included in the proposal complementing the oral content.

Continuing with this one to one relationship, this concept was explored again in the exhibition "Childhood" using other resources. In this case, the content was a collection of portraits made by Spanish photographer Isabel Muñoz. UNICEF commissioned her to photograph children all around the world to show their lives and the objects they owned. This work would show how different and unfair childhood can be. This exhibition travelled all around Spain for years, and the success comes from the created experience. The mirrored walls and the size of the pictures were creating a new landscape where users were seeing their reflection in the mirror, surrounded by these children. In this way, whether they like it or not, visitors were constantly comparing themselves with the children. This situation provoked a self consciousness through the visual comparison.

Sometimes exhibitions do not have interact with viewers, and curators and designers just have to show an artistic reality, as it is the case of the exhibition "Alberto Campo Baeza, the creation tree." The Spanish architect was chosen by

Tadao Ando to be exposed first in Tokyo, and later in Rome, at MAXXI Museum. Alberto Campo Baeza is well known for his sketches. He does not use computers during the designing process. He uses the sketches to manifest his thoughts. The exhibition had to be shown in Tokyo and all the sketches were used to create a blossom tree. Every branch corresponded to a different project where users could see the evolution of the building the architect was designing and the pink papers included all the information referred to the project. Although models, drawings, pictures and an interview were included, what is relevant to highlight is how recreating a landscape, defined by the blossom tree and the large-scale picture, the experience of learning from "the creation tree" was also producing the image of the exhibition.

The other selected example is an exhibition hold in the Royale Palace of Madrid called "Great Bindings in the Royale Libraries." The resources used for the bindings were also present in other objects, such as furniture, decoration, textiles...so one of the spaces focused on relating objets and bindings, facilitating the comparison to identify trends. In this exhibition, each space explained different types of binding, so the displays provided different alternatives. A circular showcase was used for serial books placing them in the same position, spinning around from the center, the user could see the different parts of the binding; front, lateral, and back. Another cabinet had to show the delicate work of the lateral of the book, what had to be highlighted was framed by using different kinds of glasses.

After meeting the director of the Royal Library who was also the curator of the exhibition, as we were fascinated by the way she manipulated the books, explaining them, we decided to film her and include this experience in a double-screen device, shaped in black, just showing her hands, the books and her explanations. This artifact is evidence that many of the solutions come from real experiences.

The most important thing for Centro Superior de Diseño de Madrid is to make students understand how important it is to focus on the relevance of the physical channels when showcasing a fashion work. It is the only chance to let users and possible customers to know the designer's work live, the quality of the fabrics. The most relevant brands and designers are conscious of this fact and that is the reason why they think about how they are going to show the costumes even in the early stages of the creating process. They will surely use the fashion show, but also exhibitions and window displays. The universe created by the designers must complete their proposal beyond the costume. In this sense, the CSDMM has been participating in a local competition where different teams must design

1

2

3

1/2/3. Great Bindings in the Royale Library Royale Palace of Madrid,
Spain. 2012

1

3

2

4

1. *Great Bindings in the Royale Library*
   Royale Palace of Madrid, Spain. 2012

2. *Shopping window.*
   Designer: Lebor Gabala
   Madrid. 2017. Designed by: Teresa Borrego, Laura
   Fernández Cavia, Lucía Gonzalez, Carla Maderuelo,
   Cristina Martín, Isabel Villar

3. *Shopping window.*
   Designer: Juana Martín
   Madrid. 2017. Designed by: Adela Alfaro, Sara
   Cerezo, Armando Embarba, Dafne Fernández, Ana
   González, María Goujon, Patricia Romero, María
   Sánchez

4. *Shopping window.*
   Designer: Beatriz Peñalver
   Madrid. 2017. Designed by: Cristina Arredondo,
   Beatriz Castro, Cristina Coleto, Rocío Colino,
   Carmen Díaz, Yu You

a window display to showcase looks designed by famous Spanish fashion designers. This competition was created by the organization in charge of the Madrid Mercedes-Benz Fashion Week.

This competition is a great chance because theoretical work has the opportunity to become a real professional experience. We added some conditions to make the exercise more interesting and get the best of the students; they have a limited budget of 70 dollars and all the materials have to be bought in Ikea. They have to decontextualize the Ikea product and transform it into something new, a building element with a solution linked to the concept behind the collection to be shown. In this way, the abstract altar in the figure above was made with these white objets designed to store plastic bags. Inside, golden papers linked to the reference of the sacred spaces from Indian culture used by fashion designer Lebor Gabala. The sticks permitted to get a structural solution for the whole and were also used to hang some garments.

Another selected work shows a dress of a Sevillian designed by Juana Martín. Usually, these dresses include small dots all around the fabric. But this one did not, so the students took the most iconic Ikea pieces of furniture and included the missing dots in them, all black and white getting a strong coherent proposal. In this way, the proposal was linking the designer's work and Ikea´s best sellers creating a coherent ensemble. The proposal is to create the cheapest window display possible. The cardboard boxes used as bricks cost five cents each and the rest of the elements can be gotten for free in any Ikea store, like paper measuring tape or pencils.

The proposal show in page 322 (above) aimed to create the atmosphere of a Hawaiian night, the concept behind this collection designed by Juan Vidal, famous fashion designer and also professor at our university. The main elements are pleated blinds from Ikea, which were quite adequate to recreate this palm tree-like scenario manipulating them and also incorporating green light to produce this specific atmosphere.

The window display (see p. 322, below) showed one look of the collection designed by Ana Locking, also professor at CSDMM, inspired by Western American culture in which the American flag is such a relevant symbol. Students made their own flag using Ikea bed bases to knit the stripes with Ikea blankets. Once again, all these proposals had a limited budget and the lack of manual help. Students had to create these shopping windows by their own in three hours.

1

2

1. *Shopping window.*
   Designer: Juan Vidal, Madrid. 2018.
   Designed by: Laura Fernández Cavia, Laura Ruiz Campos, Soraya Fernández, Inés Gabardos

2. *Shopping window.*
   Designer: Ana Locking, Madrid. 2018.
   Designed by: Laura Fernández Cavia, Laura Ruiz Campos, Soraya Fernández, Inés Gabardos

Shopping window.
Designers: Juan Vidal, Ana Locking and ManéMané, Madrid. 2018.
Design by: Patricia Arenal, Noelia Escaño, María Guardia, Jorge Rodríguez

For the last edition, students had to make a bubble proposal (see above). On this occasion, students collected aluminium pipes used in air conditioning installations. This material was perfect to create the scenario for the selected bright looks. The form, seen as a totem was the perfect claim to attract attention. Three different designers were going to be together sharing the same space, so the solution had to incorporate, in some way, an abstract element able to relate to every selected look.

All these projects all together can be considered as valuable content. Different approaches and different results manifest how powerful space can be to create a connection between contents and users. Works developed in the professional field and others made from the academic field should never take for granted what an exhibition or a window display are. Understanding the space as an ally will help build a stronger proposal. It is not just about creating an appealing visual display, but generating an experience that will transcend the object and will complete the proposal with contents that should be present in the value of the object to be shown. All these experiences show that these proposals go beyond and include themes related to architecture, scenography, sociology, technology, or audiovisuals.

CHAPTER

5

CONCLUSION

The Future Is Now and the Making of Things

Elizabeth FISCHER

Professor, Dean of Fashion and Jewellery Design, HEAD—Genève School of Art and Design, HES-SO Geneva, Switzerland.

Fashion, accessories, and jewellery are inscribed in the cultural and industrial fabric of society at various levels and scales: from a collective industry, producing huge amounts of goods that travel all over the world, to regional brands and small-scale workshops, and makers who produce on a reduced scale. There is the scandal of fast fashion on the one hand, with the necessary steps to take on a global level to change the pollution and misery generated by this industry. [1] On the other hand, there is the joy offered by a beautiful item, handcrafted or manufactured, that has been kept over time and handed down to the next generations, whether in the family circle or sold at auction. The panel of lecturers who spoke at the 2018 WoSoF symposium more often than not focused on what lies at the core of the design of garments, accessories, and jewellery: the human being and the human body. Design is about conceiving and making things for someone else, for the other. At one end of the spectrum stand the designers and makers, at the stage of ideation and production. At the other end are the consumers, who will buy and wear the items, keep them and cherish them or discard them after a while.

Most of the essays in the symposium's proceedings highlight the fact that human beings hold on to the things that shape their identity and everyday life—some, who live on the poorer side of society, out of sheer necessity. In a 2017 campaign report on fashion, Greenpeace argued that "design for longer life and promoting extended use of clothing are the most important interventions to slow down the material flow," emphasizing the importance of the technical and emotional durability of clothing. [2] As Chiara Scarpitti points out in her essay in this publication: "We should not forget that a jewel is a device with a strong symbolic power that binds the wearer to his/her emotional and perceptive sphere and amplifies it. Jewel, subject, and thought are connected when there is an exchange of energy...According to this research perspective...technology is not only used for an aesthetic or functional optimization, but it becomes itself a tool for an envisioning and the establishment of a new relationship—corporeal and intellectual—with the human being." Several of the lecturers underlined how a design-driven approach is needed to create emotional value and a vital relationship between design, product, and user. Volker Koch, founder of the sustainable leatherware brand Silentgoods, conveys the same idea from the designer's perspective: "While the material choices have a significant

---

1. "Fashion at the Crossroads." Greenpeace, 18 Sept. 2017, http://www.greenpeace.org/international/en/publications/Campaign-reports/Toxics-reports/Fashion-at-the-Crossroads/
2. Ibid.

effect on the environment, we are however aware that the biggest impact we as a designer-manufacturer have, is dependent on the relationship formed between the product and the wearer." By essence, in an ideal world, design is about making things of good quality, which benefit the user and stand the test of time—as recently advocated by Lucie and Luke Meier, current co-creative directors of Jil Sander. [3]

This echoes what Richard Sennett wrote in 2008: "we can achieve a more humane material life, if only we better understand the making of things" (Sennett, 2008). Designers and users can both benefit from this knowledge about "the making of things." During the recent COVID-19 pandemic that halted the world economy, many people rediscovered the act of making things, whether food, clothes, domestic objects, or simply taking time to do mending and repairs. This kind of activity is often undervalued because it is not "profitable" in capitalistic terms. However, it is an indication of something precious in that it shows how much care we actually bestow on our material surroundings if given the time and leisure to do so. Making things also brings us back to a more humane level and gets us back in touch with the materiality of the business of living: the total sensory experience of making things provides grounding and reassurance in times of uncertainty. It also reminds us of the consideration we need for the makers and producers and that the garment workers or gold miners in poor economies need our active support to earn a decent living wage. Doing justice to the human component of fashion, from the designer via the production means to the consumer, in an inclusive and multidisciplinary way, is what the lectures gathered here have touched upon. Now, more than ever, it is time to step back and take stock. Li Edelkoort has hailed this crisis as a moment for rethinking and rebooting. "Therefore, if we are wise—which sadly we now know we aren't—we will start up again with new rules and regulations, allowing countries to get back to their knowhow and specific qualities, introducing cottage industries that would flourish and grow into an arts-and-crafts century, where manual labor is cherished above everything else. A regulated shut down of production plants for two months a year could be part of this concept, as are collective creative studios that would produce ideas for several brands at a time, bringing about an economy of scale with a much lighter environmental footprint. Local industries and activities would gain momentum and people-

3. Lucie and Luke Meier, "Human Nature/Mother Nature," A Magazine Curated by xxx issue 21, 2020 https://amagazinecuratedby.com/collection/lucie-and-luke-meier/

4. Li Edelkoort interviewed by Marcus Faires for Dezeen 9 March 2020, https://www.dezeen.com/2020/03/09/li-edelkoort-coronavirus-reset/

based initiatives will take over with bartering systems and open tables, farmers markets, and street events, dance and singing contests and a very dominant DIY aesthetic. My future forecast for the Age of the Amateur seems to come much faster than I anticipated." [4] Are we able to take this holistic and more humane approach? In "Lessons we should learn" during the symposium, Elizabeth Shaw highlights the tailor-made production of prosthetics by the Australian engineer Mat Bowtell with 3D printers, under creative commons license that allows people to download the designs but not sell or make a profit from them. Bowtell is a prime example of the "Age of the Amateur" Edelkoort has predicted, in which home makers are able to answer pressing needs, for specific parts of the population, from their own studio—albeit on a small scale—in this case using electronics and computer science. Thanks to the internet the goods can be shown worldwide yet produced in a regional framework.

As Maarten Versteeg advocates, it is time to approach artifacts and wearables on the human body with a multidisciplinary approach. This involves combining the design process of fashion and the engineering of products, as well as the social and personal perspectives of these disciplines, doing away with the ideal Westernized fashion body that has ruled the field for far too long, rather opening up to the variety of morphologies and cultural contexts in the world. Alternative practices, sharing knowledge and skills, as well as accessibility to open source data, with collective and inclusive teams at the helm of design and production units, are key factors in a forward-thinking process. The contributions to the symposium provide insight into the issues that we, as a global society, have to deal with now in order to provide more resilience, inclusivity, and equity, not for the future, but for the populations living in today's world. Design, ideation, and making—the mind and the hand—have a part to play in offering more agency to human beings in more user-centered processes. We are facing major challenges. Other than impending pandemics, most importantly climate change and migratory movements already have a deep impact on our way of living and entail an unavoidable mixing of cultures and societies. In other words, we will necessarily encounter the "other,"—a human being—right on our doorstep. Design, just like art, provides experiences of otherness. By thinking through otherness and the making of things for the other, we can prepare for the challenges lying ahead.

Reference

Sennett, R. 2008. *The Craftsman*. New Haven/London: Yale University Press.

ABOUT THE EDITORS

Jie SUN

Jie SUN is the National Distinguished Expert (Awarded by the Ministry of Education of China), Professor of Design at the College of Design and Innovation (D&I), Tongji University in Shanghai; Head of New Center of Contemporary Jewellry and Fashion Culture (NoCC); Deputy-Chairman at Art and Design Academic Committee in Tongji University; Chairman and Curator at TRIPLE PARADE International Biennial Organization Committee; Director of SxV Museum of Modern Arts in Qingdao (SV MoMA); Director at the Institute of Design and Creative Industries in Guangzhou (CDC).

Porf.SUN is one of the most influential experts on fashion, jewellery and design in the Greater China. Over the past few years, he has worked on major collaborative and curatorial projects worldwide, actively engaged in both European and Asian design culture. Porf.SUN advocates that by adhering to the concept "Fashion & Design +" innovation and integration of culture, fashion, lifestyle, design, aesthetics, and business, the design should be understood within the context of contemporary, humanized experience, and sustainable development of regional consumption and industrial upgrading. In the aspect of social innovation, he proposed an innovative theoretical model driven by design and oriented by the development of urban cultural innovation: "A Model of Cultural Activity Driven by Art and Design."

Elizabeth FISCHER

Elizabeth FISCHER is professor in charge of the Fashion, Jewellery, and Accessories Design Department at the HEAD—Geneva University of art and design. She was responsible for opening the BA study program to industry and to jewellery related fields such as product and accessory design. She contributed to the launch of the MA study program and was the chair in watch design in 2014. Holder of an MA in art history specialized in the interpretation of dress, textiles, and jewellery in paintings, she has worked in education and with museums as a scientific collabo¬rator and curator for over 25 years. She is member of the scien¬tific committee of MuMode Swiss fashion Museum, in charge of defining its new cultural and scientific program (Yverdon-les-Bains).

Professor Fischer lectures and writes on the cultural history of dress in the broad sense—fashion, jewellery, accessories, body ornaments, and textiles. Her research at HEAD—Geneva explores the relationship of the contemporary body with accessories and dress as well as gender issues. She is scientific consultant on various other research projects at HEAD—Geneva.

Published by Tongji University Press and ORO Editions

www.oroeditions.com

info@oroeditions.com

Authors: Jie SUN, Elizabeth FISCHER
Graphic Designer: Qing LIU
Managing Editor: Jake ANDERSON
Executive Editor: Jialin(Crisie) YUAN

10 9 8 7 6 5 4 3 2 1 First Edition
ISBN: 978-1-951541-76-7
Color Separations and Printing: ORO Group Ltd.
Printed in China.

ORO Editions makes a continuous effort to minimize the overall carbon footprint of its publications. As part of this goal, ORO Editions, in association with Global ReLeaf, arranges to plant trees to replace those used in the manufacturing of the paper produced for its books. Global ReLeaf is an international campaign run by American Forests, one of the world's oldest nonprofit conservation organizations. Global ReLeaf is American Forests' education and action program that helps individuals, organizations, agencies, and corporations improve the local and global environment by planting and caring for trees.

Special thanks to: College of Design and Innovation/Tongji University, Shanghai College of Design and Innovation, New Center of Contemporary Jewellery and Fashion Culture (NoCC), HEAD—Genève School of Art and Design, swissnex China.